Syntactic Carpentry

An Emergentist Approach to Syntax

Syntactic Carpentry

An Emergentist Approach to Syntax

William O'Grady
University of Hawai'i

2005

LAWRENCE ERLBAUM ASSOCIATES, PUBLISHERS
Mahwah, New Jersey   London

The camera copy for the text of this book was supplied by the author.

Lawrence Erlbaum Associates, Inc., Publishers
10 Industrial Avenue
Mahwah, New Jersey 07430

Cover design by Kathryn Houghtaling Lacey

Library of Congress Cataloging-in-Publication Data

O'Grady, William D. (William Delaney), 1952-
    Syntactic carpentry : an emergentist approach to syntax / William O'Grady
        p. cm.
    Includes bibliographical references and index.
    ISBN 0-8058-4959-9 (c : alk. Paper) — ISBN 0-8058-4960-2 (pb : alk Paper)
        1.   Grammar, Comparative and general—Syntax. I. Title.

P291.O36 2005
415—dc22

                                                          2004054148

Books published by Lawrence Erlbaum Associates as printed on acid-free paper,
And their bindings are chosen for strength and durability.

Printed in the United States of America
10 9 8 7 6 5 4 3 2 1

What of architectural beauty I now see, I know has gradually grown from within outward, out of the necessities and character of the indweller, who is the only builder . . .

— Henry David Thoreau (*Walden,* 1854)

For Miho

Contents

Preface

Since the 1960s, work on syntactic theory has been dominated by the view that the defining properties of the human language faculty are the product of autonomous grammatical principles. The strongest and best developed versions of this thesis focus on the development of a theory of Universal Grammar, an inborn system of linguistic categories and principles that is taken to determine the essential characteristics of human language.

In recent years, significant opposition to this sort of approach has begun to organize itself around the idea that the key properties of language are shaped by more basic nonlinguistic forces ranging from attention, memory, and physiology to pragmatics, perception, and processing pressures. At this time, there is no definitive list of possible explanatory factors, and there is no more than a preliminary understanding of how such factors might contribute to an explanation of the many puzzles associated with the nature and use of language.

The primary objective of this book is to advance the emergentist thesis by applying it to a difficult and important set of problems that arise in the syntax of natural language. The particular idea that I explore is that the defining properties of many important syntactic phenomena arise from the operation of a general efficiency-driven processor rather than from autonomous grammatical principles. As I will try to explain in much more detail in the pages that follow, this sort of approach points toward a possible reduction of the theory of sentence structure to the theory of sentence processing.

The proposal is an extreme one, I acknowledge, and I may well have pushed it too far. Nonetheless, the exercise may still prove useful. The periodic assessment of even seemingly unassailable assumptions, such as the need for grammar, can yield new insights into the workings of nature's mysteries, even if it does not definitively solve them.

I recognize that not all readers will wish to delve into the details of syntactic analysis to the same degree. For those seeking a more general synopsis of the emergentist program for syntax, there are two possibilities. One is to focus on the following chapters and sections.

Chapter 1
Chapter 3, Sections 1 – 3
Chapter 4
Chapter 6, Sections 1 – 3
Chapter 8, Sections 1 & 2
Chapters 9 – 11

The other is to consult my paper, "An emergentist approach to syntax," which is available at my Website (http://www.ling.hawaii.edu/faculty/ogrady/) and which summarizes the principal points of my proposal.

I wrote the first draft of this book in the spring of 1997, while on sabbatical leave from the University of Hawai'i. I used the draft the following semester in a syntax seminar that I co-taught with my late colleague and friend, Stan Starosta. Over the next few years, I made periodic attempts to revise the manuscript and prepare it for publication, but administrative responsibilities and commitments to other projects made it impossible to complete the process until the fall of 2003, when I once again was able to take a one-semester sabbatical leave.

During the past several years, I have benefited from the feedback of students, colleagues, and members of audiences to whom I have presented parts of this work. I am especially grateful to Brian MacWhinney, who took the time to read and comment on several drafts. My sincere thanks also go to Kevin Gregg, Mark Campana, and Woody Mott, each of whom commented extensively on earlier drafts of the mauscritpt. I also owe a debt of gratitude to John Batali, Karl Diller, Fred Eckman, Jung-Hee Kim, Colin Phillips, Amy Schafer, Stan Starosta, the students in two of my syntax seminars, and several anonymous referees for their questions and suggestions. My daughter Cathleen Marie helped in the preparation of the index, for which I am also very grateful.

Special thanks are also due to Cathleen Petree, Sondra Guideman, and the editorial team at Lawrence Erlbaum Associates for their wonderful support and assistance during the preparation of the final version of this book.

Finally, and most of all, I thank my wife Miho, proofreader and editor extraordinaire, for her invaluable help with every part of this project.

—*William O'Grady*

Chapter 1

Language Without Grammar

1. INTRODUCTION

The preeminent explanatory challenge for linguistics involves answering one simple question—how does language work? The answer remains elusive, but certain points of consensus have emerged. Foremost among these is the idea that the core properties of language can be explained by reference to principles of grammar. I believe that this may be wrong.

The purpose of this book is to offer a sketch of what linguistic theory might look like if there were no grammar. Two considerations make the enterprise worthwhile—it promises a better understanding of why language has the particular properties that it does, and it offers new insights into how those properties emerge in the course of the language acquisition process.

It is clear of course that a strong current runs in the opposite direction. Indeed, I acknowledge in advance that grammar-based work on language has yielded results that I will not be able to match here. Nonetheless, the possibilities that I wish to explore appear promising enough to warrant investigation. I will begin by trying to make the proposal that I have in mind more precise.

2. SOME PRELIMINARIES

The most intriguing and exciting aspect of grammar-based research on language lies in its commitment to the existence of Universal Grammar (UG), an inborn faculty-specific grammatical system consisting of the categories and principles common in one form or another to all human languages. The best known versions of this idea have been formulated within the Principles and Parameters framework—first Government and Binding theory and more recently the Minimalist Program (e.g., Chomsky 1981, 1995). However, versions of UG are found in a variety of other frameworks as well, including most obviously Lexical Functional Grammar and Head-driven Phrase Structure Grammar. In all cases, the central thesis is the same: Universal Grammar makes human language what it is. I reject this idea.

Instead, I argue that the structure and use of language is shaped by more basic, nonlinguistic forces—an idea that has come to be known in recent years as the *emergentist thesis* (e.g., Elman 1999, MacWhinney 1999, Menn 2000).[1] The

---

[1]Emergentism belongs to the class of theories that I referred to as 'general nativist' in earlier work (e.g., O'Grady 1997:307ff).

particular version of the emergentist thesis that I put forward here is that the core properties of sentences follow from the manner in which they are built. More specifically, I will be proposing that syntactic theory can and should be subsumed by the theory of sentence processing. As I see it, a simple processor, not Universal Grammar, lies at the heart of the human language faculty.

Architects and carpenters

A metaphor may help convey what I have in mind. Traditional syntactic theory focuses its attention on the *architecture* of sentence structure, which is claimed to comply with a complex grammatical blueprint. In Government and Binding theory, for instance, well-formed sentences have a deep structure that satisfies the X-bar Schema and the Theta Criterion; they have a surface structure that complies with the Case Filter and the Binding Principles; they have a logical form that satisfies the Bijection Principle; and so on (e.g., Chomsky 1981, Haegeman 1994). The question of how sentences with these properties are actually built in the course of speech and comprehension is left to a theory of 'carpentry' that includes a different set of mechanisms and principles (parsing strategies, for instance).

My view is different. Put simply, when it comes to sentences, there are no architects; there are only carpenters. They design as they build, limited only by the materials available to them and by the need to complete their work as quickly and efficiently as possible. Indeed, as I will show, efficiency is *the* driving force behind the design and operation of the computational system for human language. Once identified, its effects can be discerned in the form of syntactic representations, in constraints on coreference, control, agreement, extraction, and contraction, and in the operation of parsing strategies.

My first goal, pursued in the opening chapters of this book, will be to develop a theory of syntactic carpentry that offers satisfying answers to the questions traditionally posed in work on grammatical theory. The particular system that I develop builds and interprets sentences from 'left to right' (i.e., beginning to end), more or less one word at a time. In this respect, it obviously resembles a processor, but I will postpone discussion of its exact status until chapter nine. My focus in earlier chapters will be on the more basic problem of demonstrating that the proposed sentence-building system can meet the sorts of empirical challenges presented by the syntax of natural language.

A great deal of contemporary work in linguistic theory relies primarily on English to illustrate and test ideas and hypotheses. With a few exceptions, I will follow this practice here too, largely for practical reasons (I have a strict page limit). Even with a focus on English though, we can proceed with some confidence, as it is highly unlikely that just one language in the world could have its core properties determined by a processor rather than a grammar. If English (or any other language) works that way, then so must every language—even if it is not initially obvious how the details are to be filled in.

I will use the remainder of this first chapter to discuss in a very preliminary way the design of sentence structure, including the contribution of lexical properties. These ideas are fleshed out in additional detail in chapter two. Chapter three deals with pronominal coreference (binding), chapters four and five with the form and interpretation of infinitival clauses (control and raising), and chapter six with agreement. I turn to *wh* questions in chapter seven and to contraction in chapter eight. Chapters nine and ten examine processing and language acquisition from the perspective developed in the first portion of the book. Some general concluding remarks appear in chapter eleven. As noted in the preface, for those interested in a general exposition of the emergentist idea for syntax, the key chapters are one, three (sections 1 to 3), four, six (sections 1 to 3), eight (sections 1 & 2), and nine through eleven.

Throughout these chapters, my goal will be to measure the prospects of the emergentist approach against the phenomena themselves, and not (directly) against the UG-based approach. A systematic comparison of the two approaches is an entirely different sort of task, made difficult by the existence of many competing theories of Universal Grammar and calling for far more space than is available here. The priority for now lies in outlining and testing an emergentist theory capable of shedding light on the traditional problems of syntactic theory.

3. TWO SYSTEMS

In investigating sentence formation, it is common in linguistics, psychology, and even neurology to posit the existence of two quite different cognitive systems, one dealing primarily with words and the other with combinatorial operations (e.g., Pinker 1994:85, Chomsky 1995:173, Marcus 2001:4, Ullman 2001).[2] Consistent with this tradition, I distinguish here between a conceptual-symbolic system and a computational system.

The conceptual-symbolic system is concerned with symbols (words and morphemes) and the notions that they express. Its most obvious manifestation is a lexicon, or mental dictionary. As such, it is associated with what is sometimes called *declarative* memory, which supports knowledge of facts and events in general (e.g., Ullman 2001:718).

The computational system provides a set of operations for combining lexical items, permitting speakers of a language to construct and understand an unlimited number of sentences, including some that are extraordinarily complex. It corresponds roughly to what we normally think of as syntax, and is arguably an instance of the sort of *procedural* cognition associated with various established motor and cognitive skills (Ullman ibid.).

---

[2]The distinction is not universally accepted. Some psycholinguists reject it (e.g., Bates & Goodman 1999:71) in favor of a single integrated system, as do some linguists (Goldberg 1995:4, Croft 2001:17).

Don't be misled by the term *computational*, which simply means that sentence formation involves the use of operations (such as combination) on symbols (such as words). I am not proposing a computer model of language, although I do believe that such models may be helpful. Nor am I suggesting that English is a 'computer language' in the sense deplored by Edelman (1992:243)—'a set of strings of uninterpreted symbols.'

The conceptual-symbolic and computational systems work together closely. Language could not exist without computational operations, but it is the conceptual-symbolic system that ultimately makes them useful and worthwhile. A brief discussion of how these two systems interact is in order before proceeding.

3.1 The lexicon

A language's lexicon is a repository of information about its symbols—including, on most proposals, information about their category and their combinatorial possibilities. I have no argument with this view,[3] and I do not take it to contradict the central thesis of this book. As I will explain in more detail below, what I object to is the idea that the *computational system* incorporates a grammar—an entirely different matter.

Turning now to a concrete example, let us assume that the verb *carry* has the type of meaning that implies the existence of an entity that does the carrying and of an entity that is carried, both of which are expressed as nominals. Traditional category labels and thematic roles offer a convenient way to represent these facts. (V = verbal; N = nominal; ag = agent; th = theme.)

(1)   *carry*:   V, <N N>   (e.g., *Harry carried the package.*)
              ↑   ag th
         category   ↑
         of the   arguments in
         word   'grid' form

Carry thus contrasts with *hop*, which has the type of meaning that implies a single participant.

(2)   *hop*: V, <N>   (e.g., *Rabbits hop.*)
                    ag

I will refer to the elements implied by a word's meaning as its *arguments* and to the argument-taking category as a *functor*, following the terminological practice common in categorial grammar (e.g., Wood 1993). Hence *carry* is a functor that demands two arguments, while *hop* is a functor that requires a single argument.

---

[3]This is more or less the standard view of the lexicon, and I adopt it for the sake of exposition. There are perhaps alternatives though; see, for instance, Elman (2004).

In accordance with the tradition in categorial grammar (e.g., Steedman 1996, 2000), I assume that functors are 'directional' in that they look either to the left or to the right for their arguments. In English, for example, a verb looks to the left for its first argument and to the right for subsequent arguments, a preposition looks rightward for its nominal argument, and so forth. We can capture these facts by extending a functor's lexical properties as follows, with arrows indicating the direction in which it looks for each argument. (P = preposition; loc = locative.)

(3) a. *carry*: V, <N N>   (e.g., *Harry carried the package.*)
                ag th
                ← →

   b. *hop*: V, <N>   (e.g., *Rabbits hop.*)
                ag
                ←

   c. *on*: P, <N>   (e.g., *on the table*)
                loc
                →

Directionality properties such as these cannot account for all aspects of word order, as we will see in chapter seven. However, they suffice for now and permit us to illustrate in a preliminary way the functioning of the computational system.

3.2 The computational system

By definition, the computational system provides the combinatorial mechanisms that permit sentence formation. But what precisely is the nature of those mechanisms? The standard view is that they include principles of grammar that regulate phenomena such as structure building, coreference, control, agreement, extraction, and so forth. I disagree with this.

As I see it, the computational system contains no grammatical principles and does not even try to build linguistic structure per se. Rather, its primary task is simply to resolve the lexical requirements, or *dependencies*, associated with individual words. Thus, among other things, it must find two nominal arguments for a verb such as *carry* and one nominal argument for *hop*.

The resolution of dependencies is achieved with the help of a *Combine* operation that, in the simplest case, brings together a functor and an adjacent argument,[4] as depicted in (1) for the intransitive sentence *Harvey left*.

---

[4]A combinatorial operation of this type has long been posited in categorial grammar under the name of *functional application* (e.g., Wood 1993:9 and the references cited there). More recently, a similar operation—dubbed *Merge*—has been posited in the Minimalist Program (Chomsky 1995). However, as we will see in the next chapter, Combine can operate on more than just functor-argument pairs.

(1)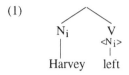

As illustrated here, the resolution of a dependency is indicated by copying the index of the nominal into the verb's argument grid, as in Stowell (1981), Starosta (1994), and Sag & Wasow (1999), among others.[5]

There is nothing particularly 'grammatical' about the Combine operation—it could just as easily be a processing mechanism. The only way to determine its status is to identify more fully its properties and those of the computational system of which it is a part.

The intuition that I wish to develop in this regard is this: the Combine operation is in fact a processing mechanism, and its character can best be understood by recognizing that it is part of a computational system whose operation is subject to the following simple imperative.

(2)   Minimize the burden on working memory.

Following Carpenter, Miyake, & Just (1994), I take working memory to be a pool of operational resources that not only holds representations but also supports computations on those representations. It is, as Lieberman (2000:62) states, 'the neural "computational space" in which the meaning of a sentence is derived.' Jackendoff (2002:200) suggests a related metaphor—'working memory is a dynamic "workbench" or "blackboard" on which processors can cooperate in assembling linguistic structures.'

Some researchers believe that there is a specialized working memory for syntax (e.g., Caplan & Waters 1999, 2001, 2002). Others believe that a single working memory may subserve a wider range of linguistic activities (e.g., Just & Carpenter 1992, Just, Carpenter, & Keller 1996). It has even been suggested that working memory is just an abstraction that allows us to talk about the ability of a network of neurons to process information (e.g., MacDonald & Christiansen 2002).

None of this matters for now. The point is simply that there is an advantage to reducing the burden on working memory, whatever its nature and whatever its capacity, and that the effects of this advantage can be discerned in the way that sentences are built. Let us consider this point in more detail by considering some sample instances of sentence formation.

---

[5]Here and elsewhere, I typically do not use category labels for phrasal categories, since this information is predictable from more general considerations (e.g., O'Grady 1997:312ff, Ninio 1998). A phrase formed by specifying an event's arguments or properties (*eat it*, *run quickly*) still denotes an event and is therefore verbal. (Hence clauses too are verbal projections.) Similarly, a phrase formed by specifying the properties of an object (e.g., *tall building*) still denotes an object and is therefore a nominal.

4. HOW SENTENCES ARE BUILT

An obvious consequence of seeking to minimize the burden on working memory is that the computational system should operate in the most efficient manner possible, promptly resolving dependencies so that they do not have to be held any longer than necessary. This is in fact a standard assumption in work on processing, where it is universally recognized that sentences are built in real time under conditions that favor quickness (e.g., Frazier 1987:561, Hagoort, Brown, & Osterhout 1999:275, Pickering 1999:124).

What this means for the computational system, I propose, is that its operation is constrained by the following simple requirement:

(1)　　*The Efficiency Requirement:*
　　　　Dependencies are resolved at the first opportunity.

No particular significance should be assigned to the term 'efficiency.' 'Promptness,' 'quickness,' or 'expediency' would do just as well. The essential point is simply that dependencies should be resolved rather than held, consistent with the charge to reduce the burden on working memory.

I take the computational system (or at least the part of it that I consider here) to be identical in the relevant respects for both production and comprehension. (A similar position is adopted by Kempen 2000; see also Sag & Wasow 1999:224, Jackendoff 2002:198-203, and Garrett 2000:55-56.) This is not to say that production and comprehension proceed in exactly the same way—clearly they do not (e.g., Wasow 1997, Townsend & Bever 2001:37). The claim is simply that regardless of whether the computational system is creating a sentence or interpreting one, it seeks to complete its work as quickly as possible. This much at least is widely accepted (Hagoort, Brown, & Osterhout 1999:275).

For expository reasons, I typically take the perspective of comprehension in discussing how the computational system goes about the task of sentence formation. This is because comprehension is both arguably less complicated (the task of selecting the appropriate lexical items falls to the speaker) and far better studied (see chapter nine).

Building a simple transitive clause

As a preliminary illustration of how an efficiency driven computational system works, let us consider the formation of the simple sentence *Mary speaks French*, whose verb has the lexical properties summarized below. (I drop thematic role labels where they are irrelevant to the point at hand.)

(2)　　*speak*: V, <N, N>
　　　　　　　　← →

As noted above, the computational system must resolve the verb's dependencies (in the order given in its lexical entry) at the first opportunity. For the sake of concreteness, let us say that an opportunity to resolve an argument dependency arises if the following condition is met:

(3)   An opportunity for the computational system to resolve an argument dependency arises when it encounters a category of the appropriate type in the position stipulated in the functor's lexical entry.

In the case of *Mary speaks French* then, an efficiency driven computational system has no choice but to begin by combining *speak* with *Mary*. The lexical properties of the verb require a nominal argument to the left. The nominal *Mary* occurs in that position, so it must be used to resolve the verb's first argument dependency.

(4)   Step 1: Combination of the verb with its first argument:

N_i V
| $<N_i N>$
Mary   speaks

The computational system then proceeds to resolve the verb's second argument dependency by combining the verb directly with the nominal to its right, giving the result depicted below.[6]

(5)   Step 2: Combination of the verb with its second argument:

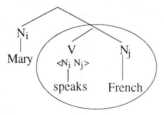

Here again, there is no alternative for the computational system. The verb *speak* seeks a nominal argument to its right. The nominal *French* occurs in that position, so it must be used to resolve the verb's argument dependency.

---

[6]Consistent with the charge to reduce the burden on working memory, the computational system combines the nominal just with the verb, rather than with the phrase consisting of the verb and its first argument.

The status of syntactic representations

The representations produced by our computational system manifest the familiar binary branching design, with the subject higher than the direct object—but not as the result of an a priori grammatical blueprint like the X' schema.[7] Rather, 'syntactic structure' is the byproduct of a sentence formation process that proceeds from left to right, combining a verb with its arguments one at a time at the first opportunity in the manner just illustrated. A sentence's design reflects the way it is built, not the other way around.

Syntactic representations, then, are just a fleeting residual record of how the computational system goes about its work. The structure in (4) exists (for a moment) as a reflex of the fact that the verb combines with the nominal to its left at a particular point in time. And the structure in (5) exists only because the verb then goes on to combine with the nominal to its right.

A more transparent way to represent these facts (category labels aside) might be as follows:

(6)

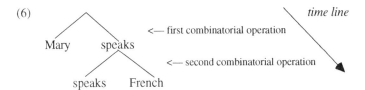

The time line here runs from top to bottom, with each 'constituent' consisting of the functor-argument pair on which the computational system has operated at a particular point in time. This in turn points toward the following *routine*—a frequently executed sequence of operations. (The symbol $\perp$ indicates combination.)

(7)   Computational routine for transitive clauses:

   i. $N_1 \perp V$

      (combination of a transitive verb with the nominal to its left)

  ii. $V \perp N_2$

      (combination of a transitive verb with the nominal to its right)

      In brief: $N_1 \perp V$; $V \perp N_2$

---

[7]The X' schema, a staple of traditional work on Universal Grammar, stipulates the following architecture for phrase structure.

(i)

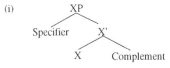

More recently, the effects of the X' schema are derived from more general and more abstract principles (e.g., Chomsky 1995).

Computational routines are not just grammatical rules under another name. Routines correspond to real-time *processes*, whereas rules describe *patterns* of elements (Jackendoff 2002:57). Rules say what the structure is (ibid.: 31); routines say how it is built. These are not the same thing, as the literature on grammatical analysis itself repeatedly emphasizes (e.g., Jackendoff 2002:197).

As we will see in more detail in chapter ten, the emergence and strengthening of routines not only facilitates processing, it sheds light on the nature of the developmental changes associated with language acquisition.

A second example

Consider now a second example, this one involving a motion-denoting verb.

(8)   Jerry dashed to safety.

I assume that *dash* has the lexical properties depicted in (9); 'DIR' stands for 'directional.'

(9)   *dash*: V, $<N\ P_{DIR}>$
                  $\leftarrow\ \rightarrow$

Consistent with the idea that selection is a 'head-to-head' relation (Baltin 1989:6, Chomsky 1995:173), the verb's second argument in (8) is not the prepositional phrase, but rather the preposition *to*, whose lexical properties are summarized in (10).

(10)   *to*: P, $<N>$
                  $\rightarrow$

The computational system will therefore proceed as follows. (A check mark indicates resolution of the verb's dependency on its prepositional argument.)

(11)   Step 1: Combination of *dash*   Step 2: Combination of *dash*
            with its first argument: with its second argument:

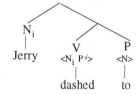

Step 3: Combination of *to* with its argument:

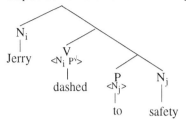

The computational routine for forming intransitive motion clauses can therefore be summarized as follows:

(12) i. $N_1 \perp V$

 (combination of the verb with the nominal to its left)

 ii. $V \perp P$

 (combination of the verb with the preposition to its right)

 iii. $P \perp N_2$

 (combination of the preposition with the nominal to its right)

 In brief: $N_1 \perp V;\ V \perp P;\ P \perp N_2$

Examples such as these illustrate only the bare workings of the computational system with regard to structure building, I realize, but the picture will be extended somewhat in chapter two and developed in more detail in later chapters.

Word order again

There is reason to think that the directionality properties of the functors we have been considering are not arbitrary. As noted by Hawkins (1990, 1994), the direction in which a functor looks for its argument(s) is designed to reduce the space between it and the heads of the various phrases with which it must combine. Thus it makes sense for languages such as English to have prepositions rather than postpositions, since this allows the head of the PP to occur adjacent to the verb that selects it.

(13) **V [P** NP] (e.g., *go to Paris*)
 (cf. **V** [NP **P**])

By the same reasoning, it makes sense for a verb-final language such as Korean to have postpositions rather than prepositions.

(14)   [NP **P**]   **V**   (e.g., Korean *Paris-ey ka*, lit. 'Paris-to go')
         (cf. [**P** NP] **V**)

Although this suggests that lexical properties can be shaped by processing considerations (a view with which I concur), this is not my concern here. My point is that the computational system functions in the most efficient manner *permitted by the lexical properties of the words on which it operates.* If those properties facilitate processing, so much the better. If they do not, then the computational system still does the best it can with the hand that it is dealt, seeking to resolve whatever dependencies it encounters at the first opportunity.

5. THE PROGRAM

The existence of an intimate connection between syntax and processing is not in doubt. There is a long tradition of work that proposes processing mechanisms for production and/or comprehension that complement particular syntactic theories (e.g., Levelt 1989 and Frazier & Clifton 1996, among many others). In addition, it is frequently suggested that particular grammatical phenomena may be motivated by processing considerations of various sorts (e.g., Givón 1979, Berwick & Weinberg 1984, Kluender & Kutas 1993, Hawkins 1999, Newmeyer 2003a, and many more).

It has even been proposed that the grammatical operations of particular syntactic theories can be used for the left-to-right processing of sentence structure—see MacWhinney (1987) for Dependency Grammar, Pritchett (1992) for Government and Binding theory, Steedman (1996, 2000) for Categorial Grammar, Kempson, Meyer-Viol, & Gabbay (2001) for Dynamic Syntax, Hausser (2001) for Left-Associative Grammar, Sag & Wasow (1999:218ff) for Head-driven Phrase Structure Grammar, and Phillips (1996) and Weinberg (1999) for the Minimalist Program.

These approaches differ from each other in many ways, including the precise nature of the grammatical mechanisms that they posit. Steedman draws on the resources and representations of Categorial Grammar, whereas Phillips employs those of the Minimalist Program. In Pritchett's theory, the processor relies on grammatical principles that exist independently of the left-to-right algorithms responsible for structure building. In the theories put forward by Kempson et al. and Hausser, on the other hand, the grammatical rules are designed to operate in a left-to-right manner and are therefore fully integrated into the processor.

My proposal goes one step further in suggesting, essentially, that there is no grammar at all; an efficiency driven processor is responsible for everything. Methodologically, this is an attractive idea, since processors are necessary in a way that grammars are not. There could be no cognition or perception without a way to process sensory input, but the case for grammar is not so straightforward.

In a way, the existence of conventional grammar has already been challenged by the Minimalist Program, with its emphasis on simple operations (Move, Merge, Agree) that are subject to conditions of locality and economy. Indeed, Marantz (1995:380) optimistically declares that minimalism marks 'the end of syntax.'

I am skeptical about this for two reasons. First, the notions in terms of which locality and economy are implemented in the Minimalist Program and its predecessors (e.g., governing category, bounding node, cycle, phase, and so forth) are rooted in grammatical theory, not processing. Second, it is far from clear that the Minimalist Program has succeeded in putting an end to syntax. As Newmeyer (2003b:588) observes:

> ...as many distinct UG principles are being proposed today as were proposed twenty years ago. I would go so far as to claim that no paper has ever been published within the general rubric of the minimalist program that does not propose some new UG principle or make some new stipulation (however well motivated empirically) about grammatical operations that does not follow from the bare structure of the [Minimalist Program].

As noted at the outset, the particular reductionist idea that I am pursuing is part of the larger research program known as *emergentism*—so-called because it holds that the properties of language 'emerge' from the interaction of more basic, non-linguistic forces. This calls for an additional comment.

Emergentism has come to be associated with connectionism, an approach to the study of the mind that seeks to model learning and cognition in terms of networks of neuron-like units (e.g., Elman 1999, Christiansen & Chater 2001, Palmer-Brown, Tepper, & Powell 2002). In its more extreme forms, connectionism rejects the existence of the sorts of symbolic representations (including syntactic structure) that have played a central role in work on human language. (For a critique of this sort of 'eliminativist' program, see Marcus 1998, 2001. Smolensky 1999 and Steedman 1999 discuss ways to reconcile traditional symbolic approaches to language with connectionism.)

I accept the traditional view that linguistic phenomena are best understood in terms of operations on symbolic representations.[8] At the same time though, I reject the standard view of linguistic representations, which attributes their properties to autonomous grammatical principles, such as those associated with Universal Grammar in the Principles and Parameters tradition. On the view I propose, these and other properties of language follow from something deeper and more general—the efficiency driven character of the computational system which is the focus of this book.

---

[8] However, I leave open the possibility that these representations might be 'symbolic approximations' in the sense of Smolensky (1999:594)—that is, abstract, higher-level descriptions that approximate the patterns of neuronal activation that connectionist approaches seek to model.

6. CONCLUSION

If the approach we have been considering is on the right track, then the syntax of natural language reflects a compromise between two sorts of demands.

On the one hand, the computational system must combine symbols in a way that respects their lexical properties (e.g., transitive verbs look to the left for their first argument and to the right for their second argument). On the other hand, it must deal with the fact that spoken language unfolds on a temporal axis that requires words to be produced and perceived one at a time, subject to significant constraints on working memory.

The human mind has arguably hit on a reasonable compromise for dealing with these demands, which is simply to resolve dependencies at the first opportunity, in accordance with the Efficiency Requirement.

This in turn has various consequences for the way language is. For instance, sentences that are formed by an efficiency driven computational system end up with a binary branching syntactic representation in which the subject is higher than the direct object. Such properties are important, but they are not grammatical primitives. Rather, they emerge from the way in which the computational system carries out its responsibilities—by combining words as efficiently as possible one at a time. A sentence's design reflects the way it is built, not the other way around. There are no architects, just carpenters.

The question that now arises has to do with just how far this can be taken. Quite far, I believe. As I will show in the next several chapters, the emergentist approach to syntax not only sheds light on the core properties of phenomena such as coreference, control, agreement, contraction, and extraction, it does so in a way that essentially subsumes the theory of sentence structure under the theory of sentence processing. This in turn yields promising insights into how language works and how it is acquired.

Before these matters can be considered though, it is first necessary to examine certain aspects of structure building in a bit more detail. Chapter two is devoted to these questions.

Chapter 2

More on Structure Building

1. INTRODUCTION

Although the primary focus of this book is on 'second-order' phenomena such as coreference, control, agreement, contraction, and extraction, chapter one raised a number of points relating to structure building that call for additional comment and development. I will briefly discuss three potentially relevant issues.

The first of these issues relates to the status of the representations produced by the computational system. In the examples considered in chapter one, representations were more or less isomorphic with traditional tree structures. It turns out, however, that this is not always the case and that the fleeting residual record that the computational system leaves behind as it forms sentences sometimes departs in interesting and important ways from the tree structures associated with more traditional approaches to syntax.

A second matter involves the precise manner in which the computational system goes about resolving argument dependencies. When adjacent words enter into a functor–argument relationship with each other, as happens in a subject–verb pattern such as *John left*, matters are straightforward—combination takes places, and the argument dependency is resolved immediately. However, things do not always work this way. There is no functor–argument relationship between *John* and *quickly* in *John quickly left*, for example, or between *a* and *tall* in *a tall man*. How exactly does the computational system proceed in such cases?

A third point has to do with what happens if the computational system errs at some point in the sentence formation process. Given the simplicity of the structure-building mechanism, this is a real possibility, raising important questions about whether and how the computational system can recover from missteps that it might make.

Although each of these issues is of considerable inherent interest, they are somewhat tangential to the main themes of this book. Readers interested in moving forward immediately are invited to proceed to chapter three.

2. ANOTHER LOOK AT REPRESENTATIONS

In the case of the sentences we have considered so far, the computational system builds representations that resemble familiar tree structures. To a certain extent, this is a positive result, since it provides an emergentist computational explanation for various basic features of sentence structure, including their binary constituency and the structural prominence of subject arguments—properties that were first observed in the pregenerative era (e.g., Fries 1952:264ff, Gleason 1955:128ff).

On the other hand, it is important not to lose sight of the fact that the approach I adopt rejects the existence of traditional syntactic structure. The representations that I have been using are not grammatical objects per se—they are just residual records of the manner in which sentences are built by the computational system as it seeks to combine words and resolve dependencies at the first opportunity.

If this is so, then we might expect there to be cases in which the representations left by the computational system depart in significant ways from traditional tree structures. One place where this appears to happen involves the formation of sentences containing a ditransitive (or 'double object') verb such as *teach*.

2.1 Double object patterns

According to widely held assumptions, *teach* has three nominal arguments—an agent, a goal, and a theme, arranged in that order in its argument grid (e.g., Hoekstra 1991, Radford 1997:377).

(1)   *teach*: V <N N N>
                    ag go th

The computational system builds the sentence *John taught Mary French* by combining the verb with its arguments one at a time in the sequence specified in its grid—agent first, then goal, then theme.

(2)   Step 1: Combination of the verb with its first argument (the agent):

N_i V
  | <N_i N N>
 | |
John   taught
(agent)

Step 2: Combination of the verb with its second argument (the goal):

N_i
  |
John   V N_j
     <N_i N_j N> |
         |
       taught   Mary
                    (goal)

Step 3: Combination of the verb with its third argument (the theme):

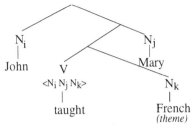

A striking feature of the structure produced in this final step is that it contains a 'discontinuous constituent'—the nonadjacent words (*taught* and *French*) form a phrase.

As the steps above illustrate, this outcome is a consequence of building sentences by means of a linear computational procedure that combines a functor with its arguments one by one, as they are encountered. Thus the representations in (2) capture the fact that the verb combines with its first argument (*John*), then with its second argument (*Mary*), and finally with its third argument (*French*)—in that order. (Because the sentence formation process takes place in real time, it follows that *John* precedes *Mary* and that *Mary* precedes *French*.)

The combinatorial operations that take place here can be represented even more transparently as follows, with each of the relevant functor-argument pairs depicted in sequence of occurrence.

(3)

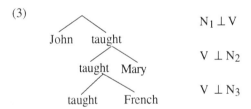

But is this the right computational history for the sentence? That is, are sentences containing ditransitive verbs really built in this way? If they are, there should be independent evidence that the verb and its third argument form a phrase in the predicted manner. One such piece of evidence comes from idioms.

Evidence from idioms

Idioms are essentially pieces of sentences that have been preserved as complex lexical entries with a meaning that is not predictable from the meaning of their component parts. On the structural side, idioms manifest a potentially helpful property—there is a very strong tendency for single-argument idioms to consist of the verb and its innermost or lowest argument (O'Grady 1998). Thus there are countless idioms consisting of a transitive verb and its object argument (*hit the road, bite the dust, lose it*), but virtually none consisting of a transitive verb and its subject (e.g., Marantz 1984:27ff).

Returning now to ditransitive verbs, our analysis of the double object pattern makes a straightforward prediction: there should be idioms consisting of the verb and its third argument (the theme), parallel to the phrase *taught (x) French* in (2). This seems to be exactly right—the idiom *teach X a lesson* 'make x see that s/he is wrong' has just this form, as do many other idiomatic expressions (Hudson 1992, O'Grady 1998).

(4)   give X a hard time   lend X a hand
      give X a piece of one's mind   promise X the moon
      give X a wide berth   read X the riot act
      give X the cold shoulder   show X the door
      give X the creeps   show X the light
      give X the green light   show X the ropes
      give X the shirt off one's back   teach X a thing or two
      give X the slip   tell X a thing or two
      give X X's due   tell X where to get off
      give X X's walking papers   throw X a curve
      etc.

In contrast, idioms consisting of a ditransitive verb and just its second argument (the goal) seem not to exist (Hudson 1992, O'Grady 1998).

This fit between idioms and structure suggests that the computational system does in fact operate in the proposed way, combining the verb with its arguments one at a time in the manner illustrated in (2) and (3).

Evidence from negative polarity

Additional evidence for the structure of double object patterns comes from so-called 'c-command[1] asymmetries,' including those involving negative polarity items such as *any*.

A defining feature of negative polarity items is that they must be licensed by a higher element in the syntactic representation, usually a negative word such as *no* or *not* (e.g., Adger & Quer 2001:112). The sentences in (5) illustrate the phenomenon in simple transitive sentences.

(5) a.   The negative is structurally higher than the polarity item:
         No one saw *anything*.

---

[1] I use this term for the sake of descriptive convenience only; it has no role in the theory I propose. One element c-commands another if it is higher in the syntactic representation. (More technically, X c-commands Y if the first phrase above X contains Y.)

b. The negative is not structurally higher than the polarity item:
    *Anyone saw nothing.

The acceptability of the (a) sentence in contrast to its (b) counterpart confirms that a
transitive verb's first argument is higher than its second argument, consistent with
the sort of representations we have been building. For example:

(6)

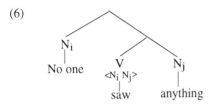

Interestingly, as Barss & Lasnik (1986) note, comparable asymmetries are
found between the verb's second and third arguments in 'double object'
constructions.

(7) a. I told no one anything.
    b. *I told anyone nothing.

In these sentences, an element in the second argument position can license a
negative polarity item in the third argument position—but not vice versa. This
suggests that the second argument is structurally more prominent than the third,
exactly as we predict.

Asymmetries involving idioms and negative polarity constitute genuine puzzles
for syntactic theory and have helped fuel the rush toward ever more abstract
grammatical analyses. An example of this is Larson's (1988) 'layered VP,' which
came to be widely accepted both in Government and Binding theory and in the
Minimalist Program. The example below is based on Hoekstra's (1991) adaptation.

(8)

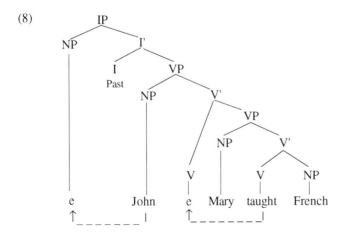

As depicted here, the verb's second argument is more prominent than the third, consistent with the facts involving negative polarity and idioms. Subsequent movement operations, indicated by arrows, give the correct linear order. (See also Kayne 1994.)

In fact, though, there is another explanation for these asymmetries. As we have seen, they appear to reflect the way in which an efficiency driven linear computational system does its work, resolving a functor's dependencies by combining it with its arguments one at a time, from left to right, at the first opportunity.

2.2 Other patterns

If the analysis that I have proposed for double object patterns is right, then similar effects should be found in other patterns as well. In particular, we would expect to find evidence that in any pattern of the form Verb–X–Y, the verb should combine first with X and then with Y, yielding a representation in which X is structurally higher than Y.

(1)   Step 1:   Step 2:

This seems to be right for a range of patterns, including prepositional datives, instrumentals, locatives, and time expressions. As the examples below illustrate, for instance, a negative in the position of X can license a negative polarity item in the position of Y in all of these patterns (Larson 1988, Stroik 1990, Hoekstra 1991).

(2)   Prepositional dative pattern:
        Harry said *nothing* [to *anyone*].

(3)   Instrumental pattern:
        The doctor treated *no one* [with *any* unapproved drugs].

(4)   Locative pattern:
        He said *nothing* [at *any* of the meetings].

(5)   Temporal pattern:
        Jerry said *nothing* [at *any* time during his visit].

This is just what one would expect if the verb combines first with the argument to its immediate right and then with the element to the right of that argument, as depicted in (1).

Once again, facts that seem mysterious and appear to call for an exotic analysis are emergent. They follow from the manner in which the computational system goes about resolving dependencies—from left to right and one step at a time, consistent with the Efficiency Requirement.

3. COMBINE AND RESOLVE

In the sorts of sentences considered so far in this book, the functor and its argument(s) have occurred in a continuous string, permitting resolution of dependencies without delay. Such examples make it difficult to discern that two separate operations are involved here. The first, which we have called Combine, brings two words together. By itself though, this does not resolve an argument dependency; it simply creates the conditions under which this can happen. The actual *Resolve* operation, whose effects we have been representing by index copying, involves matching the nominal with the corresponding argument requirement in the functor's grid. For instance:

(1)   Input: Combine: Resolve:

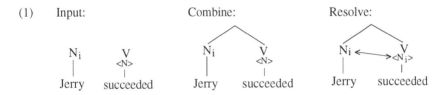

In this and many other examples, Combine and Resolve apply in tandem, making it difficult to distinguish their separate effects. But this is not always the case, as we will see next.

3.1 Combine without Resolve

The sentence *Jerry quickly succeeded* offers an instructive puzzle for the approach to sentence building that we have been pursuing in that its first two words are a noun and an adverb, neither of which exhibits a dependency on the other. (The nominal has no arguments, and the adverb seeks a verbal argument.[2]) How is the computational system to proceed in such cases?

There are two options—either hold the nominal and the adverb in working memory while awaiting some future opportunity to start building the sentence, or combine the two immediately even though no dependency can be resolved. I propose that the computational system adopts the latter option, and that the sentence is built as follows.

---

[2]Recall that I use the term *argument* to refer to any expression required by a functor (e.g., Wood 1993:8), not just nominals that carry a thematic role.

(2)   Step 1: Combination of the nominal and the adverb; no dependencies are resolved at this point:

Step 2: Combination of the verb with the adverb; resolution of the adverb's dependency on a verbal category: (I return shortly to the question of how the verb's argument dependency is resolved.)

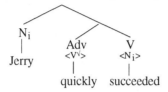

What are we to make of the fact that the computational system initially combines two words—a noun and an adverb—that bear no semantic relationship to each other? In particular, how can this lighten the load on working memory?

A long-standing assumption in work on information processing is that one of the ways to minimize the burden on working memory is to structure the input as expeditiously as possible. In the words of Frazier & Clifton (1996:21), the processor 'must quickly structure material to preserve it in a limited capacity memory' (see also Deacon 1997:292-293 & 337 and Frazier 1998:125). Immediate combination of adjacent elements is nothing if not an instance of quick structuring.

In addition, by proceeding in this way, the computational system begins to build the sort of hierarchically structured binary representation that is eventually necessary anyhow. As the representations in (2) indicate, a strict adherence to the principle of immediate combination, even when no argument dependency is resolved, yields precisely the right syntactic representation in the end.

Interestingly, there appears to be phonological evidence that the computational system does in fact operate in this manner.

Some evidence from phonology

A key assumption underlying my view of phonology is that phonological operations take place in real time, as the words making up a sentence combine with each other. On this view, assimilatory processes are iconic, reflecting the phonological merger that accompanies syntactic combination.

Take, for example, the process of flapping that converts a /t/ into a [D] when it occurs intervocalically in English (e.g., Bybee & Scheibman 1999, Gregory, Raymond, Bell, Fosler-Lussier, & Jurafsky 1999).

(3)   t —> D / V_V

The effects of this process are widely attested not only within words (as in *hitter*), but also across word boundaries.

(4)   right arm (pronounced 'righ[D]arm')

Clearly, we want to say that combination of *right* and *arm* creates the conditions (V_V) under which flapping can apply.

Now consider a sentence such as (5), in which the /t/ at the end of the subject nominal can be flapped.

(5)   **It** actually worked. (pronounced 'I[D]actually')

The obvious explanation for this is that combination of *it* and *actually* creates the conditions for flapping, just as the proposed analysis leads us to expect.

(6)   tree diagram: N_i (It) and Adv (actually)   ← flapping takes place here

N_i Adv

It   actually

A common morphophonological phenomenon illustrates the same point. As is well known, the indefinite article in English has two allomorphs—*an* when the next word begins with a vowel and *a* when it begins with a consonant. The alternation is completely straightforward when it involves determiner–noun juxtapositions, as in *an ox* versus *a horse*, since determiners clearly combine with nouns to form a phrase.

But what about patterns such as *an old car* versus *a blue car*, in which the first segment of the adjective dictates the form of the determiner, although neither is an argument of the other? Intuitively, we want to say that the determiner combines with the adjective as the sentence is being built, and that this is why the form of the determiner is sensitive to the adjective's initial segment. The proposed computational system captures this intuition by immediately combining the determiner and the adjective, as depicted below.

(7)   Step 1: Combination of the   Step 2: Combination of the
       determiner and the adjective: adjective and the noun:

Det   A

an   old

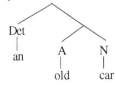

Det

an   A   N

         old   car

3.2 Feature passing

Returning now to the sentence *Jerry quickly succeeded*, there is still a question to address—how is the nominal able to resolve the verb's argument dependency? Evidently, there must be a way other than direct combination to link a functor to its argument, a further indication that Resolve is distinct from Combine.

The simplest assumption seems to be that the verb's argument dependency can be passed upward through the previously formed representation to the point where it makes contact with the required nominal. I will refer to this as *feature passing*. (The terms *inheritance* and *percolation* have also been used for this sort of operation.)

(1)

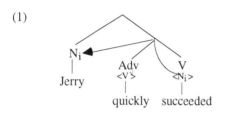

This is obviously a complication, and it might well be 'better' if English adverbs could not occur preverbally (i.e., if they could not look to the right for their verbal argument). However, as noted in chapter one (p. 12), there is no requirement that lexical properties facilitate the operation of the computational system. They often do so of course, but this is not necessary—the lexicon is primarily concerned with concepts and contrasts, not efficiency.[3]

Efficiency *is* the primary concern of the computational system though, and the computational system does what it is supposed to do, even in subject–adverb–verb sentences. The adverb's dependency on a verb is resolved the instant the two elements combine, and the verb then immediately resolves its argument dependency with the help of feature passing. There are no delays, and both dependencies are resolved at the first opportunity permitted by the lexical properties of the elements involved. As always, the computational system plays the hand that it is dealt in the most efficient manner possible.

4. SELF-CORRECTION OF ERRORS

A computational system as simple as the one I have proposed will encounter many problems as it seeks to form and interpret the sentences of a language. This is to be expected. After all, it is not a grammatical system, and it has no access to grammatical principles. The crucial question has to do with whether errors can be uncovered and corrected over the course of time.

---

[3]By permitting preverbal adverbs, English is able to express the subtle semantic contrast exemplified by the difference between *John quickly spoke* (= 'John was quick to start speaking') and *John spoke quickly* (= 'John spoke at a rapid rate'); see Bolinger (1952), Sangster (1982), and Costa (1997) for discussion.

A simple sentence illustrates the challenge.

(1)   Friends of John arrived.

Working from left to right, the computational system will first form the phrase *friends of John*.

(2) a.   Combination of *friends* and *of*:   b.   Combination of *of* and *John*:

                                       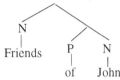

So far, so good, but what prevents the computational system from combining the verb with just the nominal *John* rather than with the larger phrase *friends of John*?

(3)

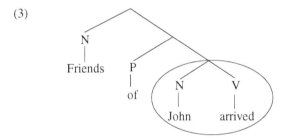

This sort of mistake would be unlikely in a grammar-based system of sentence building, but it is a real possibility in the system I propose.[4] How can such an error be uncovered and corrected?

One possibility is that sentences formed in the manner of (3) leave no role for the nominal *friends*. It ends up functioning as neither an argument nor a modifier; it is simply superfluous. Although this sort of anomaly is traditionally addressed via grammatical constraints that require nominals to carry a thematic role or Case, a more general solution is perhaps possible.

In particular, errors like this may be detected and subsequently avoided because superfluous elements are not tolerated—they frivolously *add* to the burden on working memory and are thus fundamentally incompatible with the mission of the computational system, which is to minimize this burden. (A similar intuition is expressed in Chomsky's (1995:130) Principle of Full Interpretation.)

---

[4]In fact, such errors may underlie some of the comprehension miscues associated with agrammatism (Caplan & Futter 1986:125) and child language (Booth, MacWhinney, & Harasaki 2000:991), in which the nominal *the man* in (i) is interpreted as the subject of *climb*.

(i)   The bear [that chased the man] climbed a tree.

A somewhat different problem arises in sentences such as (4).

(4)   They put the books [on shelves].

Here the PP *on shelves* must combine with the verb *put*, which requires a locative argument. In other superficially similar sentences, on the other hand, the prepositional phrase combines with the noun to its left. Thus *by Hemingway* in (5) is interpreted as a modifier of *books*, not *read*.

(5)   They read the books [by Hemingway].

In still other sentences, the PP can combine with either the noun or the verb, giving the familiar ambiguity illustrated in (6).

(6)   They saw the men [with the binoculars].

How can the computational system ensure a correct result in each case?

Once again, the answer lies in what happens if the right operation is not executed. Unless the prepositional phrase combines with the verb in (4), the verb's argument requirements will not be fully satisfied. And unless it combines with the nominal in (5), the sentence will not have a pragmatically plausible interpretation.

In sum, the computational system *will* err from time to time, even on simple sentences. (I discuss more complex 'garden path' sentences in chapter nine.) However, this need not be a serious problem, provided that errors have detectable consequences—a nominal is superfluous, a dependency is left unresolved, an interpretation is implausible, and so forth.

The detection of such flaws helps eliminate faulty computational routines and strengthens those that avoid such problems (e.g., routines that combine a verb with the entire nominal phrase to its left rather than with just the nearest N, routines that satisfy argument requirements, and so on). Played out over time, self-correcting modifications like these contribute to the emergence of a smoothly functioning computational system, permitting it to do the work that might otherwise fall to grammatical principles. We will return to this theme many times in the chapters that lie ahead.

5. CONCLUSION

Despite its spare simplicity, the computational system that we have been considering is arguably a plausible engine for sentence building. In particular, it does the two things that one expects of a system of this sort—it forms sentences, and it assigns them a structure.

The structures are not always conventional, it is true. Because they arise as a record of the step-by-step operation of the computational system, they include both temporary constituents (e.g., *it* initially combines with *actually* in *It actually works*) and discontinuous phrases (e.g., *teach French* in *teach Mary French*). Crucially, however, there is independent support for proceeding in this way, as we have already seen and as we will see in more detail in later chapters.

There is much more that needs to be said about how sentences of various types are formed and about the workings of the combinatorial system. However, I will put these matters aside for now, so that we can begin our investigation of the phenomena that constitute the principal concern of this book. I will begin by examining constraints on coreference.

Chapter 3

Pronoun Interpretation

1. INTRODUCTION

As I see it, sentence formation is based on a simple idea: words drawn from the lexicon introduce dependencies which the computational system proceeds to resolve in the most efficient manner possible—at the first opportunity.

Thus far, I have focused on dependencies that are resolved by the combination of two categories (for instance, an intransitive verb with a nominal argument). A quite different sort of dependency relation is illustrated in (1) and (2), where anaphors such as the reflexive pronoun *himself* and the reciprocal pronoun *each other* depend on another nominal for their interpretation. I will henceforth refer to this relation as a *referential dependency*. (The more traditional term is *binding*.)

(1)   Harry overestimates himself. (himself = Harry)

(2)   The boys admire each other. (each other = the boys)

For the sake of exposition, I will use letters drawn from the end of the alphabet (x, y, z) to represent a referential dependency. I indicate that a referential dependency has been resolved by replacing its index with the index of the nominal that determines its interpretation, as illustrated in (3).

(3) $Harry_i$ overestimates $himself_{x \rightarrow i}$.

The central theme of this chapter is that the familiar constraints on the resolution of referential dependencies, including the 'binding principles' of traditional grammatical theory, simply follow from efficiency considerations. In other words, the constraints are emergent—they reflect the operation of more basic, nonlinguistic forces.

I will begin my discussion by considering the interpretation of *anaphors*—that is, reflexive and reciprocal pronouns that require a nearby antecedent. Section 3 focuses on the interpretation of 'plain pronouns' such as *he* and *him*, which are typically in complementary distribution with anaphors. Section 4 investigates the conditions under which anaphors and plain pronouns can occur in apparent free variation, while section 5 deals with patterns in which neither type of pronoun is permitted.

2. HOW ANAPHORS ARE INTERPRETED

It has been believed for several decades that the resolution of referential dependencies is sensitive to two factors, one involving prominence and the other involving locality. Let us begin with a preliminary characterization of each, so as to better understand the descriptive and explanatory challenges that an emergentist account must confront.

2.1 The classic account of binding

As the contrast between the following sentences shows, an anaphor in English typically must be bound—that is, have a more prominent (i.e., 'c-commanding') antecedent.

(1)   Anaphor with a c-commanding antecedent:
        The men$_i$ admire themselves$_i$.

(2)   Anaphor with a non-c-commanding antecedent:
    a. *[A friend of *the men$_i$*] admires themselves$_i$.
    b. *[*The men's$_i$* friend] admires themselves$_i$.

In (1), the anaphor in direct object position gets its reference from the structurally more prominent subject. In the unacceptable sentences in (2), in contrast, the intended antecedent is embedded inside the subject phrase and hence not more prominent than the anaphor. Let us temporarily use the following generalization to describe these contrasts.

(3)   *The Prominence Constraint:*
        An anaphor requires a c-commanding antecedent.

The interpretation of anaphors in English is also sensitive to locality considerations. As illustrated in the following sentences, an anaphor normally requires an antecedent in the same minimal clause or noun phrase.

(4) a. Antecedent in the same minimal clause:
        Mary thinks that [*the boys$_i$* admire themselves$_i$].

    b. Antecedent outside the minimal clause:
        *The boys$_i$ think that [Mary admires themselves$_i$].

(5) a. Antecedent in the same noun phrase:
        Mary dismissed [*Bob's$_i$* criticism of himself$_i$].

    b. Antecedent outside the noun phrase:
        *Bob$_i$ dismissed [Mary's criticism of himself$_i$].

As a first and temporary approximation, we can describe these contrasts with the help of the following generalization. (For now, we can take a *domain* to be the smallest clause or noun phrase containing the anaphor.)

(6)   *The Locality Constraint:*
        An anaphor requires an antecedent in the same domain.

Taken together, the Prominence Constraint and the Locality Constraint give something like the traditional version of Principle A (cf. Chomsky 1981:188).

(7)   *Principle A:*
        An anaphor requires a c-commanding antecedent in the same minimal domain.

My goal is to derive the generalizations embodied in Principle A from more fundamental nongrammatical considerations, consistent with the emergentist program that we are pursuing.

2.2 How referential dependencies are resolved

What does the computational system outlined in chapter one have to say about coreference? I will begin by describing the basic system and illustrating its operation with a few simple examples. Subsequent sections offer a more in-depth consideration of how the emergentist theory can contribute to our understanding of binding and the constraints to which it is subject.

As we have seen, pronouns introduce referential dependencies, which are represented as indices (x, y, z) on the pronominal element. The key idea underlying my proposal is that the syntax of coreference emerges from the manner in which these dependencies are resolved by the computational system.

Our starting point must be the Efficiency Requirement, which guides the functioning of the computational system for language.

(1)   *The Efficiency Requirement:*
        Dependencies must be resolved at the first opportunity.

For the sake of concreteness, let us assume that an opportunity to resolve a referential dependency arises under the following circumstances.

(2)   An opportunity for the computational system to resolve a pronoun's referential dependency arises when it encounters the index of another nominal.

Consider in this regard the prototypical pattern of coreference found in a sentence such as *Harvey admires himself.*

The structure-building process begins with the combinatorial operation depicted in (3), which resolves the verb's first argument dependency. The index of *Harvey* is then copied into the first argument slot in the verb's grid, in accordance with the practice adopted in chapter one.

(3)
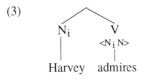

Next comes combination of the verb with its second argument, the reflexive pronoun *himself.*

(4)
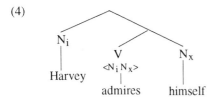

This resolves the verb's second argument dependency, but leaves untouched the referential dependency associated with the reflexive pronoun (represented by the index *x*). Intuitively, this dependency must be resolved by the index associated with *Harvey*. But how and when is this accomplished?

Because the computational system encounters the index of *Harvey* in the grid of *admire* at the point at which it combines the reflexive pronoun with the verb, resolution of the referential dependency can and should be immediate.

(5)
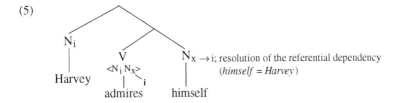

Given the Efficiency Requirement, there is no alternative. The computational system has the opportunity to resolve the pronoun's referential dependency when it encounters the index of *Harry* in the grid of the verb, so it must do so. Anything else would be inefficient.[1]

Feature mismatch

Now consider what happens in an anomalous sentence such as the following.

(6) *Boys admire herself.

The intuition here is that 'efficiency' and 'opportunity' are understood in a totally procedural manner. Consistent with the notion of opportunity outlined in (2), the computational system is compelled to resolve the reflexive pronoun's referential dependency the instant it encounters the index of another nominal, without regard for the end result. At the point at which *herself* combines with the verb in (6) then, the index of *boys* in the grid of *admire* triggers an attempt to resolve the referential dependency.

(7)

N_i | Boys

V $<N_i N_x>$ $_i$ | admire

N_x → i; attempt to resolve the referential dependency | herself

If the referential dependency is resolved in this way, a semantic anomaly arises due to the gender and number mismatch—*boys* is masculine plural, and *herself* is feminine singular. On the other hand, if the referential dependency is *not* resolved in this way, the Efficiency Requirement is violated. Either way, the sentence is unacceptable.

A case of referential ambiguity

Next consider the following sentence, in which the reflexive pronoun has two interpretations—one in which *himself* refers to Marvin and one in which it refers to John.[2]

---

[1] This is not the same thing as requiring that a reflexive pronoun be an argument of the same predicate as its antecedent, as in the 'co-argument analysis' put forward by Pollard & Sag (1992), for example. In (i), the reflexive pronoun is a pure adjunct—yet it is still coreferential with the subject.

(i) John dozes off himself at times, so he shouldn't criticize others for having a nap.

At the point where *himself* combines with the verb, the index of *John* is available to resolve its referential dependency. The Efficiency Requirement therefore permits no other interpretation.

[2] The first interpretation is brought to the fore by adding 'so he wouldn't forget what John looked like,' and the second interpretation is highlighted by adding 'so John would realize how ridiculous he looked.'

(8)   Marvin$_i$ described John$_j$ to himself$_{i/j}$.

Just before the reflexive pronoun makes its appearance, the sentence has the structure depicted in (9), with the indices of *Marvin* and *John* both already recorded in the verb's argument grid.

(9)

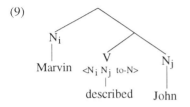

Because a reflexive pronoun's referential dependency is resolved by an index in the verb's grid (rather than by a nominal per se), both interpretive options (*i* and *j*) are equally available at the point at which *to himself* combines with the verb. The fact that the nominal *Marvin* is farther from the reflexive than is the nominal *John* is not relevant here; what matters is that the indices of both nominals occur together in the grid of the verb with which the pronoun combines.

(10)   Marvin$_i$ described John$_j$ [to himself$_x$].
          <N$_i$ N$_j$> |
         ↑_____|

From a computational perspective then, the sentence is ambiguous; contextual considerations alone decide between the two potential antecedents—exactly the right result.

2.3 How prominence and locality fall out

The computational approach to referential dependencies sheds important light on the nature of traditional constraints on the interpretation of reflexive pronouns, particularly those involving prominence and locality. Let us consider each in turn.

Prominence

As previously noted, the reflexive pronoun in a sentence such as (1) can refer to Mary's sister, but not to Mary.

(1)   [Mary's$_i$ sister]$_j$ overestimates herself$_{*i/j}$.

This contrast has traditionally been interpreted as evidence that the antecedent must be structurally higher (the Prominence Constraint that makes up part of Principle A, as explained above). But there is another way to look at this.

In particular, there are independent reasons why an efficiency driven computational system cannot access the genitive nominal in (1). To see this, we need only
consider how the sentence is formed.

(2)   Steps 1 & 2: Combination of the genitive nominal *Mary's* with *sister*;
       combination of the resulting phrase with the verb:

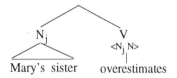

Step 3: Addition of the verb's second argument, the reflexive pronoun
herself:

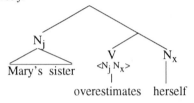

Because the nominal *Mary's sister* functions as the verb's first argument, its index
is copied into the verb's grid when the two are combined (step 1 above). This is
then the only index in the grid at the point at which the reflexive pronoun combines
with the verb, and it provides the first opportunity to resolve the accompanying
referential dependency. The computational system therefore cannot but opt for this
interpretation.

(3)

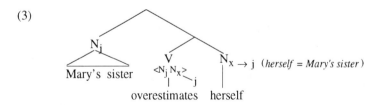

On this view then, the reflexive pronoun is not searching for a c-commanding
antecedent per se; it is simply complying with the requirement that its referential
dependency be resolved at the first opportunity. This gives the *appearance* of a
sensitivity to c-command when, in fact, the computational system cares only about
efficiency.

Locality

Now consider the locality requirement on binding, the part of Principle A that ensures the proximity of the antecedent. The sentence in (4) illustrates the crucial contrast.

(4)   John$_i$ thinks [Jerry$_j$ overestimates himself$_{*i/j}$].

Clearly, *himself* can refer only to Jerry in this sort of sentence, but this doesn't mean that a principle of Universal Grammar is at work. Once again, there is another way to look at things.

The first opportunity to resolve the referential dependency associated with the reflexive pronoun in a sentence such as (4) arises when *himself* combines with the verb *overestimate*, whose grid contains the index of its subject argument *Jerry*.

(5)

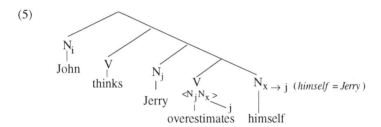

As demanded by the Efficiency Requirement, the index of *Jerry* in the grid of *overestimate* is used to resolve the pronoun's referential dependency, ruling out the possibility of a more distant antecedent.

Things work the same way in patterns such as (6), which contains a complex noun phrase rather than an embedded clause.

(6)   Harry$_i$ listened to [Ralph's$_j$ criticism of himself$_x$].

The reflexive pronoun in this sentence combines with the functor noun *criticism*, whose grid already contains the index of the nominal *Ralph*. Once again then, there is only one possibility—the referential dependency introduced by the reflexive pronoun must be resolved by the index of *Ralph*. Anything else would violate the Efficiency Requirement; no principle of grammar need be invoked.

There are other patterns to consider of course, including the interpretation of reflexive pronouns that occur in infinitival clauses, which will be dealt with in the next chapter. For now though, it seems that the interpretation of reflexive pronouns comes down to the following computational routine.

(7) i.   F $\perp$ N-$self_x$
            $<N_i ...N_x>$

            (combination of the reflexive pronoun with a functor whose grid contains
            the index of another element)

    ii.   N-$self_{x \rightarrow i}$

            (resolution of the pronoun's referential dependency by the index already in
            the functor's argument grid)

The idea here is strikingly simple and involves nothing more than the general
computational requirement that dependencies be resolved at the first opportunity. If
there is an index in the grid of the category with which the anaphor combines, that
index must be used to resolve the referential dependency. As we have seen, the
familiar prominence and locality effects then simply fall out; they need not be stated
as autonomous grammatical constraints.

3. PLAIN PRONOUNS

There is a general consensus that the use and interpretation of plain pronouns (e.g.,
he, *him*) is in some sense secondary to that of reflexive pronouns. Put simply, plain
pronouns are generally used where reflexive pronouns cannot be. Why should
things work this way?

3.1 Three accounts of plain pronouns

Three proposals about the distribution and interpretation of plain pronouns are of
special relevance to our discussion. The first is the highly regarded grammatical
account based on Principle B of the binding module of Universal Grammar. The
second is a pragmatic account that has been put forward in response to this
analysis, and the third is an efficiency-based computational account designed to
supplement the analysis of reflexive pronouns that I have just outlined.

A grammatical account

A long-standing insight in work on coreference is that plain pronouns are in (near)
complementary distribution with reflexive pronouns. Thus, a plain pronoun cannot
have a c-commanding antecedent in its minimal domain, as shown by the ungram-
maticality of the sentences in (1).

(1) a.   *$John_i$ admires him_i.
    b.   *$Marvin_i$ described $John_j$ to $him_{i/j}$.

As expected though, a plain pronoun does permit a non-c-commanding antecedent
in the same clause, or even a c-commanding antecedent in a higher clause.

(2) a. A non-c-commanding antecedent in the same clause:
        [*John's*$_i$ sister] admires him$_i$.

    b. A c-commanding antecedent in a higher clause:
        John$_i$ thinks that [Mary admires him$_i$].

And, of course, a plain pronoun can look outside the sentence for its antecedent.

(3)   I saw him.

The traditional account of these facts is summarized in Principle B, the major constraint on the interpretation of plain pronouns in Government and Binding theory (e.g., Chomsky 1981:188).

(4)   *Principle B:*
        A plain pronoun cannot have a c-commanding antecedent in the same domain.

This constraint correctly rules out the patterns in (1), where the plain pronoun has a structurally higher antecedent in the same clause, while at the same time permitting the patterns in (2) and (3).

The success of Principle B in accounting for such facts has led to a great deal of additional research, including exploration of the possibility that its content might follow from pragmatic considerations.

A pragmatic account

Pragmatic accounts of Principle B effects have been put forward by a number of scholars, including Reinhart (1983:166) and Levinson (1987:410). The intuition is that a reflexive pronoun is more informative (in the sense of having fewer potential antecedents) than a plain pronoun.

As we have seen, a reflexive pronoun takes a local antecedent, whereas a plain pronoun doesn't even require an antecedent in the same sentence. Given Gricean principles for rational and efficient language use, it makes sense to employ the reflexive pronoun where it is permitted, reserving the less specific plain pronoun for cases where the anaphor is not allowed. Levinson states the principle as follows:

(5)   *The Informativeness Principle* (= Grice's Second Maxim of Quantity):
        Be as informative as possible.

As a concrete illustration of how this works, consider a contrast such as the following.

(6)   John$_i$ overestimates himself/*him$_i$.

Because the referential dependency introduced by the reflexive pronoun can only be resolved by the index of *John*, use of *himself* to indicate coreference in this sentence is highly informative. In contrast, the plain pronoun would be much less informative. Even if its possible referents includes John, it permits too many other interpretations to be as informative as the reflexive pronoun when coreference is intended. Its use is therefore barred in this situation—the very result stipulated by traditional versions of Principle B.

A computational account

The pragmatic approach is very promising, but for reasons that will become clearer in the next section, I will construct a parallel computational account. Like the pragmatic account, it rejects the existence of Principle B. Instead, it proposes that the unacceptability of the plain pronoun in a sentence such as (6) stems from considerations of computational efficiency. In particular, use of the reflexive pronoun offers an opportunity to resolve a referential dependency immediately via the computational system, whereas use of the plain pronoun does not.

If this is right, then the basis for the contrast between reflexive pronouns and plain pronouns lies in the fact that reflexive pronouns are used to introduce referential dependencies that can be resolved by the computational system at the first opportunity. By imposing no such requirement, plain pronouns are *computationally* less efficient. Their use is therefore shunned where the more efficient alternative is available.

At this point, one might ask why languages have plain pronouns at all. The answer seems obvious—communication demands reference to distant and extra-sentential antecedents. Pronouns are therefore tolerated of necessity, but their interpretation lies outside the reach of the computational system.

This is in essence another way of stating the long-standing intuition that the interpretation of plain pronouns is regulated by principles very different from those used for reflexive pronouns. For instance, traditional binding theory stipulates precisely where to find an antecedent for a reflexive pronoun (i.e., in the same 'minimal domain'), but offers no comparable guidance for the interpretation of plain pronouns—saying only where its antecedent cannot be. Other approaches make a similar distinction, as does the theory I propose.

3.2 How plain pronouns are interpreted

How then is the referential dependency introduced by a plain pronoun resolved? It is well known that pronominal coreference is sensitive to a variety of factors, including topicality, coherence, recency, empathy, perspective, and the like—factors which fall beyond the scope of the sentence-level computational system. The following example from Winograd (1972) helps illustrate this.

(1) a. The city council denied the demonstrators the permit because they advocated violence.

b. The city council denied the demonstrators the permit because they feared violence.

As noted by Kehler (2002) and Wolf, Gibson, & Desmet (2004), listeners interpret the pronouns in such sentences in a way that makes the discourse coherent. Hence *they* is taken to refer to *the demonstrators* in (1a) but to *the city council* in (1b), consistent with general assumptions about groups that might advocate or fear violence.

This does not mean that plain pronouns are always harder to interpret than reflexive pronouns—they need not be (Piñango, Burkhardt, Brun, & Avrutin 2001, Runner, Sussman, & Tanenhaus 2003). It just means that their interpretation is mediated by considerations other than the drive for quickness that guides the computational system. Indeed, entire frameworks have been developed to deal with the myriad of factors that enter into the interpretation of plain pronouns, including Discourse Representation Theory (Kamp & Reyle 1993, Gordon & Hendrick 1998), Centering Theory (Gordon, Grosz, & Gillion 1993), and Coherence Theory (Kehler 2002). (For a psycholinguistic perspective, see Garrod & Sanford 1994.)

Evidently then, the traditional intuition is right: the task of interpreting plain pronouns lies outside the purview of the computational system. For the sake of exposition, I will use the term *pragmatic system* to refer to the body of principles and strategies (whatever they turn out to be) that determine the reference of plain pronouns.

We can represent the transfer of responsibility for a pronoun-related referential dependency from the sentence-level computational system to the pragmatic system with the help of the symbol '$\rightarrow$ Prag,' as follows.

(2) a.   b.

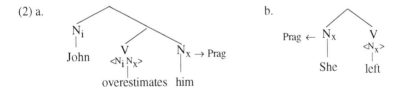

If this is right, then the computational routine for interpreting plain pronouns can be summarized as follows.

(3) i. $F \perp \text{ProN}_x$, or $\text{ProN}_x \perp F$
(combination of a functor with a plain pronoun)

ii. $\text{ProN}_x \rightarrow \text{Prag}$
(responsibility for the pronoun's referential dependency is passed to the pragmatic system)

Pronominal antecedents

Although the referential dependency associated with a plain pronoun is resolved pragmatically, its index can still play a role in the *computational* resolution of other referential dependencies. Consider in this regard a pattern such as *He admires himself*, in which the plain pronoun *he* serves as antecedent for the reflexive. During the first step in the sentence formation process, the pronoun combines with the verb, its index is copied into the verb's argument grid, and the referential dependency it introduces is passed to pragmatic mechanisms for resolution.

(4)

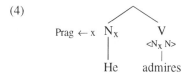

Next, the verb's object argument is added and the referential dependency that it introduces is immediately resolved by the index of the plain pronoun, which is already in the verb's argument grid.

(5)

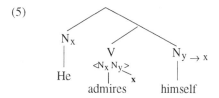

This gives an interpretation in which the referent of *himself* is identical to the referent of *he*—whoever pragmatic considerations determine this to be. Intuitively, this is exactly the right result.

4. NON-LOCAL ANAPHORS

Returning now to reflexive pronouns, we have so far considered only cases in which the referential dependency introduced by the anaphor can be resolved immediately, typically by an argument of the same predicate.

As is well known, however, things do not always work this way. In a sentence such as (1), for instance, the reflexive pronoun is distant from its antecedent.

(1)   Larry$_i$ thinks [that there are [pictures of himself$_i$] on the table].

The puzzle is further compounded by the fact that reflexive pronouns in such contexts can alternate with plain pronouns.

(2)   Larry$_i$ thinks [that there are [pictures of *him*$_i$] on the table].

How can this be?

4.1 'Picture NPs'

As the structure below illustrates, it is not possible to immediately resolve the referential dependency associated with a reflexive pronoun in an NP such as *pictures of himself*. (For now, I treat *of* as a case marker rather than a preposition. I will consider the status of prepositions in section 4.4.)

(1)

$$N \qquad\qquad N_y$$
$$\text{<of-}N_y\text{>}$$

pictures   of-himself

Because the argument grid of *picture* contains no index other than that of *himself*, there is no opportunity to resolve the pronoun's referential dependency here.[3]

I propose that under these circumstances, the computational system passes responsibility for resolution of the referential dependency to the pragmatic system, which will locate an antecedent at the first opportunity using criteria such as topicality, contextual plausibility, and so forth. The antecedent is then selected from elsewhere in the sentence or even from a different sentence in the discourse.

(2)   Antecedent inside the same sentence:
  a. *Howard$_i$* insisted that [a picture of himself$_i$] is hanging in City Hall.
  b. *John's$_i$* diary contains [several pictures of himself$_i$].
  c. [The picture of herself$_i$] delighted *Mary$_i$*.

(3)   Antecedent outside the sentence:
   Larry$_i$ had left his room in a terrible state. Pictures of himself$_i$ lay on the floor, the dishes had not been washed, and the bed was unmade.

The computational routine that is invoked in such cases can be summarized as follows.

(4) i.   F $\perp$ N-*self$_x$*
        $\text{<}N_x...\text{>}$
        (combination of the reflexive pronoun with a category whose grid does not already contain an index)

---

[3]It is standardly assumed that the reflexive pronoun in sentences such as *John saw [Jerry's picture of himself]* must take *Jerry* as its antecedent, but this may not be right. If, as is sometimes suggested (e.g., Grimshaw 1990:56), possessors are not arguments, the index of *Jerry* will not appear in the grid of the noun *picture*, opening the door to a pragmatic interpretation that could select *John* as the antecedent. Interestingly, Runner, Sussman, & Tanenhaus (2003) report that native speakers of English frequently opt for this interpretation. See also Runner (2003).

ii.   N-*self*$_{x \rightarrow Prag}$

(responsibility for the pronoun's referential dependency is passed to the pragmatic system)

Free variation with plain pronouns

As we have just seen, a reflexive pronoun that occurs inside a picture NP can get its interpretation from a nominal inside or outside the sentence. Moreover, when the antecedent is inside the sentence, it is sometimes in a structurally higher position (as in (2a)) and sometimes not (as in (2b,c)).

The existence of such a range of options can only reduce the computational advantage normally enjoyed by reflexive pronouns, which more typically occur in structures where their referential dependency can be resolved immediately and unambiguously by the computational system. This in turn leads to an interesting prediction.

According to the efficiency-based account of Principle B put forward in section 3, reflexive pronouns are preferred to plain pronouns only because their referential dependency can usually be resolved immediately by the computational system. Given that this does not happen in picture-NP patterns, we predict that plain pronouns should be able to compete with reflexive pronouns in these constructions. A reflexive pronoun should be possible because the referential dependency that it introduces is resolved at the first opportunity (although not immediately and not by the computational system). And a plain pronoun should be possible too, since it is arguably no less efficient than a reflexive pronoun whose referential dependency cannot be instantly resolved. The prediction seems to be correct, as the following examples help illustrate.

(5) a.   Howard$_i$ insisted that [a picture of *himself/him*$_i$] is hanging in City Hall.
     b.   John's$_i$ diary contains [several pictures of *himself/him*$_i$].
     c.   [The picture of *herself/her*$_i$] delighted Mary$_i$.

(6)   Larry$_i$ had left his room in a terrible state. Pictures of *himself/him*$_i$ lay on the floor, the dishes had not been washed, and the bed was unmade.

The free variation between reflexive and plain pronouns observed here provides strong evidence that Principle B effects follow from computational considerations, as assumed in the efficiency-based account.

The key claim, recall, is that a plain pronoun is not normally used when a reflexive pronoun is permitted, since the latter element can be dealt with more efficiently by the computational system—its reference can usually be determined immediately without the need to consider external factors.

However, matters are quite different when the computational system cannot resolve a reflexive pronoun's referential dependency right away. Because the computational advantage of reflexive pronouns erodes under these circumstances, the door is opened to competition with plain pronouns—which is exactly what we observe.

TABLE 3.1
Reflexive and Plain Pronouns in English

How the Referential Dependency is Dealt With	Type of Pronoun
Immediate resolution by the computational system	Reflexive pronoun is obligatory; plain pronoun is forbidden
No opportunity for immediate resolution by the computational system; recourse to the pragmatic system	Reflexive pronoun and plain pronoun may alternate with each other

This in turn sets the stage for the development of semantic contrasts between the two forms. One such contrast may involve 'perspective,' with the reflexive being used for reference to the entity from whose point of view an event is seen (Kuno 1987, Speas & Tenny 2003, MacWhinney 2003). Consider in this regard the following examples.

(7) a. John heard a story about him/himself.
   b. John told a story about *him/himself.

MacWhinney suggests that there are two perspectives in (7a), one corresponding to the referent of the subject (John) and the other corresponding to the storyteller. Because either perspective could be adopted, reference to John is possible via either the reflexive (reflecting John's perspective) or the plain pronoun (the storyteller's perspective). Not so in (7b), where the referent of the subject is also the storyteller and there is therefore only one perspective—forcing use of the reflexive pronoun.

I take no position on the precise nature of these contrasts other than to suggest that they arise in contexts where reflexive and plain pronouns are both permitted for computational reasons.

4.2 Anaphors that function as first arguments

Another case in which referential dependencies cannot be resolved immediately arises in constructions where the anaphor functions as subject of a clause, as in (1a), or as specifier of a noun, as in (1b).[4] (I take a genitive to be a functor that takes a nominal argument.)

---

[4]Patterns such as (1a) are marginal for some speakers, but a Google search reveals many comparable examples. For instance:

(1) a. *The boys*ᵢ wonder [whether each other ⱼ succeeded].

   b. *The boys*ᵢ admire [each other's ⱼ cars].

As the representations below help illustrate, the verb *succeed* in (1a) contains only the index of the anaphor, whereas the noun *cars* in (1b) does not even have an argument grid since it is not a functor.[5]

(2) a.

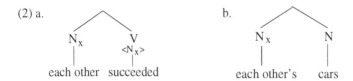

each other   succeeded   each other's   cars

Immediate resolution of the referential dependency is thus precluded in these patterns, although it arguably does still take place *at the first opportunity*.

As in the cases of picture NPs, there are a variety of places to look for a potential antecedent. It can be in a structurally higher position in the same sentence, as in (1); it can be in a non-c-commanding position inside the same sentence, as in (3); or it can be in another sentence altogether, as in (4).

(3)   Non-c-commanding antecedent in the same sentence:
      [The agreement that [*Iran and Iraq*]ᵢ reached] guaranteed [each other's ᵢ trading rights] in the disputed waters until the year 2010. (Pollard & Sag 1992:264)

(4)   Antecedent in another sentence:
      By 1999, there was tension between [*Iran and Iraq*]ᵢ. The agreement guaranteeing [each other's ᵢ trading rights] was about to expire and negotiations for a new agreement had broken down.

Predictably, this erodes the computational advantage normally enjoyed by anaphors, opening the way for the appearance of plain pronouns (although minus the sense of reciprocality, of course).

(5) a. The boysᵢ wonder [whether *they*ᵢ succeeded].

   b. The boysᵢ admire [*their*ᵢ cars].

(i)   ... and have an equal inventory and have it verifiable, so that we'll know whether each other is cheating.

(ii)   We don't have to agree with everything that each other teaches.

[5]Reflexive pronouns fail to occur in these positions (*...*themselves succeeded*, *...*themselves' cars*) for morphological reasons—they lack nominative and genitive forms (Pollard & Sag 1992:290).

In sum, anaphors that function as first arguments behave just like anaphors in other positions—they introduce referential dependencies that are resolved at the first opportunity. This opportunity arises immediately in cases where the reflexive pronoun or reciprocal combines with a category that contains the index of another nominal in its grid. In other cases, the referential dependency is simply resolved as quickly as practical via recourse to pragmatic resources, with the consequences we have just seen.

4.3 Coordinate structures

Coordinate structures constitute yet another example of a pattern in which the referential dependency introduced by a reflexive pronoun cannot be immediately dealt with.

(1) I_i bought [Mary and myself$_i$] tickets for the big concert.

That is because the semantics of coordination first requires the union of the referential indices on all conjuncts, as depicted in (2).

(2)

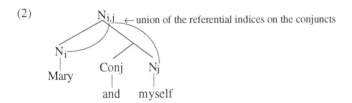

Thanks to this union operation, a coordinate structure that contains only singular nominals typically ends up counting as a plural (but see chapter six).

(3) a.   [Bob and Mary] are/*is outside.
    b.   [Paul and Jerry] overestimate themselves/*himself.

Because the referential dependency introduced by the reflexive pronoun in a coordinate structure can therefore not be *immediately* resolved, it is handed over to the pragmatic system—which creates a variety of options. One possibility is that the antecedent lies in a higher position in the same clause, as in (1), or in a higher clause, as in (4) from Reinhart & Reuland (1991:315).

(4)   *John$_i$ thinks that [I mistrust [Mary and himself$_i$]].

It even seems possible to have a non-c-commanding antecedent or a sentence-external antecedent in some cases.

(5) a.   Non-c-commanding antecedent:
         ?*My*$_i$ proposal is that you pick [Mary and myself$_i$].
         (cf. *My proposal is that you pick myself.)

    b.   Sentence-external antecedent:
         ?The proposal is that you pick [Mary and myself].
         (cf. *The proposal is that you pick myself.)

Because non-immediate resolution of the referential dependency undermines the computational advantage of reflexive pronouns, we predict that the contrast with plain pronouns should be weakened, paving the way for competition between the two forms. This too is correct.

(6)   John$_i$ thinks that [I mistrust [Mary and *himself/him*$_i$]].

(7)   The Queen$_i$ compared [the King and *herself/her*$_i$] to Jerry and his wife.

I return to the interpretation of reflexive pronouns in coordinate structures in chapter six, section 4.

4.4 Prepositional phrases

The interpretation of pronouns that lie within a prepositional phrase provides further evidence that reflexives can enter into free variation with plain pronouns in cases where their referential dependency cannot be immediately resolved. Consider in this regard the following examples, from Kuno (1987:65ff).

(1) a.   Harvey$_i$ pulled the rope [toward *himself/him*$_i$].
    b.   Mary$_i$ hid the book [behind *herself/her*$_i$].
    c.   Max$_i$ wrapped the blanket [around *himself/him*$_i$].

As depicted in (2), corresponding to (1a), there is no index in the grid of the preposition that can help interpret the pronoun that combines with it.

(2)

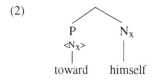

Immediate resolution of the referential dependency is therefore not feasible, opening the way for use of a plain pronoun in these contexts as well—which is just what we see in (1).[6]

Why, then, is the plain pronoun not permitted in the prepositional phrases in the following sentences?

(3) a. Harvey$_i$ gave a gift [to *himself/*him$_i$*].
    b. Mary$_i$ thinks [about *herself/*her$_i$*] too much.
    c. Max$_i$ looked [at *himself/*him$_i$*] in the mirror.

The answer, I believe, lies in the solution to another puzzle involving prepositional phrases and coreference.

Referring prepositional phrases

Consider in this regard the following sentence.

(4) Mary talked to Henry$_i$ about himself$_i$.

How is the nominal *Henry*, which occurs inside a prepositional phrase, able to serve as antecedent for a reflexive pronoun? Put more technically, how can we ensure that the index of *Henry* will appear in the grid of *talk*, where it can satisfy the referential dependency introduced by the reflexive pronoun?

The solution to this puzzle lies in the fact that certain prepositional phrases have a peculiar status. Instead of referring to locations (as *behind the bench* does) or directions (as *to the store* does), they denote entities whose thematic role they simultaneously indicate. Thus the denotation of the PP *to Henry* in (4) is not a direction; it is the individual Henry, the goal argument.

This opens the door to the suggestion that the antecedent of the reflexive pronoun in (4) is not the nominal *Henry*, but rather the prepositional phrase *to Henry*, which simultaneously refers to the individual Henry and identifies him as the goal. (Suggestions along these lines have been put forward by Bach & Partee 1980:5-6, Reinhart 1981:631, 1983:177, and Pollard & Sag 1992:286, among others.)

If this idea is on the right track, then prepositional phrases such as *to Henry*, *about himself*, and so on carry the referential index on which the computational system operates.[7]

---

[6]However, in contrast to what was observed for other patterns in which reflexive pronouns alternate with plain pronouns, nonlocal antecedents are at best only marginally possible.

(i)   ?* *Mary$_i$* asked me [to wrap a blanket around herself$_i$].

[7]A similar idea has been put forward by Sag & Wasow (1999:156), who propose that the index on the nominal 'percolates' up to the prepositional phrase.

(5) a.   b.

I will henceforth refer to prepositional phrases of this type as *referring prepositional phrases*.

When a referring prepositional phrase combines with a verb, as happens in a sentence such as *Mary talked to Henry about himself*, its index appears in the verb's argument grid in accordance with the usual conventions.

(6)

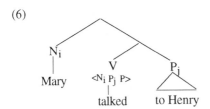

When the verb's third argument, the referring prepositional phrase *about himself*, is added to this sentence, the referential dependency that it introduces is immediately resolved by the index of *to Henry*, which is already in the verb's argument grid— exactly the right result.

(7)   Mary$_i$ talked [to Henry]$_j$ [about himself]$_x$.
         $<N_i \, P_j \, P_x>$
                    $\downarrow$
                    j

We can now return to the puzzle presented by the sentences in (3), repeated here as (8).

(8) a.   Harvey$_i$ gave a gift [to himself/*him$_i$].
    b.   Mary$_i$ thinks [about herself/*her$_i$] too much.
    c.   Max$_i$ looked [at himself/*him$_i$] in the mirror.

Because expressions such as *to himself*, *about himself*, and *at himself* are referring prepositional phrases, they carry their own referential dependency. Upon combination with the verb, this dependency is immediately resolved by the index of the subject nominal, as illustrated in (9) for (8c).

(9)

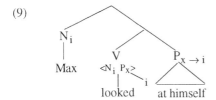

Because the referential dependency is resolved *immediately*, reflexive pronouns enjoy a clearcut computational advantage over plain pronouns in these cases, which in turn rules out patterns such as *Max_i looked at him_i.

In sum, there are two types of prepositional phrases. On the one hand, we have phrases such as *to x* and *about x*, which resemble noun phrases in being able to denote individuals and which therefore carry their own referential index. Reflexives of this type (e.g., *to himself, about themselves*) are subject to immediate interpretation for the usual reasons when they combine with a functor whose grid already contains an index.

On the other hand, we also have phrases such as *near x* and *toward x*, which denote locations and directions rather than individuals. The reflexive pronoun inside such phrases carries an index corresponding to an individual of course. But the referential dependency that this index represents cannot be immediately resolved, since the grid of the preposition with which the pronoun combines does not contain the index of another nominal.

(10)

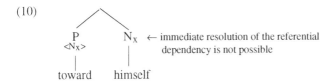

This in turn leads to a potentially broader range of antecedents and possible free variation with plain pronouns.

4.5 Long-distance anaphora in Asian languages

So far, I have deliberately focused my attention on English. In fact though, the most notorious cases of referential dependencies that are not immediately resolved come from other languages, especially Japanese, Korean, and Chinese. The following example is from Japanese. (Top = topic, Nom = nominative, Acc = accusative, Pst = past, Comp = complementizer.)

(1)   [Sam-wa$_i$ [Harry-ga$_j$ *zibun-o*$_{i/j}$ seme-ta-to]   it-ta.]
        Sam-Top Harry-Nom self-Acc blame-Pst-Comp say-Pst
        'Sam$_i$ said that Harry$_j$ blamed self$_{i/j}$.'

Notice that the reflexive pronoun can look to either the nearby nominal *Harry* or the more distant nominal *Sam* for its interpretation. How is this possible?

The most straightforward solution, and the one that I adopt for now, is that reflexive pronouns such as *zibun* and its counterparts in other languages are polysemous (e.g., Hirose 2002, Pollard & Xue 1998). On the one hand, they have a true reflexive use which is very much like that of their English counterparts. When employed in this way, they require a local antecedent and are in strict complementary distribution with plain pronouns. Thus if we replace *zibun* in (1) by *kare* 'him,' coreference with *Harry* is no longer possible.

(2)   [Sam-wa$_i$ [Harry-ga$_j$ *kare-o$_{i/*j}$* seme-ta-to]   it-ta.]
         Sam-Top Harry-Nom him-Acc blame-Pst-Comp say-Pst
         'Sam$_i$ said that Harry$_j$ blamed him$_{i/*j}$.'

On the other hand, *zibun* and its counterparts are also used to indicate logophoricity and viewpoint. In this latter use, I suggest, *zibun* is a type of plain pronoun, whose interpretation therefore falls to the pragmatic system rather than to the efficiency driven computational system. It is this use that permits the long-distance interpretation in (1).

5. Principle C effects

Consider now the following classic contrast.

(1) a.   John$_i$ said [he$_i$ won].
     b. *He$_i$ said [John$_i$ won].

The unacceptability of the second of these sentences is traditionally attributed to Principle C, a component of Universal Grammar.

(2)   *Principle C:*[8]
         A pronoun cannot c-command its antecedent.

Does this constraint have to be stipulated as a principle of grammar, or can its effects be derived from something more basic?

---

[8]In its more usual form, Principle C is stated as 'An R-expression (roughly a lexical noun phrase) must be free (not c-commanded by a coreferential expression).' On this formulation, Principle C also rules out patterns such as *Larry$_i$ lost Larry's$_i$ wallet*, with the second instance of *Larry* c-commanded by the first. However, this particular pattern is not universally prohibited (it is permitted in Thai, for instance; see Lasnik 1989) and is perhaps not totally unacceptable even in English (e.g., Gordon & Hendrick 1997). I believe that it should be treated separately from cases such as **He$_i$ lost Larry's$_i$ wallet*, which no language permits.

Since the interpretation of plain pronouns falls to the pragmatic system, an emergentist account of Principle C effects must focus on this side of the interpretive process. Two ideas are crucial.

First, I suggest that the pragmatic system can base its inferences about a pronoun's interpretation not only on the discourse and context in which an utterance occurs, but also (as seems reasonable) on the syntactic representation formed by the computational system. Of special importance in the latter regard, I propose, is the possibility that the pragmatic system can use feature passing to link a pronoun with a potential antecedent within the same sentence.

Second, I adopt the principle in (3), which restates an idea first put forward by Reinhart (1983:167).

(3)   *Preference Principle:*
        When a pronoun and its antecedent lie within the same sentence, they are best arranged in a way that permits resolution of the referential dependency via upward feature passing, if possible.

This makes good sense from a processing perspective. Feature passing dramatically narrows the set of interpretive options to which the pragmatic system has access, since it has access only to nominals in structurally higher positions. Consider in this regard the following example, corresponding to (1a). (I consider the status of clausal complements in more detail in chapter seven.)

(4)

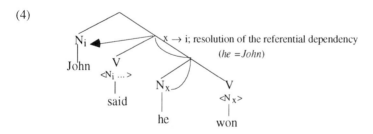

As can be seen here, the referential dependency introduced by the pronoun can be passed upward through the syntactic representation by the pragmatic system for eventual resolution by the index on the nominal *John*.

Crucially though, this can happen only if the antecedent is in a structurally higher (i.e., c-commanding) position, as unresolved referential dependencies are passed *upward*. If the position of the pronoun and the intended antecedent were reversed—as in (5), corresponding to (1b)—feature passing could not assist in the resolution of the referential dependency.

(5)

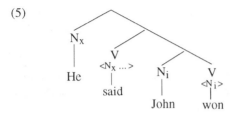

On the intended interpretation (with *he* and *John* coreferential), this sentence is in violation of the Preference Principle. This is because the pronoun and its antecedent are needlessly arranged in a way that does not permit upward feature passing. By reversing their positions, the referential dependency introduced by the pronoun could have been resolved by feature passing, as in (4), with no need for the pragmatic system to venture beyond the sentence containing the pronoun.

Now consider the pair of sentences in (6).

(6) a.   John's$_i$ mother said he$_i$ won.
    b.   His$_i$ mother said John$_i$ won.

From a structural perspective, neither of these sentences is preferable to the other. That is because neither permits resolution of the referential dependency via feature passing—not even the 'forward' pattern of coreference exemplified by (6a).

(7)

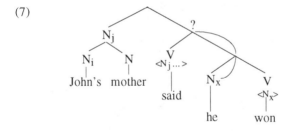

Even if the referential dependency associated with *he* is passed up through the syntactic representation by the pragmatic system, it does not have the opportunity to make contact with the index associated with *John*, which is embedded inside a larger noun phrase. Because feature passing is useless here, nothing is lost by reversing the position of the pronoun and its antecedent. Which is precisely why the 'backward' pattern of coreference in (6b) is also permitted.

Thus, Principle C effects are real, but Principle C is not. Speakers' aversion to sentences in which a pronoun c-commands its antecedent stems from the fact that there is an alternative way to express the same meaning which places less burden on the pragmatic system.

Length effects

Implementation of the Preference Principle demands considerable pre-planning of a sentence's structure, which could be difficult, especially in longer sentences. Indeed, lapses appear to be common in both spoken and written discourse, leading to sentences such as the following.

(8)   *He* was shot in the arm when, police say, *Sua* lunged at them. [report on the Channel 8 News, Honolulu, February 7, 1997]

(9)   President Boris Yeltsin today canceled all meetings for this week because of medical tests for his upcoming heart surgery. *He* also punished a former bodyguard who said *Yeltsin* was too sick to govern. [AP story in the *Honolulu Star-Bulletin*, Oct. 28, 1996]

(10)   *He* reserved special scorn for a critic who wrote that *Balthus* had been deeply influenced by the art of Germany, during a youthful period spent in that country. ['The Balthus Enigma' by Nicholas Weber, *The New Yorker*, Sept. 6, 1999, p. 36]

(11)   Lawrence crammed for Miami as if it were a final exam: *he* hired a Spanish tutor, who placed new words on little note cards around *Lawrence's* house... ['The Herald's Cuban Revolution' by Mimi Swartz, *The New Yorker*, June 7, 1999, p. 40]

(12)   *He*'s far enough ahead that, if everything fell just right, *Jarret* could be the champion when the checkered flag waves at the end of the 500-kilometer, 312-lap race. [AP story in the *Honolulu Advertiser*, Nov. 7, 1999, p. C11]

In all these cases, the pronoun is structurally higher than its antecedent, rather than vice versa. Crucially though, these examples all have something else in common—the antecedent follows the coreferential pronoun by some distance.

This suggests a processing problem—the sentences are so long that at the point where the pronoun is used, the speaker cannot anticipate the need for a nominal later in the utterance to reactivate the referent. Or, alternatively, by the time the speaker reaches the part of the sentence where the nominal is used, he or she can no longer recall having used a pronoun earlier in the utterance.

In any case, there is no reason to think that the constraints on coreference associated with Principle C reflect the operation of a grammatical principle. The roots of this phenomenon lie in deeper pragmatic and computational considerations.

6. CONCLUSION

There are no binding principles per se—that is, no autonomous grammatical constraints on coreference. The interpretive effects for which such principles have traditionally accounted reflect the interaction of more fundamental computational and pragmatic factors, consistent with the emergentist thesis.

As I have tried to show, the constraints embodied in Principle A (which requires anaphors to be bound in a minimal domain) simply follow from the Efficiency Requirement. Anaphors are just words whose referential dependencies must be resolved at the first opportunity. The familiar c-command and locality requirements fall out automatically, as we have seen.

An obvious advantage of anaphors is that the computational system is often able to resolve the referential dependency they introduce not just at the first opportunity, but *immediately*. Considerations of efficiency therefore preclude the use of a form whose referential dependency cannot be dealt with so expeditiously in the same context. This in turn allows us to derive as a corollary the constraint embodied in the traditional version of Principle B, which places plain pronouns more or less in complementary distribution with anaphors.

In addition, we correctly predict that in patterns where reflexive pronouns lose their computational advantage (i.e., where their referential dependency cannot be resolved immediately), they end up in free variation with plain pronouns. This yields the following set of contrasts.

TABLE 3.2
The Contrast Between Reflexive and Plain Pronouns in English

Type of pronoun	Conditions of use
Reflexive pronoun	Obligatory when the referential dependency can be immediately resolved by the computational system; optional otherwise
Plain pronoun	Forbidden when the referential dependency can be immediately resolved by the computational system; optional otherwise

There is also an alternative explanation for the facts that traditionally fall under Principle C. As we have seen, syntactic representations in which the antecedent is higher than the pronoun permit the pragmatic system to resolve the pronoun's referential dependency via upward feature passing—a process that dramatically restricts the set of interpretive options and that can be initiated as soon as the pronoun is encountered.

Of course, implementation of this preference requires significant advance planning, since a speaker has to be able to 'see' far enough ahead to know whether the sentence under construction is going to contain both a lexical nominal and a pronoun, and whether the nominal could be placed in a structurally higher position. Not surprisingly, 'violations' of the Preference Principle seem to increase with the length and complexity of the sentence. Even good carpenters fail to foresee details sometimes, especially when they have to plan as they build.

Referential dependencies have a role to play in more than just the interpretation of pronouns. As we will see in chapter four, they are also vital to our understanding of how the computational system forms and interprets certain patterns containing covert arguments. We will begin our discussion of this matter by considering the syntax of infinitival verbs in English.

Chapter 4

Control

1. INTRODUCTION

This chapter focuses on the status and interpretation of so-called *control* structures—patterns like (1) in which an infinitival phrase functions as second argument of the matrix verb.

(1)   Mary hopes [to succeed].

A salient feature of infinitival phrases in English is that they lack a visible 'subject' (first argument). Compare (1) with (2), in which the verb in the embedded clause takes an overt subject.

(2)   Mary hopes [she will succeed].

The meaning of *succeed* clearly entails an agent argument in both patterns. Yet no such argument is visible in the infinitival construction.

A further puzzle arises when we consider the interpretation of the unexpressed first argument in the infinitival pattern. Unlike its pronominal counterpart in (2), this element can refer only to the matrix subject (dubbed its *controller*). Understanding why this is so has been a major goal of traditional syntactic analysis for many years.

The principal goal of this chapter is to outline a theory of the representation and interpretation of subjects in infinitival constructions that is compatible with the emergentist approach to syntax proposed in the preceding chapters.[1]

2. MATTERS OF REPRESENTATION

The signpost of English infinitival patterns is the morpheme *to*, which I take to make up a special one-member category that I will dub 'TO.' Instances of this category seek out a 'bare' (uninflected) verb as their sole argument.

---

[1] I deliberately restrict my remarks here to infinitival verbs, setting aside gerundives (e.g., *Going there is a bad idea*). The latter forms are more noun-like than infinitivals are, and it is not clear that their first argument is represented and/or interpreted in the same way as that of a true verbal category.

(1)   *to*: TO. <V>
         ↑   ↑
        category argument grid

If this is right, then a verb such as *try* has the properties in (2), with the symbol N standing for its first argument (the subject) and TO for its second argument.

(2)   *try*: V, <N TO>

The sentence *Mary tried to leave* is formed in the following manner.

(3)   Step 1: Combination of *try* with its first argument, the nominal *Mary:*

N_i V
        <N_i TO>
| |
Mary   tried

Step 2: Combination of *try* with its second argument, the infinitival morpheme *to:*

N_i
| V   TO
Mary   <N_i TO'>   <V>
          | |
         tried   to

Step 3: Combination of *to* with its verbal argument, *leave:*

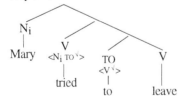

N_i
| V
Mary   <N_i TO'>   TO   V
                      <V'>
          | | |
         tried   to   leave

Two considerations favor this approach. First, selection is stated in a maximally simple manner as a relationship between two lexical items—the matrix verb *try* and the infinitival marker *to*.

Second, on the assumption that *to*'s dependency on a verbal argument can sometimes be resolved pragmatically, we have a simple way of forming sentences such as *Mary tried to* (as in response to the question, 'Did anyone leave?'). Such sentences are simply the product of the second step in the sentence formation process outlined above.

Covert subject arguments

This brings us to the problem of how an infinitival verb's first argument is represented. The commonly held view is that control patterns include a null pronoun, such as the PRO of Government and Binding theory and more recent work, but I reject this. As I see it, syntactic structure is simply a residual record of the combinatorial operations carried out by the computational system. Because combinatorial operations apply only to actual words, there is no room for PRO in the type of representations I propose.

The key idea that I will seek to develop is that there are two ways to express or 'project' an argument requirement. The first and most common (in English) is to represent it as a *categorial dependency*— that is, as a dependency on a category of a particular type. This is what happens in the case of finite verbs in English. As illustrated below, such verbs combine with a nominal to satisfy their first argument requirement.

(4)

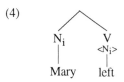

$$N_i \qquad V$$
$$\qquad\quad <N_i>$$
$$Mary \quad left$$

Something else is required in the case of infinitival verbs, however, since they are unable to take a nominal as their first argument.

(5)   *We hope [Mary to leave].

If an infinitival verb's first argument is not projected as a categorial dependency, how is it expressed? I propose that it is represented as a referential dependency— the other type of dependency found in our computational system (see chapter three).

If this is right, then the nonfinite form of *leave* has the properties depicted in (6), with the first argument projected as a referential dependency, represented by the index x.[2]

(6)   *leave* (-Fin): $<x>$
                        ag

As things now stand then, verbs such as *leave* or *buy* require an agent argument regardless of whether they are finite or nonfinite—their meaning permits nothing less. However, this argument requirement can be projected in two very different

---

[2] A version of this idea can be found in Starosta (1994, 1997), who also uses an index to represent the subject argument in infinitival clauses; see also Sag & Pollard (1991) and Jackendoff & Culicover (2003).

ways. Where the verb is finite, the requirement is manifested as a categorial dependency that must be satisfied by combination with a nominal element.

(7)   *leave* (+Fin): <N>   *buy* (+Fin): <N N>
                      ag   ag th

In contrast, where the verb is nonfinite, its first argument is expressed as a referential dependency.

(8)   *leave* (-Fin): <x>   *buy* (-Fin): <x N>
                      ag   ag th

The relationship between the argument grids of the finite and nonfinite forms of a verb can therefore be captured as follows.

(9) $V_{+finite} \Leftrightarrow V_{-finite}$
        <N ...>   <x ...>

As is perhaps already evident, the idea that an infinitival verb's subject argument is projected as a pure referential dependency is in some ways similar to the traditional idea that it is expressed as a null pronoun (PRO, in Government and Binding theory). In both cases, after all, the end result is a 'null argument.' However, there are also important differences.

Whereas the traditional theory posits the existence of an actual position in the syntactic representation that is filled by PRO, I posit no such position, as the representation in (3) above helps illustrate. Instead, the referential dependency expressing the infinitival verb's subject argument resides in the argument grid of the verb, and only there.

This brings us to the question of how such referential dependencies are resolved—that is, of how they are interpreted with the help of information elsewhere in the sentence or discourse. I turn to this matter in the next section.

3. MATTERS OF INTERPRETATION

Traditional control theory offers two important generalizations concerning the interpretation of covert subject arguments (e.g., Chomsky 1981, Manzini 1983, Hornstein 1999). Although each has proven somewhat controversial, they none-theless constitute a useful starting point for our analysis.

(i)   The covert subject of an infinitival clause in complement position is coreferential with an argument of the immediately higher verb—with *Mary*, but not *Tim*, in the following sentence.

        Tim_i thinks that [$Mary_j$ tried [$PRO_{*i/j}$ to leave]].

(ii)   The covert subject of an infinitival clause in subject position is interpreted pragmatically. Thus the sentence below can have the interpretation 'for anyone to leave now' or 'for us to leave now.'

[PRO$_i$ to leave now] would be impolite.

In the computational system adopted here, there is of course no PRO. Instead, as we have seen, the first argument of an infinitival verb is expressed as a referential dependency. Crucially, this is all that is needed to derive the principal facts of control theory from the Efficiency Requirement ('Resolve dependencies at the first opportunity').

3.1 The core cases

As we saw in chapter three, language manifests at least two types of referential dependencies—those that can be resolved at the first opportunity (and often immediately) by the computational system and those that must be handed over to the pragmatic system for resolution by other means. In the case of pronouns, separate forms are typically used for each type of referential dependency—reflexive pronouns such as *himself* and *herself* for the former case, and plain pronouns such as *he*, *she*, *him*, and *her* for the latter.

There is reason to think that a parallel contrast is found in the case of the unexpressed referential dependencies introduced by infinitival verbs, even though it cannot be expressed overtly. In order to see this, we must first ask under what conditions an opportunity arises to resolve dependencies of this sort.

It is widely believed that lexico-semantic properties of individual matrix verbs have a major role to play in the interpretation of the unexpressed subject of an infinitival verb. The notorious contrast in many varieties of North American English between *promise* and *persuade* provides one indication of this. As the examples below illustrate, the 'controller' of the infinitival verb corresponds to the first argument of *promise*, but the second argument of *persuade*.

(1)   *Harvey* promised Max [to leave].

(2)   Harvey persuaded *Max* [to leave].

How can this contrast be captured?

There is more or less a consensus, with which I concur, that verbs with an infinitival complement designate which of their arguments is the controller, based on semantic factors (e.g., Ladusaw & Dowty 1988, Sag & Pollard 1991, Jackendoff & Culicover 2003). We can represent the contrast between *promise* and *persuade* as follows, with the underline indicating which of the verb's arguments is to resolve the referential dependency introduced by the infinitival verb.

(3) a. *promise*: V, <<u>N</u> N TO>
    b. *persuade*: V, <N <u>N</u> TO>

If this is right, then the computational system encounters an opportunity to resolve the referential dependency introduced by an infinitival verb under the following conditions.

(4)   An opportunity for the computational system to resolve the referential dependency introduced by an infinitival verb arises when it encounters the index of a designated argument.

Given the Efficiency Requirement, such an opportunity must of course be exploited without delay.

Consider first a case such as *Mary decided to leave*, in which the matrix verb's sole nominal argument is designated as the controller.

(5)   *decide*: V, <<u>N</u> TO>

At an intermediate stage in its formation, the sentence has the representation depicted below. (For ease of exposition, I will henceforth not represent the grid of *to*.)

(6)

```
         Nᵢ
          |
        Mary      V        TO
               <Nᵢ TO>      |
                  |
               decided     to
```

Addition of the infinitival verb gives the representation depicted in (7).

(7)

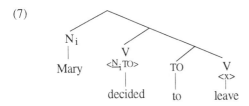

There is now an opportunity to resolve the referential dependency introduced by the infinitival verb. As illustrated in (8), the dependency can be passed upward and resolved immediately by the index of *Mary*, the designated argument in the grid of *decide*.

(8)

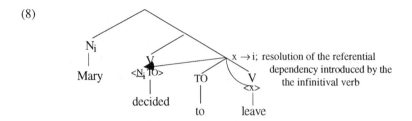

This is the only result compatible with the Efficiency Requirement, which demands that dependencies be resolved at the first opportunity. Long-distance or sentence-external antecedents are thus automatically ruled out—which is why *Tim* is not a possible controller in the following sentence.

(9)   Tim$_i$ thinks that [Mary$_j$ decided [to leave]].
                                      <$\underline{N_j}$ TO>   <x>
                                       ↑_____⌐

Because there is an immediate opportunity to resolve the referential dependency via an index in the grid of *decide*, no other option is permitted. The requirement that there be a local controller in these patterns (the first generalization of traditional control theory—see p. 59) therefore simply falls out, with no need for reference to a grammatical principle.

The computational routine associated with the interpretation of an infinitival complement can be summarized as follows.

(10) i.   N$_i$ ⊥ V
           <$\underline{N_i}$ TO>
           (combination of the matrix verb with its first argument)

     ii.   V ⊥ TO
           <$\underline{N_i}$ TO>
           (combination of the matrix verb with *to*)

     iii. TO ⊥ V
           <x ...>
           (combination of *to* with its verbal argument)

     iv.   x → i
           (resolution of the referential dependency by the index of the designated argument in the grid of the matrix verb)

Promise and *persuade* again

Matters work essentially the same way in the case of *promise* and *persuade*, except that the matrix verb has a second nominal argument. And of course, unlike *persuade* and virtually every other verb with two nominal arguments (e.g., *tell*, *force, advise, signal,* etc.), *promise* selects its first argument (the subject) as controller.

(11) a. *Harvey* promised Max [to leave].
   b. Harvey persuaded *Max* [to leave].

This is an affront to locality as it is traditionally conceived. (The earliest formulation of the locality condition on control, Rosenbaum's (1967:6) 'Minimal Distance Principle,' required that PRO be controlled by the nearest c-commanding NP.)

From the perspective adopted here though, the *promise* pattern is not computationally different from the *persuade* pattern—both manifest the immediate resolution of the referential dependency introduced by the infinitival verb. As can be seen in (12), the indices corresponding to both the agent argument and the goal argument are in the grid of the matrix verb at the point at which the infinitival phrase is added to the sentence.

(12)

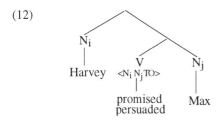

The computational system therefore has only to associate the referential dependency introduced by the infinitival verb with the index of the designated argument in the verb's grid—the first argument in the case of *promise* and the second one in the case of *persuade*.

(13) a. [Harvey$_i$ promised Max$_j$ [to leave].
      $<\underline{N_i}$ N$_j$ TO> $<x>$
      ↑_____|

   b. [Harvey$_i$ persuaded Max$_j$ [to leave].
      $<$N$_i$ $\underline{N_j}$ TO> $<x>$
      ↑_____|

Prepositional phrase controllers

In the patterns considered so far, the designated argument has always been (informally speaking) the subject or the direct object of the matrix verb. But things do not always work this way, as the next examples help show.

(14) a. Sue signaled [to *Bob*] [to leave].
   b. Jerry pleaded [with *Max*] [to stay].

Such patterns are challenging for theories that require the controller to be a c-commanding nominal, but they create no problem for the approach I adopt. That is because the PPs in question are referring prepositional phrases (see chapter three, pp. 47-49). They therefore carry their own referential index, which is copied into the grid of the matrix verb at the point where combination takes place. This index is then used to resolve the referential dependency introduced by the infinitival verb, as illustrated below.

(15)   Jerry$_i$ pleaded [with Max]$_j$ [to stay].
          <N$_i$ P$_j$ TO>   <x>

In some cases, the PP argument in this sort of control pattern is unexpressed. A common example of this involves verbs of communication, as Jackendoff & Culicover (2003:532-533) observe.

(16) a. John shouted [to leave].
           (cf. John shouted *to Sally* [to leave].)

     b. Jerry signaled [to bail out].
           (cf. Jerry signaled *to Bob* [to bail out].)

The controller in these patterns is the unexpressed addressee argument of the matrix verb—the person to whom John shouted in (16a) and the person to whom Jerry signaled in (16b).

One way to account for this is to assume that the addressee (goal) argument in these cases is itself represented as a referential dependency that is resolved pragmatically. The grid of *shout* in *John shouted to leave* therefore contains the information depicted in (17), with the referential dependency underlined to indicate that it corresponds to the designated controller argument.

(17)   <N x TO>
          ag go

If this is right, then the computational system can immediately resolve the referential dependency introduced by the infinitival verb in patterns such as (16) by linking it to the matrix verb's goal argument, even where that argument is not overtly expressed.

Control and anaphora

Once resolved, the referential dependency that expresses an infinitival verb's first argument is itself available to help resolve other dependencies. This is just what happens in sentences such as (18).

(18)   Mary decided [to criticize herself].

As illustrated below, the referential dependency corresponding to the first argument of *criticize* is resolved by the index of *Mary* in the grid of *decide*.

(19)

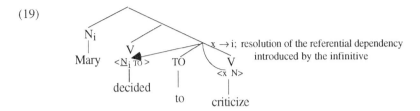

Once interpreted, the infinitival verb's subject argument then plays a role in interpreting the referential dependency introduced by the reflexive pronoun that serves as the verb's second argument. In (20), for instance, the index (now *i*) representing the infinitival verb's subject argument is used to resolve the referential dependency introduced by the reflexive pronoun.

(20)

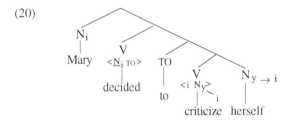

This gives exactly the desired result (*herself = Mary*), with resolution of both referential dependencies taking place locally and immediately in accordance with the Efficiency Requirement.

Summary

The assumption that the first argument of an infinitival verb is expressed as a referential dependency accounts for a number of important facts, as we have seen, but it also begs an important question—which sort of referential dependency? The sort associated with reflexive pronouns that is resolved by the computational system, or the sort associated with plain pronouns that is resolved pragmatically?

The cases we have considered so far manifest the first type of referential dependency. Because the grid of the matrix verb with which the infinitival phrase combines includes a designated controller argument, there is an immediate opportunity to resolve the referential dependency, and the computational system has no choice but to do so. We thus end up with a single, local, c-commanding controller—duplicating the results of the first generalization of traditional control theory (see p. 59).

As we will see next, however, computational resolution of the referential dependency in infinitival patterns is not always possible.

3.2 Pragmatic control

There are a variety of patterns in which there is no immediate opportunity to resolve the referential dependency introduced by the infinitival verb. When this happens, the computational system reacts just as it does in the case of pronouns that introduce a similar sort of referential dependency (see chapter three)—it passes the dependency to the pragmatic system for resolution there, as this presents the best opportunity to see the dependency resolved expeditiously. The end result is the possibility of a nonlocal interpretation, including interpretations that look beyond the sentence (again just as we find with pronouns). Let us consider some actual cases.

Infinitival phrases that function as subjects

The prototypical case of a pragmatically resolved referential dependency involves the occurrence of an infinitival phrase in subject position.

(1)   [To leave early] embarrasses the hosts.

Following combination of the infinitival phrase with the matrix verb, we end up with the representation depicted below. (I assume that the first argument of *embarrass* in (1) is a *to* phrase.)

(2)

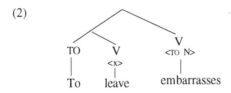

There is clearly no opportunity for the immediate computational resolution of the referential dependency here—the matrix verb's grid contains no index at all at this point.

As we have already seen, the computational system deals only with referential dependencies that it can resolve right away. Because no such opportunity arises in the case of matrix verbs that take an infinitival phrase as their first argument, a designated controller would be pointless in such cases. The pragmatic system offers the best opportunity to resolve the referential dependency.

This leads to a simple prediction: no verb whose first argument is an infinitival phrase can designate a controller for the computational system. This seems to be right in the case of (1) and similar patterns, where only pragmatically derived interpretations are possible. As illustrated below, the unexpressed first argument of the infinitival verb can correspond to a referent mentioned elsewhere in the sentence; it can be interpreted as the speaker and/or addressee (a 'logophoric' reading); or it can be assigned a generic reading.

(3)   Mary noted that [to leave early] would violate the rules.
        (= 'for Mary to leave...;' 'for us to leave...;' 'for anyone to leave...')

Similar interpretations are also found when the matrix verb takes an expletive argument.

(4)   Mary noted that [*it* would violate the rules [to leave early]].
        (= 'for Mary to leave...;' 'for us to leave...;' 'for anyone to leave...')

It is evidently the case that if the verb does not designate a controller argument before the expletive is added to its argument grid, it will not designate one afterward either.[3]

So far, so good, but Jackendoff & Culicover (2003:535) note an apparent counterexample.

(5)   [To call Ernie at 3:00 a.m.] would be rude of Bert.

Here only one interpretation is possible—the caller must be Bert. But does this mean that *rude* designates a controller argument for the computational system, undermining the prediction that we have made? I don't think so.

As Jackendoff & Culicover note (p. 540), adjectives such as *rude* ascribe the same property to an actor as they do to his or her actions. So, if phoning someone in the middle of the night is rude, so is the person who does it. And since Bert cannot be considered rude because of someone else's actions, it follows that he must be the early-morning caller in (5).

Crucially though, these facts are the result of pragmatic reasoning and have nothing to do with the sentence's structure per se, contrary to what Jackendoff & Culicover propose. (Their idea is that predicates such as *rude* designate a unique controller for an action-denoting infinitival argument in subject position.) As the next example shows, the facts are the same even when there is no head–argument relation between *rude* and either the infinitival clause or the controller.

(6)   [To call Ernie at 3:00 a.m.] would require real rudeness on Bert's part.

In (6), the caller can only be Bert. Yet neither the infinitival clause nor the nominal *Bert* is an argument of *rude(ness)*.

---

[3]In fact, even matrix predicates whose first argument is always an expletive (e.g., *It's time to leave*) do not designate a controller. This is presumably because expletives lack a referential index and therefore are not able to participate in the resolution of referential dependencies.

A similar case involves the expression *take time*.

(7)   [To paint that house] would take Jerry a lot of time.

Here it is clear that Jerry is the painter, presumably because someone else's activity cannot literally consume Jerry's time. But once again this has nothing to do with the structure of the sentence per se. The same interpretation is required in (8), where *Jerry* is not an argument of *take*.

(8) a.   [To paint that house] would take a lot of Jerry's time.
    b.   [To paint that house] would take up a lot of the time that Jerry had set aside
         for his vacation.

This is very different from what happens in the case of infinitival clauses in complement position, where a designated argument of the matrix verb must serve as controller.

In sum then, there is no reason to think that the computational system is responsible for resolving the referential dependency associated with an infinitival verb that functions as subject of the matrix verb. Like the referential dependencies associated with plain pronouns, such dependencies are simply passed to the pragmatic system.[4]

Infinitival phrases that function as modifiers

Patterns with infinitival subjects are not the only type of construction in which the referential dependency introduced by an infinitival verb cannot be immediately resolved and must therefore be passed to the pragmatic system. Another set of cases illustrating the same point involves the use of infinitival phrases as modifiers—a common occurrence in English.

(9) a.   Purpose clause (e.g., Bach 1982):
         Sally bought several things [to read while on vacation].

    b.   *In order to* clause:
         [In order to get a permit], John first must take a course.

The infinitival purpose clause in (9a) combines with a category (the noun *things*) that does not even have an argument grid. And although the *in order to* clause in

---

[4]This may also shed light on a crucial property of so-called '*tough* constructions' such as *John is tough [to find]*, in which the unexpressed first argument of the infinitival verb must be interpreted generically. Crucially, predicates such as *tough* also occur in patterns where they take the infinitival phrase as their first argument (e.g., *[To find John] is tough*). This suggests that they do not designate a controller argument, leaving recourse to the pragmatic system as the only option for interpreting the unexpressed subject of the infinitival phrase.

(9b) is a type of adverbial modifier, its positioning (typically at the beginning or the end of the sentence) rules out direct combination with the verb.

In the absence of an immediate opportunity to resolve the dependency introduced by the infinitival clause, recourse to the pragmatic system is the only option. This may result in the selection of a sentence-internal referent—both purpose clauses and *in order to* clauses tend to be strongly agent-oriented, as the examples in (9) illustrate. But there is no general requirement that the referential dependency be resolved sentence-internally, and minor changes in the choice of lexical items can lead to a radically different result. We therefore find patterns such as the following, in which the pragmatic system looks outside the sentence to resolve the referential dependency associated with the modifier clause.

(10) a. Purpose clause:
   Sally recommended several things [to read while on vacation].
   (= 'for us to read;' 'for everyone to read')

   b. *In order to* clause:
   [In order to succeed in the business world], tenacity is a must.
   (= 'for one to succeed in the business world')

This is what we would expect if the computational routines for such patterns pass the referential dependencies to the pragmatic system rather than attempting to resolve them internally.

Wh infinitival clauses

Finally, let us consider patterns such as the following, in which the infinitival complement begins with a *wh* word.

(11) a. Paul asked Sally [how to fix a flat tire].
   b. Mary asked Fred [what to do if someone asks for money].

As noted by Manzini (1983:429) and Jackendoff & Culicover (2003:551), these sentences have two interpretations—one where the second argument of the matrix verb is the controller and one involving a generic interpretation (e.g., 'Paul asked Sally how *one* fixes a flat tire,' 'Mary asked what *one* does if asked for money'). This suggests that the resolution of the referential dependency has been left to the pragmatic system, which then chooses between the addressee argument of the matrix verb and a generic interpretation. But why was the referential dependency left for the pragmatic system to resolve in the first place?

The answer is in fact straightforward. The referential dependency introduced by the infinitival verb cannot be immediately resolved by the computational system. As we will see in chapter seven, *wh* words such as *how* and *what* introduce a type of dependency that must be resolved when the embedded verb is encountered. The resolution of this dependency evidently delays the resolution of the referential dependency associated with the infinitival verb, causing the computational system to transfer responsibility for it to the pragmatic system just as it does in the case of plain pronouns.

Summary

At least as a first approximation, it seems that the core properties of control theory may follow from the workings of the same computational system that is used to build sentences and to resolve the sorts of referential dependencies associated with pronouns. The idea is strikingly simple—the conceptual-symbolic system introduces dependencies (categorial and referential) and the computational system seeks to resolve them in the most efficient manner possible.

Where the computational system can resolve a dependency immediately, it does so. This is what happens in the case of most infinitival verbs that appear in complement position. As we have seen, the referential dependency corresponding to their first argument is resolved by an index of a designated argument in the grid of the matrix verb. Where immediate resolution is not feasible, because no such index is available, the computational system passes the dependency to the pragmatic system, which typically produces a generic or logophoric interpretation.

The following table summarizes the workings of the control phenomenon in English.

TABLE 4.1
Control in English

Type of Opportunity to Resolve the Referential Dependency Introduced by the Infinitival Verb	Consequence (Type of Control Pattern)
The computational system has immediate access to the index of a designated controller	Resolution by the computational system (= 'obligatory control')
The computational system lacks immediate access to the index of a designated controller	Interpretation yielded by the pragmatic system (= 'pragmatic control')

4. COMPLEMENTS OF DEVERBAL NOUNS

Next, let us consider how control works in infinitival verbs that serve as complements of nouns, beginning with the pattern exemplified in (1).

(1)   The decision [to leave] struck me as unwise.

As illustrated in (2), there is no index in the argument grid of *decision* at the point at which the infinitival verb is added to the sentence.

(2)

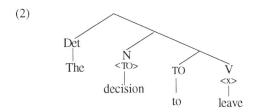

In the absence of a timely opportunity for the computational system to deal with the referential dependency introduced by the infinitival verb, it is resolved pragmatically. This in turn accounts for the availability of the logophoric reading ('...for us to leave') and of the generic interpretation ('... for everyone to leave').

Such patterns contrast with constructions such as (3), in which the nominal has a genitive argument.

(3)   Tim's decision [to leave] struck me as unwise.

In structures such as these, the index corresponding to the genitive nominal is in the argument grid of the noun at the point at which the infinitival complement is incorporated into the sentence. The Efficiency Requirement therefore forces an interpretation in which the understood subject of *leave* refers to Tim.[5]

(4)   Step 1: Combination of *decision* with its first argument, the genitive nominal *Tim:*

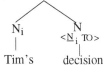

Step 2: Combination of *decision* with its second argument, the infinitival morpheme *to:*

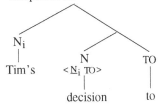

---

[5]An interesting intermediate case here involves patterns such as *the American decision [to restrict potato imports]*. Assuming that *American* is an adjective and does not carry a referential index, its presence assists the pragmatic system, not the computational system, in identifying the first argument of the infinitival verb.

Step 3: Combination of *to* with its verbal argument; resolution of the referential dependency representing the infinitival verb's subject argument:

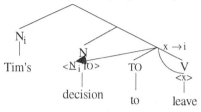

Tim's   <N̲ᵢ͟t̲o̲>   TO   V
               | | <x>
             decision   to   leave

As Jackendoff & Culicover (2003:533) note, the semantic considerations that determine which of a verb's arguments is designated as controller carry over to nominals. Thus the noun *promise* designates its first argument as controller, while the noun *signal* selects its second argument—just as the corresponding verbs do. (The *to*-phrases in these examples are referring prepositional phrases (see p. 64).

(5) a.   John's$_i$ promise [to Mary]$_j$ [to leave early]
         <N̲$_i$ P$_j$ TO>   <x>

   b.   John's$_i$ signal [to Mary]$_j$ [to lock the door]
        <N$_i$ P̲$_j$ TO>   <x>

This is consistent with the idea that the computational system seeks out semantically designated controllers within a 'space' that permits quick resolution of the referential dependency introduced by the infinitival verb.

5. CONCLUSION

In sum, there is good reason to think that argument requirements can be made visible to the computational system in two quite different ways—as categorial dependencies that are resolved by combination with an overt argument and as referential dependencies.

By assuming that infinitival verbs project their subject argument as a referential dependency, we derive a straightforward account for the grand generalizations of traditional control theory.

In general, infinitival verbs that occur in complement position take an argument of the matrix verb as their controller. But not because of a principle of Universal Grammar. Rather, as we have seen, the explanation lies in the interaction of two factors—the properties of individual matrix verbs (*promise* designates its first argument as controller, while *persuade* designates its second argument) and the operation of the computational system, which uses this information as it seeks to immediately resolve the referential dependency associated with the first argument of the infinitival verb.

At the same time—and here we come to the second major generalization of traditional control theory—immediate resolution of the referential dependency via the computational system is not possible when the infinitival phrase occurs in subject position, when it is a modifier, or when it is part of a *wh* clause. Under these circumstances, the pragmatic system offers the best opportunity to expeditiously resolve the referential dependency introduced by the infinitival phrase. Responsibility for the referential dependency is therefore waived by the computational system, resulting in a different and typically broader set of interpretive options.

In the end then, the facts follow from more basic computational forces, consistent with the emergentist thesis—they simply reflect the most efficient way to resolve referential dependencies. I will pursue this theme further in chapter five by examining a second type of infinitival complement pattern.

Chapter 5

'Raising' Structures

1. INTRODUCTION

English contains a second major type of infinitival complement pattern. Exemplified by the sentence in (1), it is frequently manifested with matrix verbs such as *seem* and *appear*.

(1)   Harvey seemed [to work hard].

At first glance, this pattern seems identical to the control constructions considered in the previous chapter and re-exemplified in (2).

(2)   Harvey tried [to work hard].

However, there is at least one major difference. As shown in (3), *seem*-type verbs permit an expletive subject, whereas control verbs such as *try* and *decide* do not.[1]

(3) a.   *There* seemed [to be a problem].
    b.   **There* tried [to be a problem].
    c.   **There* decided [to be a problem].

On the one hand then, *seem*-type patterns are clearly similar to their *try*-type counterparts; on the other hand, they differ in a significant way. This raises the obvious question—where do these similarities come from, and why are there differences? The answer that I will propose is that the similarities come from the operation of the computational system, and that the differences arise from lexical properties of the items on which that system operates.

More ambitiously, I will try to show that the defining properties of *seem*-type patterns, like the core features of control, follow from the efficiency driven character of the computational system, not from principles of grammar in the traditional sense.

---

[1] A parallel contrast holds for another type of non-referring nominal, namely idiom chunks such as *the cat* in the following example.

(i)   The cat seems to have gotten out of the bag. (= 'The secret has apparently been revealed.')
(ii)   *The cat decided to get out of the bag. (* on the idiomatic interpretation)

2. *SEEM*-TYPE VERBS

The classic analysis of *seem*-type verbs makes two claims. The first claim, with which I concur, is that *seem*-type verbs do not assign a thematic role to their subject.

(1)   *seem*: V, <N TO>

In this, they differ from control-type verbs such as *try*.

(2)   *try*: V, <N TO>
                       ag

The most direct reflex of this difference is the property alluded to above: *try* cannot take an expletive subject, presumably because *there* is incompatible with a conventional thematic role such as agent, theme, or goal.[2]

The second claim of the classic analysis is that the subject of a *seem*-type verb 'raises' from within the embedded clause. (For this reason, these constructions are often called *raising* patterns.)

(3)   Harvey seemed [_ to work hard].
          ↑_____|

The prima facie evidence for this is that the thematic role of the matrix subject is determined by the infinitival verb. Thus if the subject of *seem* is an agent, it is because the embedded verb requires an agent subject; if the subject of *seem* is an expletive, it is because the embedded verb calls for a subject of this type; and so on (ag = agent; ex = expletive).

(4) a.   Before raising:
           seemed [Harvey to work hard]
                              <ag>

    b.   After raising:
           Harvey seemed [_ to work hard].
              ↑_____| <ag>

(5) a.   Before raising:
           seemed [there to be a problem]
                         <ex N>

---

[2]*Seem*-type verbs have a second use, not relevant here, in which they take a tensed clause as their second argument (*It seems that John left early*). On this use, *seem* requires an expletive first argument (**Harry seems that John left early*).

b. After raising:
   There seemed [_ to be a problem].
   ↑_____| <ex N>

2.1 An alternative analysis

My analysis consists of three principal points. First, like everyone else, I acknowledge that *try*-type verbs and *seem*-type verbs differ with respect to whether they provide a thematic role for their first argument. As observed above, *try* assigns a thematic role to its first argument, whereas *seem* doesn't.

Second, I maintain that the infinitival verb's first argument is expressed as a referential dependency in *seem*-type patterns, just as it is in *try*-type patterns. In accordance with the usual practice, this dependency must be resolved at the first opportunity, with consequences that we will consider shortly.

Finally, I hold that like *try*-type verbs, *seem*-type verbs designate their first argument as controller (an idea dating back at least to Bresnan 1982:377). This further constrains the operation of the computational system by providing a designated argument to which it can look to resolve the referential dependency introduced by the infinitival verb.

I therefore reject the raising analysis of *seem*-type patterns, proposing instead that a sentence such as *John seemed to win* is formed in the following manner.

(1)   Step 1: Combination of *seem* with *John:*

Step 2: Combination of *seem* with *to:*

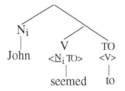

Step 3: Combination of *to* with its verbal argument:

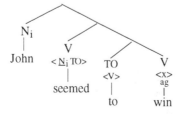

Step 4: The referential dependency expressing the infinitival verb's agent argument is resolved by the index of *John* in the grid of *seem*, in accordance with the Efficiency Requirement:

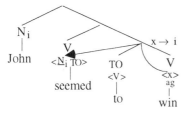

This gives the interpretation in which the agent argument of *win* corresponds to *John*, as desired.

2.2 Some other properties of raising patterns

So far so good, but what about other familiar properties of raising patterns? (Although I reject the raising analysis of *seem*-type patterns, I will continue to use the term 'raising' as a convenient descriptive label.) I will focus here on two phenomena—the impossibility of long-distance raising and the manner in which *seem*-type patterns license an expletive subject. The goal in each case is to show that the relevant facts follow from the operation of the computational system on lexical items with particular properties; no reference is made to grammatical principles.

Long-distance raising

As the sentence below illustrates, raising patterns permit neither a long-distance interpretation nor a sentence-external interpretation—the worker in (1) can only be Mary.

(1)   John thinks [Mary seems [to work hard]].

Given the opportunity to resolve the referential dependency by the index of *Mary* in the grid of *seem*, the Efficiency Requirement permits no other interpretation— exactly the right result.

(2)   John$_i$ thinks [Mary$_j$ seems [to work hard]].
                      <N$_j$ TO>   <x>
                         ↑_____|

A long-distance relationship appears to be possible in patterns such as (3).

(3)   John seems [to tend [to win]].

But this is just an illusion. To begin, *seem* resolves its first argument dependency
by combination with the nominal *John*.

(4)

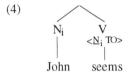

Next, *to* and *tend* are added, and the referential dependency introduced by *tend* is
resolved by the index of *John* in the grid of *seem*.

(5)

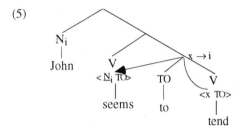

Then *to* and *win* are added, and the referential dependency introduced by *win* is
resolved by the index (now *i*) in the grid of *tend*, giving the desired interpretation—
John is the apparent usual winner.

(6)

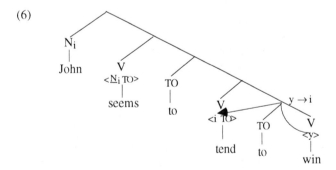

The sentence thus owes its acceptability to the fact that each dependency is resolved
at the first opportunity in accordance with the usual requirements for the operation
of the computational system.

There seem patterns

When a verb such as *be* occurs with an expletive argument in sentences such as
There is a problem, I assume that it instantiates the argument grid illustrated below.

(Remember that I use the term *argument* to refer to any expression required by a functor; arguments do not have to bear a thematic role.)

(7)   There is a problem.
        <N N>
        ex th

But what happens when the verb is infinitival and its first argument is not expressed as a categorial dependency, as in the sentence *There seems to be a problem*? In particular, how is the infinitival verb's dependency on an expletive argument to be represented and resolved?

   Intuitively, we would like to represent the dependency in the same manner as in other raising patterns—by a referential index. But can such an index be justified, given that expletives do not refer to real-world entities?

   Although expletives do not have prototypical referents, they do have an identity that the computational system must record and track. (The expletive *there* is not identical to the expletive *it*, for instance, and the two occur in different contexts— cf. *It/*There seems that John has left*). It has even been suggested that expletives designate 'abstract settings' and therefore have a 'quasi-referential' meaning (Langacker 1995:46; see also Jacobsen 1990:436).

   I propose to accommodate these considerations by employing the 'dummy' index 0 for expletive *there* and by positing the existence of a parallel dummy index, which I will write as z, for expletive arguments that are not overtly expressed. The two types of indices are exemplified in (8), where z represents the unexpressed first argument of *be*.

(8)   There$_0$ seems [to be a problem]
                 <z N>

The task of determining the identity of the z index falls to the computational system, which acts with the usual dispatch. It first combines *seem* with the expletive nominal to its left, resolving the verb's first argument dependency.

(9)

N$_0$ V
 | <N$_0$ TO>
 | |
There   seems

Then, following addition of *to* and *be*, the infinitival verb's dependency on an expletive argument is resolved by the index of the expletive in the grid of *seem*.[3]

---

[3]If the infinitival verb's first argument is not an expletive, the sentence will be anomalous—cf. *There seems to go far*, in which the non-referring expletive argument of the matrix verb has to be associated with the infinitival verb's agent argument dependency.

(10)

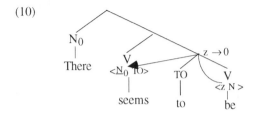

The formation of the sentence *There seems to be a problem* therefore exactly parallels that of patterns such as *John decided to solve the problem*, with a regular referring subject, as desired. However, an interesting and telling difference shows up in another pattern.

Because an expletive has no concrete real-world reference, there are limitations on how the corresponding dependency can be managed. It can be resolved computationally by the 0 index corresponding to *there* in the grid of *seem*, as we have just seen. But it cannot be interpreted by the pragmatic system, since there is nothing in the sentence-external world to which it could refer.

This in turn leads to an interesting prediction—infinitival verbs with an expletive subject should not be acceptable in positions where the covert expletive argument would have to be interpreted pragmatically. One relevant construction is the following, in which an infinitival verb with an unexpressed expletive argument functions as subject of the matrix clause.

(11)   *[To *be* three people at the door at this hour] is surprising.
        (cf. [That *there* are three people at the door at this hour] is surprising.)

Resolution of the infinitival verb's unexpressed subject argument dependency is impossible here. It cannot be resolved via the computational system, since there is no index in the grid of the matrix verb (*be surprising*). And resolution via the pragmatic system is likewise impossible, since expletives have no real-world referent. The dependency is therefore left unresolved, rendering the sentence unacceptable.

3. *EXPECT*-TYPE VERBS

Now consider the pattern exemplified in (1).

(1)   John expected Mary [to leave].

At first glance, this looks just like the control pattern in (2).

(2)   John persuaded Mary [to leave].

But there are important differences, the most obvious being that the second nominal in the *expect* pattern can be an expletive. (Other verbs that work this way include *believe, consider,* and *prove.*)

(3)   John expected *there* [to be a problem].
        (cf. *John persuaded *there* [to be a problem].)

How can this be?

3.1 An analysis of *expect*-type patterns

The classic analysis of *expect*-type patterns, developed within the Government and Binding framework during the 1980s, is that the second nominal in *expect*-type patterns functions as subject of the embedded clause, where its 'role' (agent, expletive, and so forth) is determined (e.g., Chomsky 1981:98).

(1) a. John expected [*Mary* to leave].
    b. John expected [*there* to be a problem].

In fact, however, there is good reason to believe that the second nominal in these patterns is actually in the *higher* clause, as proposed in theories ranging from Lexical Functional Grammar (Bresnan 1982:374ff, Dalrymple 2001:314ff) to Head-driven Phrase Structure Grammar (Pollard & Sag 1987:20) to Dependency Grammar (Starosta 1997).

One piece of evidence for this conclusion comes from Postal's (1974:146) observation that an adverb with scope over the matrix clause, can occur *after* the postverbal NP. (See also Authier 1991:729.)

(2) a. We expect the committee, *unfortunately*, to stick with its current policy.
        (= 'Unfortunately, we expect the committee to stick with its current policy.')

    b. I believed Nixon, *incorrectly*, to be interested in ending the war.
        (= 'I incorrectly believed Nixon to be interested in ending the war.')

This suggests that the adverb—and therefore the NP to its left as well—must be part of the matrix clause.

Another piece of evidence for the same conclusion comes from the distribution of negative polarity items, which must be licensed by a structurally more prominent negative word such as *no* or *not* (see chapter two, p. 18). The key observation involves sentences such as the following, from Lasnik & Saito (1991:329).

(3)   The DA proved *no one* [to be guilty] during *any* of the trials.

If the NP *no one* were in the embedded clause, as depicted in (4), it would be unable to license the negative polarity item *any*, which is clearly in the matrix clause since it is part of a PP that modifies *prove*.[4]

(4)   The DA proved [*no one* to be guilty] during *any* of the trials.
                                negative word
                                is lower than the
                                negative polarity item

However, things work smoothly if we assume that *expect*-type verbs (including *prove*) are just like *persuade*-type verbs in taking three arguments—two nominals (the second of which is the designated controller) and one infinitival *to*-phrase.

        1st arg   2nd arg   3rd arg
(5)   [The DA] proved [no one] [to be guilty].

On this view, then, *persuade*-type patterns and *expect*-type patterns are exactly alike in two respects—they both take two nominal arguments and one infinitival argument, and they both designate their second nominal argument as controller. They differ only in that *expect*-type verbs do not assign a thematic role to their second argument, which can therefore be an expletive. (In this, they are like *seem*-type verbs, which also provide no thematic role for a nominal argument.)

(6) a. *persuade*: <N N TO>
                      ag go th

    b. *expect*: <N N TO>
                    ag   th

The key facts now follow, as can be seen by considering the formation of the sentence *John expects Mary to win*.

(7)   Steps 1 & 2: Combination of *expect* with its agent argument *John* and then with its thematically unspecified argument *Mary*:

---

[4]This fact is often accommodated in the Minimalist Program by assuming that the subject of the infinitival clause raises to the higher clause (e.g., Chomsky & Lasnik 1995), which is reminiscent of Postal's (1974) raising analysis.

Step 3: Combination of *expect* with its third argument, the infinitival marker *to:* [5]

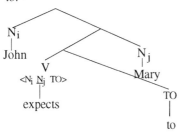

Step 4: Combination of *to* with its verbal argument, *win*: The referential dependency introduced by the verb is immediately resolved by the index of *Mary* in the grid of *expect*, in accordance with the Efficiency Requirement. This in turn allows *Mary* to be identified as the agent argument of *win*.

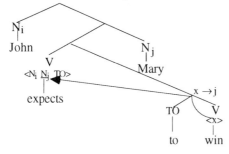

There is no other option here. The computational system has the opportunity to resolve a referential dependency upon encountering the index of the designated controller in the grid of the matrix verb, and it must do so. The possibility of a long-distance or sentence-external antecedent is precluded, just as it is in classic control patterns.

---

[5]As noted in chapter two (p. 17), the same combinatorial relationships can be more transparently represented as follows.

(i)

$N_1 \perp V$

$V \perp N_2$

$V \perp \text{TO}$

(8) a. *Expect*-type pattern:
       Susan$_i$ thinks [that John$_j$ expects Mary$_k$ to win].
                     <N$_j$ N$_k$ TO>   <x>
                        ↑_____|

   b. Classic control pattern:
       Susan$_i$ thinks [that John$_j$ persuaded Mary$_k$ to win].
                <N$_j$ N$_k$ TO>   <x>
                 ↑_____|

Once again, we see that a fundamental property of a particular sentence type follows from the efficiency driven character of the computational system that forms it. No grammatical principle is in play here; it is simply the case that dependencies must be resolved at the first opportunity.

3.2 Anaphor interpretation in *expect*-type patterns

A further advantage of this analysis of *expect*-type constructions is that it allows us to solve an otherwise puzzling fact about the use of pronouns. As illustrated below, coreference in *expect*-type patterns requires use of a reflexive pronoun, just as it does in classic control constructions.

(1) a. *Expect*-type pattern:
       John$_i$ believes himself/*him$_i$ to be a hard worker.

   b. Classic control pattern:
       John$_i$ persuaded himself/*him$_i$ to work hard.

The need for the reflexive form of the pronoun is expected if it is an argument of the matrix verb, as I have suggested. The crucial milestones in the formation of (1) are depicted in (2).

(2)   Step 1: Combination of *believe* with its first argument:

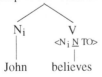

Step 2: Addition of the verb's second argument (the reflexive pronoun) and immediate resolution of the referential dependency that it introduces:

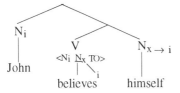

At the point where the reflexive pronoun is added to the sentence, there is already an index in the verb's argument grid—the *i* corresponding to the nominal *John*. In accordance with the usual practice, it is used to immediately resolve the pronoun's referential dependency.

This in turn rules out the use of a plain pronoun in this context. As we saw in chapter three, the reflexive form of a pronoun is required precisely in those situations where a referential dependency can be immediately resolved by the computational system.

The facts surrounding the use of reflexive pronouns in English are extraordinarily intricate. Not surprisingly, they have played a major role in the development of traditional grammatical theory, with its emphasis on autonomous syntactic principles. As I have repeatedly emphasized, however, there is perhaps another way of looking at things. Even the most complex properties of language may be emergent, reflecting the operation of a computational system whose foremost mandate is to reduce the burden on working memory.

4. THE UNIFICATION OF CONTROL AND RAISING

The similarity between raising and control is too great to be a coincidence, and it is not surprising that there have been two sorts of attempts to unify the phenomena over the years—one type that seeks to treat control as raising, and another type that analyzes raising as control.

The best known attempt to reduce control to raising has been put forward by Hornstein (1999) and Boeckx & Hornstein (2003, 2004), who suggest that control patterns such as (1) are derived by movement.

(1)   Harvey decided [_ to leave].
          ↑_____|

There have also been attempts to unify the two phenomena in the opposite direction, most notably by Starosta (1997). The analysis that I have put forward is of this type too, since it attempts to reduce raising to control by proposing that the first argument of the infinitival verb in both patterns is expressed as a referential dependency that the computational system seeks to resolve at the first opportunity.

Proposals such as these raise two sorts of questions. First, we must ask whether there is empirical evidence to distinguish between accounts that reduce control to raising and those that reduce raising to control. One candidate is the structure in (2).

(2)   Mary pleaded [$_{PP}$ with Jane] [to stay].

As Culicover & Jackendoff (2001) note, proponents of the raising account of control have to posit movement to a position within PP, an operation that is otherwise unattested in the transformational framework that they adopt.

(3)   Mary pleaded [$_{PP}$ with Jane] [_ to stay].
                                       ↑____|

In contrast, these patterns present no problem to the control-based approach that I have proposed. As explained in chapter four (p. 64), the PPs found here are referring prepositional phrases with their own referential index. Following combination, this index is copied into the grid of the matrix verb, where it is available to resolve the referential dependency introduced by the infinitival verb.

(4)   Mary$_i$ pleaded [with Jane]$_j$ [to stay].
              <N$_i$ P$_j$ TO>   <x>
              ↑_____|

The second question raised by attempts to unify control and raising is of a more fundamental sort—can either proposal for unification account for the existence of various *differences* between the two patterns?

The particular idea that I have pursued is that any such differences must reflect contrasts in the lexical properties of the matrix verbs, especially the fact that control verbs have the type of meaning that determines a thematic role for their subject argument, whereas raising verbs do not. Boeckx & Hornstein (2004:445) take an identical position.

As we have already seen, this difference accounts for why raising verbs, but not their control counterparts, can occur with expletive subjects (*There seems to be a problem* vs. **There tried to be a problem*). But there are many other facts that need to be considered.

For instance, one consequence of having a verb that assigns an agent role to its first argument, as *try*-type verbs do, is that that argument must be a nominal (since only nominals denote the types of entities that can function as agents). Raising verbs assign no thematic role to their first argument, and there is likewise no requirement that the first argument be a nominal. Rather, both its thematic role and its precise categorial properties are determined by the embedded verb. Thus if the embedded verb takes an infinitival *to*-phrase or a clause as its first argument, that type of category will appear as subject of *seem* in the raising pattern.

(5) a. [$_{TO}$ To leave early] might seem [to be impolite].
         <TO A>

 b. [$_S$ That he left early] seemed [to insult the hosts].
         <S N>

Nothing comparable is possible with control verbs, which require a nominal subject regardless of the selectional properties of their infinitival complement.

(6) a. *[$_{TO}$ To leave early] might try [to be impolite].
 b. *[$_S$ That he left early] tried [to insult the hosts].

Another illustration of how the properties of the subject of a raising predicate are determined by the infinitival verb comes from Icelandic. As (7) shows, the exceptional accusative case associated with the first argument of the verb *vantu* 'lack' shows up on the subject of the matrix verb in Icelandic raising patterns (Andrews 1982).

(7)   *Hana*   virðist [vantu peninga].
        She.Acc seems to-lack money.Acc
        'She seems to lack money.'

Nothing comparable is found in control patterns, where the matrix verb independently determines the properties of its first argument.

The fact that the properties of the first argument are wholly determined by the matrix verb in control patterns but not in raising patterns may have something to do with another difference between the two constructions. As observed by Jacobsen (1990), some control verbs permit deletion of both *to* and its verbal argument, but no raising verbs do.

(8) a. Control:
         Mary tried to succeed, and John also tried.

 b. Raising:
         *Mary seemed to succeed, and John also seemed.
         (cf. Mary seemed to succeed, and John also seemed to.)

This may be related to the fact that raising verbs rely on the complement of *to* (i.e., the infinitival verb) to license their subject. No such relationship exists in the case of control verbs.

Another difference between control and raising is even subtler. As noted by Landau (2003), certain control verbs can occur in patterns such as the following, in which the unexpressed first argument of the embedded verb refers to a set of individuals that includes, but is not restricted to, the referent of the matrix subject. (This is sometimes dubbed *partial control*.)

(9)   John wants [to get together twice a week].
        (= John wants for him and us to get together twice a week.)

In contrast, no raising verbs sound natural in these constructions.

(10)   *John seems [to get together twice a week].

From the point of view of reference too then, control verbs, but not raising verbs, appear to select a first argument with properties somewhat independent of those of the embedded verb's first argument.[6]

Still other differences remain wholly mysterious. For instance, it is well known that raising constructions differ from control constructions in not permitting nominalization.

(11) a. Control:
        John's decision to leave (cf. John decided to leave.)

     b. Raising:
        *John's appearance to leave (cf. John appeared to leave.)

Moreover, as noted by Landau (2003:491), control and raising verbs differ with respect to the acceptability of a 'floated quantifier' after the first argument of the matrix verb.

(12) a. Control:
        *One interpreter *each* tried to be assigned to the visiting diplomats.

     b. Raising:
        One interpreter *each* seems to have been assigned to the visiting diplomats.

It is unclear precisely how these contrasts should be dealt with, or whether their eventual solution will be compatible with the ideas outlined here. Although I am unable to make a concrete proposal at this time, the hope is that an eventual fuller analysis will retain the emergentist character of the proposals that I have put forward.

---

[6]This suggests that it may be necessary to fine-tune the notion of 'referential dependency' so that it need not always entail identity of reference.

5. CONCLUSION

The particular idea that I have pursued in this chapter is that the similarities between control and raising patterns come from the fact that both contain an infinitival verb whose first argument is expressed as a referential dependency that the computational system seeks to resolve at the first opportunity. Differences between the two patterns are then traced to contrasts in their lexical properties. In accordance with the standard view, control verbs have the type of semantics that determines a thematic role for their subject argument, while raising verbs do not.

If the analysis I have proposed is on the right track, the interpretation and distribution of infinitival patterns in general follows from the efficiency driven character of the computational system and from the lexical properties of the words on which it operates. There is no need for principles of grammar in the traditional sense.

I will pursue this theme still further in chapter six by examining the role of efficiency in the syntax of agreement in English and other languages.

Chapter 6

Agreement

1. INTRODUCTION

Thus far in this book I have deliberately concentrated on the manner in which the computational system for language brings together and interprets the word- and phrase-sized constituents of sentences. In many languages, though, valuable insights into the operation of the computational system can also be gleaned from sublexical phenomena, particularly inflection. Verbal agreement is a case in point.

A familiar generalization about verbal agreement is that it records a relationship between a functor and one or more of its arguments. This makes good computational sense of course, since sentences are the product of combinatorial operations involving functors and their arguments. It also helps explain why agreement is almost always 'local'—verbs typically agree with their own arguments, not with those of other functors.

But which argument does the verb agree with when there is more than one? Most commonly the subject, it seems (e.g., Croft 2003:147). Certainly, this appears to be the case in English, where verbal agreement is standardly assumed to involve person and number features of the subject.

(1)   *Harvey* visit-*s* us every day.

This chapter focuses on the question of why this should be so, and on whether the standard grammatical generalization can be derived from deeper properties of the computational system.

2. THE AGREEMENT MECHANISM

In its prototypical instantiations, agreement is a relation between sublexical features of words—number, gender, person, and the like. This seems right, but important questions arise as to the character and organization of these features. These questions are worth examining briefly, even though we will not be able to answer them fully.

2.1 Features

At first glance, the category of number conveys a simple contrast—nouns and pronouns are either singular or plural, depending on how many entities they denote. Moreover, again at first glance, that distinction appears to be straightforwardly exploited by the agreement mechanisms that determine the form of the verb.

(1) a. Singular noun—singular form of the verb:
       A book *is* on the floor.

   b. Plural noun—plural form of the verb:
      Two books *are* on the floor.

But matters are not so simple. For example, English permits sentences such as the following, in which the subject carries the plural suffix, but the verb is in the singular (see Hirtle 1982, Reid 1991, and Kim 2004 for extensive discussion).

(2) a. Twenty dolla*rs is* a lot of money when you're six years old.
   b. Egg*s* with ham or bacon *was* the staple for breakfast. (Philip Roth, cited by Reid 1991:6)

And we find nouns without a plural suffix that can nonetheless trigger the plural form of the verb.

(3) a. The *couple were* married last month.
   b. A *variety* of problems *have* arisen.
   c. A *number* of people still *haven't* signed in.

Furthermore, although *couple* can behave like a plural with respect to verbal agreement, it behaves like a singular when it comes to the form of the determiner— we say *this couple*, not **these couple*.[1] And of course, nouns like *variety* and *number* occur with the singular determiner *a*, despite their propensity to trigger plural agreement in the verb.

The problem is not restricted to English. In French, for instance, the polite form of the second person singular pronoun triggers the *plural* form of the verb, but the *singular* form of an adjective. (This example is from Stephen Wechsler; for many additional examples from a variety of languages, see Dalrymple & Kaplan 2000 and Wechsler & Zaltic 2000.)

(4) Vous êtes loyal.
     you be.Pl loyal.Sg
     'You are loyal.'

---

[1] Sauerland & Elbourne (2002) note that this contrast is more widespread in British English, where nouns such as *committee, team, group*, and *family* always take the singular form of the determiner, but can trigger the plural form of the verb.

Types of features

Nouns and pronouns can evidently carry more than one type of number feature. According to the proposal put forward by Wechsler & Zaltic (2000), it is necessary to distinguish between *index agreement*, which involves the referential indices that are part of a nominal's semantic content, and *concord*, which involves the sharing of certain morphosyntactic head features. In the case of a sentence such as *This couple were married last week*, they propose, the relation between *this* and *couple* involves concord, while the relation between *couple* and *were* is an instance of indexical agreement.

I set all of this to the side and concentrate instead on the *location* of the features that are involved in agreement relations. In particular, I will focus on the role of the computational system in determining which of the verb's arguments is capable of triggering agreement in it.

In order to do this, it is necessary to divide features of all types (both concord features and index features) into two classes. On the one hand, there are *basic features* which are intrinsic to the elements in which they occur and do not have to be externally licensed. On the other hand, there are *dependent features* which must be matched with features on an element elsewhere in the sentence. This parallels Chomsky's distinction (e.g., 2002:36) between interpretable and uninterpretable features.

In a sentence such as *John likes horses*, the third person and singular features associated with the nominal *John* as well as the third person and plural features associated with *horses* are basic. They are intrinsic to their respective nominals and do not need to be licensed by features on another element. In contrast, the third person and singular features on the verb *likes* are of the dependent type and must be matched with features on the subject nominal (hence the unacceptability of **We likes horses*). I will refer to the relationship between dependent features and basic features as an *agreement dependency*.

2.2 Resolving agreement dependencies

The dependent features involved in verbal agreement in English can reside in either of two places. On the one hand, they are found in irregular verb stems, such as first person singular *am* and third person singular *has*, which we represent as follows.

(1)   V   V
       1Sg   3Sg
        | |
       am   has

On the other hand, and more commonly, agreement features are expressed by inflectional suffixes—the suffix *-s* for third person, singular and *-Ø* for everything else. The effects of suffixation are illustrated below.

(2)

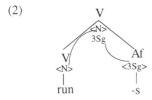

As can be seen here, the finite verb *runs* inherits its argument grid from its stem and its agreement features from its affix, as proposed by Selkirk (1982).

This brings us to the question of how agreement dependencies are to be resolved. There can be only one answer to this question—they should be resolved at the first opportunity, in accordance with the demands of the Efficiency Requirement.

(3)   *The Efficiency Requirement:*
        Dependencies are resolved at the first opportunity.

I assume that an opportunity to resolve an agreement dependency arises under the following circumstances.

(4)   An opportunity to resolve an agreement dependency arises immediately after the resolution of an argument dependency involving a feature-bearing nominal.

For instance, as we will see in much more detail shortly, an opportunity to resolve the agreement dependency introduced by the suffix *-s* in *Mary runs every day* occurs at the point where *runs* combines with *Mary*, resolving its dependency on a nominal argument.

As (4) implies, I take the resolution of agreement dependencies to be subordinate to the resolution of argument dependencies. One piece of evidence in support of this assumption comes from patterns such as the following.

(5)   Who are the boys sitting next to?
        (cf. *Who is the boys sitting next to?)

As we will see in the next two chapters, there is strong reason to believe that *who* combines with *are* in the initial stages of the formation of this sentence. Yet there is no agreement relationship between the two—*who* is singular and *are* is plural. The reason for this is straightforward on my account. In combining these two elements, the computational system does not resolve an argument dependency, since neither word is an argument of the other. (*Who* is in fact the argument of the preposition *to.*) Consistent with the assumption in (4), there is therefore no opportunity to resolve an agreement dependency—the right result.

More generally, there is ample evidence of various sorts that agreement dependencies are secondary to argument dependencies. Typologically, for instance, all languages manifest argument dependencies, but only some have agreement dependencies. (For instance, Mandarin lacks agreement, although it has no shortage of functor-argument patterns.)

A parallel developmental phenomenon illustrates the same point. In the early stages of language acquisition as well as in certain types of language disorders, sentences are formed solely by manipulating argument dependencies, without recourse to agreement. This results both in the overuse of uninflected verbs and in the omission of copulas and auxiliaries (Wexler 1996, Rice & Wexler 1996).

(6) a. He go.
　　b. She like me.
　　c. She happy with her dog.
　　d. Now she talking.

These considerations all point toward the same conclusion. Argument dependencies are primary and fundamental; agreement dependencies are secondary and subordinate.

Subject agreement

The English sentence *Harvey runs fast* offers a preliminary illustration of how agreement works. (For ease of exposition, I will not depict the verb's internal structure. Roman numerals and small caps represent basic features; Arabic numerals and regular roman type are employed for dependent features. A check mark is used to indicate that an agreement dependency has been resolved.)

(7) a. Combination leads to resolution of　　　b. Resolution of the agreement
　　　　the verb's argument dependency:　　　　　　dependency:

　　　　　　　　　　　　　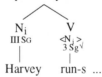

In the first step, the verb combines with the nominal *Harvey*, thereby resolving its argument dependency. Only at this point are the nominal's person and number features available to resolve the verb's third person singular agreement dependency.

(8)   Computational routine for subject-verb agreement:

i.   N$_i$ ⊥   V
        IIISG   <N$_i$>
                    3Sg

(combination of the nominal and the verb; resolution of the verb's argument dependency)

ii.   N   V
        IIISG ⇔ 3Sg$^{\surd}$

(resolution of the verb's agreement dependencies with the help of the features on its nominal argument)

Now consider a sentence such as *Harvey visits us often*, in which there are two feature-bearing nominals. The computational system proceeds as follows. (For ease of exposition, I will henceforth not represent argument dependencies.)

(9)   First steps: Combination with the nominal *Harvey* resolves the verb's first argument dependency and then its agreement dependency:

Next step: Combination of the verb with its second argument:

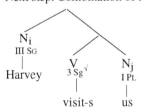

As illustrated here, the third person singular agreement dependency introduced by the inflectional suffix is resolved at the first opportunity, which occurs right after the verb resolves its first argument dependency. This essentially ensures that the verb must agree with its subject in transitive clauses. Because the first opportunity to resolve the verb's agreement dependencies arises when it combines with its first argument (the subject), agreement with the direct object is precluded on computational grounds.

Now consider a sentence such as (10), which is unacceptable in standard English.

(10)   *We visits Harvey often.

Because the computational system is compelled to resolve agreement dependencies as a matter of procedural necessity the instant it encounters a feature-bearing argument, sentences such as this one create an insurmountable dilemma. When *visits* combines with its first argument, the computational system must either violate the Efficiency Requirement by failing to resolve the verb's agreement dependencies, or it must ignore the feature clash between the first person plural subject and the third person singular verb. In either case, the result is unacceptable.

In sum, the reduction of agreement to the resolution of dependencies sheds light on the nature of so-called 'subject agreement' in English. As surprising as it may seem, the fact that agreement targets the subject has nothing to do with grammatical considerations. It simply reflects the propensity of the computational system to resolve dependencies at the first opportunity.

In the case of agreement dependencies in simple intransitive and transitive clauses, this opportunity just happens to arise when the verb combines with its first argument. As we will see next, however, something quite different can happen in other types of constructions.

3. AGREEMENT IN *THERE*-CONSTRUCTIONS

As we have just observed, an efficiency driven computational system that seeks to resolve agreement dependencies at the first opportunity creates a pattern of subject-oriented verbal agreement. From one point of view, this is a desirable result, since it provides an independent computational account for the standard grammatical generalization that English verbs agree with their subject.

From a different perspective though, the result is perhaps less than desirable, since it leaves open the possibility that the traditional grammatical account is actually correct. (If the emergentist idea is right of course, grammatical notions such as 'subject' should have no role to play in linguistic theory.) Fortunately, there are patterns that allow us to choose between the two accounts.

One such pattern involves constructions such as those in (1), where the verb's subject (first argument) is the featureless expletive *there*.

(1) a.   There was *glass* on the floor.
    b.   There were *glasses* on the floor.

There is no doubt that *there* counts as the verb's first argument here—among other things, it undergoes inversion in *yes–no* questions, just as other 'subjects' do.

(2)   Was there glass on the floor?

Yet, agreement in (1) is clearly triggered by the verb's second argument. How can this be?

Our computational system provides a straightforward explanation. Because the expletive *there* is featureless, it offers no opportunity for the verb to resolve its agreement dependencies. As illustrated in (3), the first opportunity for resolution arises at the point where the verb combines with its second argument.

(3)   Step 1: Combination with *there* resolves the verb's dependency on an expletive argument, but offers no opportunity for resolution of its agreement dependencies:

There   were

Step 2: Combination with *glasses* resolves the verb's second argument dependency and its agreement dependencies:

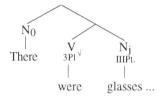

                    were   glasses ...

French contrasts in an interesting way with English in this regard. Because the expletive *il* (lit. 'it') is a third person singular pronoun, the Efficiency Requirement demands that its features be used to resolve the verb's argument dependencies. We therefore find a pattern of singular agreement, regardless of the status of the verb's second argument.

(4) a.   Singular second argument:
         Il est arrivé un homme.
         it be.Sg arrrived a man
         'There arrived a man.'

   b.   Plural second argument:
         Il est/*sont   arrivé deux hommes.
         it be.Sg/be.Pl arrived two   men
         'There arrived two men.'

A similar phenomenon can be observed in English sentences containing the third person, singular expletive *it*. As (5) illustrates, the verb must be in the singular even when the second nominal is plural.

(5)   *It* was/*were those men who did it.

In summary, the agreement pattern found in English *there* structures provides strong support for the view that agreement is driven by efficiency rather than grammatical relations. True, agreement often *appears* to target the subject in English—as in *Mary sees the boats*, where the subject nominal carries the features needed to resolve the verb's agreement dependencies. However, this is not because English has subject agreement per se; it is because the nominal that offers the first opportunity to resolve the verb's agreement dependencies just happens to be its subject (i.e., its first argument).

When the first argument carries no person and number features and therefore offers no opportunity for the resolution of agreement dependencies, the computational system has no choice but to move on. As illustrated in patterns such as *There is a man at the door*, the verb then ends up agreeing with its second argument.[2]

This is what we expect if agreement is driven by efficiency. Agreement dependencies are simply resolved at the first opportunity, regardless of the nominal's grammatical relation.

3.1 Downward feature passing

Let us turn now to the puzzlling pattern of agreement illustrated in (1).

(1) a.   There appear [to be two trees in the yard].
    b.   There appears [to be water on the floor].

The verbs in this pattern take an expletive as their first argument and an infinitival *to*-phrase as their second argument, neither of which carries person and number features. Instead, agreement is with a nominal inside the infinitival phrase—*two trees* in the first sentence and *water* in the second.

How does the computational system deal with such cases? Presumably, it simply follows the course of action that it adopts in patterns such as *There are three men at the door*, where the first argument is also unable to assist in the resolution of its agreement dependencies—it looks downward in search of another argument capable of resolving the verb's agreement dependencies.[3]

---

[2]In cases of copula contraction, English permits a sort of default singular verb form (e.g., Dixon 1977, Nathan 1981, Sparks 1984) regardless of the number features associated with the second argument.

(i)   There's a man/two men at the door.

I have nothing to say about this phenomenon here.

[3]Schütze (1999:479) reports that he permits the default singular with unstressed verbs in existential constructions but not in presentative constructions.

(i) a.   ?There appears to be two newspapers on my doorstep.
    b.   *There appears on my doorstep each morning two newspapers that endorse diametrically opposed viewpoints.

As illustrated below, the formation of sentences such as (1b) requires no more than the continuation of this search.

(2)   There appears to be water on the floor.

Step 1: Combination of *appears* with its first argument; no opportunity to resolve the agreement dependencies:

Step 2: Addition of the infinitival marker *to*; still no opportunity to resolve the agreement dependencies:

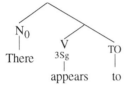

Step 3: Addition of *to*'s verbal argument:

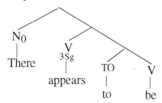

Step 4: Addition of the nominal *water*, which offers the first opportunity to resolve the agreement dependency via downward feature passing:

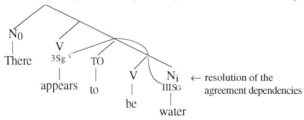

If this is right (I do not concur with the judgment), it might indicate that existential *there* differs from presentative *there* in carrying third person, singular features that immediately resolve the verb's agreement dependencies.

As illustrated here, the agreement dependency is passed down through the sentence until an opportunity arises for its resolution—in the form of the feature-bearing nominal *water*.[4]

This raises the question of why English does not permit agreement with the matrix verb's second argument in 'raising' patterns such as the following.

(3)   *There appear to the men [to be water on the floor].

The answer must be that the verb's second argument here is the prepositional phrase *to the men*, not the nominal *the men*, and that prepositional phrases do not have the type of person and number features that are relevant for verbal agreement.[5]

We see independent evidence for this in sentences such as (4), where the verb agrees with the nominal to its right, presumably because its first argument (the prepositional phrase *on the floor*) carries no person and number features.

(4)   [On the floor] were three books.

Summarizing then, there is good reason to believe that agreement in English is efficiency driven—it reflects the resolution of dependencies at the first opportunity, not the operation of a grammatical principle. In the simplest cases, such as *John works hard* or *Mary sees the boats*, the end result is the appearance of subject agreement. However, when the subject carries no person and number features, as happens in patterns such as *There is a man at the door*, agreement is with the second argument. And when neither the first argument nor the second argument carries person and number features, as happens in *There appears to be a man at the door*, agreement dependencies descend even further into the sentence, where they are finally resolved by an element that is not even an argument of the functor that carries the agreement inflection.

This is a far cry indeed from *subject* agreement, but it is perfectly in accord with the operation of an efficiency driven computational system that pays no heed to traditional grammatical notions.

---

[4]As noted earlier (p. 93), an opportunity to resolve an agreement dependency arises only after the resolution of an argument dependency involving a feature-bearing element. This is true here too— the opportunity to resolve the agreement dependencies in (2) arises only after *water* resolves the argument dependency introduced by the embedded verb *be*.

[5]Nonetheless, referring prepositional phrases do appear to have features that match those on coreferential pronouns.

(i)   I talked [to the men]$_i$ about themselves$_i$/*himself$_i$.

Of possible relevance here is the fact that agreement dependencies are resolved by (features of) the argument itself, whereas referential dependencies are resolved less directly, by an index in the grid of the verb.

4. AGREEMENT AND COORDINATION

Just as the Efficiency Requirement sheds light on the form and functioning of agreement, so agreement offers intriguing independent evidence that the computational system for language is driven by efficiency considerations. A particularly striking phenomenon in this regard arises in the case of agreement in coordinate structures. Let us begin by considering the following simple sentence.

(1)   [Water and sand] are on the floor.

The formation of the first part of this sentence proceeds in the manner depicted below. (I assume that *and* has the argument grid <X X>, which requires it to combine with two arguments of the same type. However, for the sake of exposition, I will continue to omit argument grids.)

(2)   Step 1: Combination of *water* and *and:*

Step 2: Addition of the second conjunct, leading to the creation of a plural noun phrase: (As noted in chapter three, p. 45, conjunctive coordination is additive.[6])

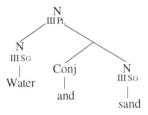

---

[6]The union of referential indices yields a plural in this case, but various puzzles remain to be solved, including the fact that both forms of the verb are permitted in sentences such as *Running and jumping is/are difficult*). Additional challenges arise when the conjuncts differ in person and/or gender features; see Corbett (1983), Pullum & Zwicky (1986), and Dalrymple & Kaplan (2000) for some discussion.

Step 3: Combination of the coordinate noun phrase with the verb: The agreement dependencies on the verb (third person, plural) are then immediately resolved by features of the coordinate subject phrase.

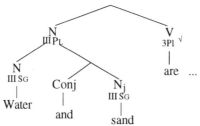

Interestingly, a quite different result is observed in cases where the coordinate phrase occurs to the right of the verb. Consider in this regard a sentence such as *There is water and sand on the floor*, in which the coordinate phrase functions as the verb's second argument.

(3)   Step 1: Combination of the verb with its first argument: Because *there* is featureless, no opportunity arises to resolve the verb's agreement dependencies here.

Step 2: Combination of the verb with the nominal *water*, which is thereby interpreted as its second argument; resolution of the verb's agreement dependencies:

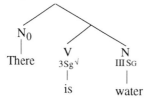

Final steps: Addition of the conjunction and of the second conjunct:

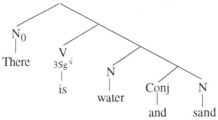

The second step is the crucial one—the verb combines with just the first conjunct of the coordinate phrase, the nominal *water*, which is thereby interpreted as its second argument. This interpretation must subsequently be partially revised with the addition of the second conjunct, but by then the agreement dependencies have already been resolved.

As noted by Munn (1999:654), agreement between the verb and the first conjunct of a coordinate phrase—dubbed *partial agreement*—is commonplace in English when the verb comes first (see also Sobin 1997 and Schütze 1999:473).

The key to understanding partial agreement lies not in some arcane exception to a grammatical rule, but rather in the manner in which sentences are formed. As depicted in the second step of (3), an opportunity to resolve the verb's agreement dependencies arises at the point where it combines with the first conjunct of the coordinate noun phrase.[7] The computational system has no choice but to take advantage of this opportunity, even though this results in singular agreement on a verb with an (eventually) plural argument.

Prescriptivist standards favor the plural form of the verb in these cases, especially in writing.

(4)   There *are* [water and sand] on the floor.

In colloquial speech though, the plural form of the verb sounds unnatural to my ear, and I am not alone in this. In a survey of twelve speakers, Sobin (1997:324) reports a mean rating of 3.58 out of 5 for the singular form of the verb in these patterns. This is clearly better than the .81 that the plural form of the verb evoked, although a bit less than the 4.03 assigned to the singular form of the verb in non-coordinate patterns such as *There is a book on the table*. (The top rating was reserved for the contracted form *There's a book on the table*.)

---

[7]A processing explanation along similar lines has been put forward independently by Deevy (1998) and Schütze (1999:472-74).

TABLE 6.1
Mean Acceptability Judgments (out of 5)

Sentence type	Mean rating
There is a book on the table.	4.03
There is a book and a pen on the table.	3.58
There are a book and a pen on the table.	0.81

See Sauerland & Elbourne (2002:292) for similar judgments.

Overall, then, the phenomenon of partial agreement provides striking evidence both for the claim that the computational system operates in a linear manner and for the proposal that agreement owes its properties to efficiency, not grammatical relations or argument structure. The verb's full second argument in a sentence such as *There is water and sand on the floor* eventually turns out to be the coordinate phrase, but agreement is triggered by just the first conjunct, in accordance with the demands of the efficiency driven computational system.

Evidence from reflexive pronouns

As we have just seen, the computational account of agreement depends crucially on the assumption that coordinate structures are built step by step and that the verb initially combines directly with the first conjunct of a coordinate phrase to its right. Interesting additional evidence for this proposal comes from the interpretation of reflexive pronouns.

As noted in chapter three (pp. 45-46), a reflexive pronoun that occurs in a coordinate structure such as (5) can have a nonlocal antecedent (Reinhart & Reuland 1991:315).

(5)   *The two commissioners*$_i$ believe [Amy admires [the mayor and *themselves*$_i$]].

In chapter two, I attributed this to the fact that *themselves* does not combine directly with the verb and therefore has no immediate opportunity to resolve its referential dependency with the help of the index of *Amy*. As a result, the referential dependency is handed over to the pragmatic system, which leads to the possibility of a nonlocal antecedent.

But now consider what happens when the reflexive pronoun is the *first* conjunct in the coordinate noun phrase.

(6)   **The two commissioners*$_i$ believe [Amy admires [*themselves*$_i$ and the mayor]].

Cowart (1991), to whom this observation is due, reports that respondents to a written questionnaire rate this pattern as less acceptable than (5)—a judgment with which I concur; see also Walther (1995). Why should there be such a contrast?

The answer lies in the step-by-step manner in which coordinate phrases are built. As illustrated below, there is a point in the formation of the embedded clause in (6) where it has the structure depicted in (7).

(7)

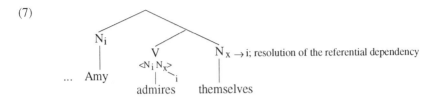

There is an immediate opportunity here to resolve the referential dependency introduced by the reflexive pronoun since it combines directly with the verb *admire*, whose grid contains the index of *Amy*. As we saw in chapter three, the Efficiency Requirement forces the computational system to take advantage of such opportunities, which leads to a feature mismatch in this case and to the unacceptability of the sentence.

Contrasts such as the one between (5) and (6) are puzzling when viewed as *grammatical* phenomena, but they make perfect sense from the perspective adopted here. In particular, they arise because the computational system builds sentences one word at a time from left to right, combining the verb directly with the first conjunct of its complement and creating an opportunity for partial agreement.

A problem in inversion patterns

There are still unsettled matters, however. Particularly problematic is the status of *yes–no* questions such as the following, in which the singular form of the verb sounds somewhat strange even though the first conjunct of the following argument is singular.

(8)   ??Is [sand and water] on the table?

Commenting on the similar sentences in (9), Morgan (1972:281) reports that neither the singular form of the verb nor the plural form is fully natural when the first conjunct is singular and the second one is plural in an inversion pattern.

(9) a.   Singular form of the verb:
         ??Is [*John* or his parents] here?

    b.   Plural form of the verb:
         ??Are [*John* or his parents] here?

Comparable results are reported in Deevy's (1998) native speaker survey of sentences such as (10), cited by Schütze (1999:471-472).[8]

(10)   Was/were [a hamburger and two sandwiches] ordered by table five?

Although the plural form of the verb was preferred, the preference was weaker when the first conjunct was singular, as it is in (10), than when it is plural (as in *Were [two sandwiches and a hamburger] ordered?*). This suggests some compulsion to resolve the agreement dependency at the first opportunity even in these patterns.

Why then does this not happen more consistently? For now, I have no answer to offer, other than to raise the possibility that unlike the corresponding *there* pattern, inversion patterns with a coordinate subject are used too infrequently to permit establishment of a strong computational routine, opening the door for extraneous influences such as the effects of pedagogical instruction.[9]

This notwithstanding, we might still expect the computational system to balk as it processes inversion patterns in which the plural form of the verb combines with a singular first conjunct. This might be detected through the study of so-called event-related potentials (ERPs), the positive and negative voltage fluctuations that are manifested in the brain during sentence processing.

Previous work has established that certain structural anomalies, including agreement mismatches such as *The men works hard*, trigger a positive-going wave form that peaks about 600 milliseconds after the anomaly is encountered (e.g., Osterhout & Mobly 1995; see chapter nine). The presence of distinctive neural activity just after the first conjunct is encountered in sentences such as (9b) could shed light on how the computational system goes about resolving agreement dependencies in inversion patterns with coordinate subjects.

5. PARTIAL AGREEMENT IN OTHER LANGUAGES

Might there be languages in which verbs frequently and consistently agree with the first conjunct of a subject argument to the right? At least two languages—Moroccan Arabic and Brazilian Portuguese—seem to exhibit this agreement profile.

---

[8]Uncertainty is also reported for locative inversion patterns such as *On the table was/were [a hamburger and two sandwiches]*.

[9]Another possibility relates to the fact that partial agreement in inversion patterns involves part of the verb's first argument, whereas partial agreement in *there* patterns involves part of its second argument. It is conceivable that more working memory resources are available in the first part of the sentence, and that this facilitates development of a computational routine that identifies the full first argument before resolving the agreement dependency.

5.1 Moroccan Arabic

As Munn (1999) notes, Moroccan Arabic manifests a clear pattern of partial agreement in verb-initial clauses. Consider in this regard the contrast between the following two sentences. (M = masculine.)

(1)   Moroccan Arabic (Aoun, Benmamoun, & Sportiche 1999:669-670):
    a. Preverbal subject triggers full agreement:
        [Ȝomar w karim] žaw.
        Omar and Karim   came.3Pl
        'Omar and Karim came.'

    b. Postverbal subject triggers partial agreement:
        ža   [Ȝomar w karim].
        came.3MSg Omar and Karim
        'Omar and Karim came.'

The formation of (1a) is unremarkable—the coordinate plural noun phrase is formed, and verbal agreement proceeds in the usual way.

(2)   First steps: Formation of the noun phrase, including union of the singular features on its conjuncts to form a plural:

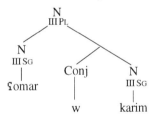

Next Step: Combination of the coordinate noun phrase with the verb; resolution of the verb's third person plural agreement dependency by the person and number features of the coordinate subject phrase:

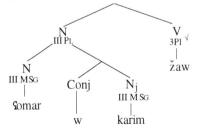

The formation of (1b) is more interesting.

(3)   First step: Combination of the verb with the (singular) first conjunct of its
       subject argument and resolution of the agreement dependency:

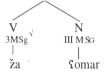

Next steps: Addition of the conjunction and of the second conjunct:

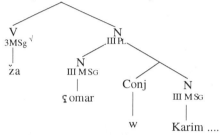

The verb thus ends up with singular agreement but a plural argument—a paradox
for which our computational system offers a straightforward explanation. As
depicted in the first step, the verb's agreement dependencies are resolved at the
point at which it combines with the singular first conjunct of its subject argument.

5.2 Brazilian Portuguese

A similar contrast is found in Brazilian Portuguese, as observed by Munn
(1999:655). As the examples in (1) illustrate, there is no partial agreement when the
coordinate subject is preverbal and is therefore fully formed before the verb
combines with it.

(1) a.   [As meninas e eu] *saímos*.
          the girls   and I   left.1Pl
          'The girls and I left.'

    b.   [Eu e as meninas] *saímos*.
          I   and the girls   left.1Pl
          'I and the girls left.'

Because all coordinate noun phrases containing a first person conjunct are treated as
first person plurals in Brazilian Portuguese, there is no reason to posit partial
agreement here. The verb simply agrees with the full noun phrase.

       However, matters are quite different when the coordinate noun phrase follows
the verb, as in (2). Under these circumstances, agreement targets just the first

conjunct. Thus the verb is third plural in the first sentence and first singular in the second.

(2) a.   3Pl   3Pl   1Sg
       Foram   [*as meninas* e eu] que compramos as flores.
       were.3Pl the girls   and I who bought.1Pl the flowers
       'It was the girls and I who bought the flowers.'

   b. 1Sg   1Sg   3Pl
       Fui   [*eu* e as meninas] que compramos as flores.
       was.1Sg I and the girls   who bought.1Pl the flowers
       'It was I and the girls who bought the flowers.'

This is just what we expect if the verb combines first with the initial conjunct of a following coordinate phrase, as already illustrated for English and Moroccan Arabic.

Brazilian Portuguese also exhibits an interesting agreement contrast in certain patterns of adjective–noun concord. When an adjective follows a coordinate noun phrase that it modifies, it agrees with the entire phrase, as illustrated in (3). (FPl = feminine plural; MPl = masculine plural.)

(3) a. as minhas [amigas   e   amigos] *famosos*
      the my.FPl friend.FPl and friend.MPl famous.MPl
      'my famous [(female) friends and (male) friends]'

   b. os   meus [amigos   e   amigas]   *famosos*
      the my.MPl friend.MPl and friend.FPl famous.MPl
      'my famous [(male) friends and (female) friends]'

Notice that the postnominal adjective *famosos* 'famous' is masculine plural in both patterns regardless of whether the second conjunct is masculine or feminine. This reflects the fact that masculine is the default gender in Brazilian Portuguese and is used to resolve gender conflicts of the sort found in the coordinate phrase in (3).

As illustrated in (4), however, a *prenominal* adjective agrees with the *first* conjunct even though it modifies the entire phrase—hence it is feminine if the first conjunct is feminine and masculine if the first conjunct is masculine. (The same is true for the determiner and for the possessive adjective 'my.')

(4) a. Feminine plural prenominal adjective with feminine plural first conjunct:
                FPl   FPl   MPl
      as minhas *velhas* [*amigas*   e   amigos]
      the my.FPl old.FPl friend.FPl and friend.MPl
      'my old [(female) friends and (male) friends]'

b. Masculine plural prenominal adjective with masculine plural first conjunct:

         MPl   MPl   FPl
os   meus   *velhos*   [*amigos*   e   amigas]
the my.MPl old.MPl friend.MPl and friend.FPl
'my old [(male) friends and (female) friends]'

This makes perfect sense if the adjective combines directly with its first conjunct, creating an opportunity for feminine plural agreement in (4a) and masculine plural agreement in (4b). In both cases, subsequent addition of the conjunction and of the second conjunct gives a coordinate phrase that is masculine plural—but this makes no difference, since the adjective's agreement dependencies have already been resolved.

In sum, the proposed sentence-building system and our theory of agreement come together in a striking way in the case of coordinate phrases, shedding light on what would otherwise be an extremely puzzling set of facts. As we have seen, verbs and adjectives are able to combine with—and therefore agree with—the first conjunct of a following coordinate phrase, but not a preceding one. This is just the result we expect if sentence structure is built by the sort of efficiency driven linear computational system I have been outlining.

6. CONCLUSION

We find in agreement strong signs of a computational influence. The particular manner in which verbal inflection works in English is especially informative, revealing that the agreement process is driven by efficiency, not grammar. In seeking an opportunity to resolve agreement dependencies, the computational system looks first to the subject, but only because that element is the verb's first argument.

Where the subject lacks person and number features, as happens in the case of *there* patterns, the computational system turns to the verb's second argument to resolve its agreement dependencies. This results in agreement with the postverbal nominal, as illustrated in sentences such as *There is a man at the door* versus *There are two men at the door.*

Further evidence for the role of efficiency in sentence formation comes from the phenomenon of partial agreement, which occurs when a functor combines directly with the first conjunct of a coordinate phrase to its right, as in *There is a pen and two pencils on the floor.* The end result—singular agreement but a plural full argument—directly reflects the linear, efficiency driven character of the sentence-building system.

Overall then, agreement fits well into the emergentist perspective that I have been trying to develop. The basic facts reflect efficiency considerations, consistent with the idea that the core properties of language follow from more basic processing-related forces.

A new set of challenges for this thesis comes from a quite different phenomenon—the 'displacement' of an argument to clause-initial position, as routinely happens in *wh* questions, for instance. I turn to this matter in chapter seven.

Chapter 7

Wh Questions

1. INTRODUCTION

This chapter focuses on the formation of English-style *wh* questions, in which a focused *wh* word appears at the beginning of the clause.

(1) a. *What* are you doing?
   b. Guess [*who* Mary saw].
   c. *Why* would someone do that?

The apparent simplicity of these patterns is deceptive—the investigation of *wh* questions has uncovered a large number of puzzles, many of which are still poorly understood. Unfortunately, I too will have to leave most of these puzzles unsolved. However, I will put forward preliminary proposals about three phenomena that are central to the syntax of *wh* questions.

The first of these phenomena involves the placement and interpretation of the *wh* word itself, especially the manner in which it comes to be associated with a functor inside the sentence. The other two phenomena involve constraints on the formation of *wh* questions that have long been attributed to grammatical principles—the well known *wh* island effect and the notorious *that*-trace effect.

2. FORMING AND INTERPRETING *WH* QUESTIONS

A salient feature of English *wh* questions that call for new information is that the *wh* word appears in initial position, as the examples above illustrate.

So far we have dealt with matters of word order only once—in chapter one, where we used lexical properties to account for the positioning of subjects and direct objects in simple declarative sentences (e.g., a transitive verb looks to the left for its first argument and to the right for its second argument). Might *wh* words have a lexical property that forces them to look rightward for an argument of some type, perhaps even a clausal argument? This seems unlikely, as there are various patterns in which *wh* words occur inside the clause (e.g., multiple *wh* questions such as *Who saw **what**?* and echo questions such as *You saw **WHO**?*).

A more promising idea is that the position of *wh* words reflects a feature of the *wh* question construction itself—or, more precisely, of the computational routines that yield that construction. To make this more concrete, let us assume that the first step in the computational routine that builds information-seeking *wh* questions is simply this:

(1)   *Wh* ⊥ X
       (A *wh* word combines with a category to its right.)

At this point, other routines take over, depending on the properties of X. In the case of a subject *wh* question such as (2), for instance, the second word in the sentence is a verb, which looks to the left for its first argument (the *wh* word itself) and then to the right for its second argument.

(2)   Who saw Mary?

But what of patterns such as those below, in which the *wh* word and the sentence-internal functor with which it is associated are not adjacent? (I deliberately avoid the effects of subject-auxiliary inversion in these and other examples by using the matrix verb *guess* to introduce the question.)

(3) a. (Guess) *what* [it *did* next].
    b. (Guess) *who* [John decided [to *see*]].

The relationship between the *wh* word and the verb in such cases is elegantly captured by the traditional transformational account, which uses a movement rule to transport a *wh* phrase from a clause-internal position (direct object of the verb in this case) to a clause-initial position (Specifier of CP).

(4)   Guess [$_{CP}$ what$_i$ [it did _ next]].
                ↑_____|

How can these facts be captured in a computational system which has no movement operations and which constructs sentences from left to right, one word at a time?

2.1 *Wh* dependencies

The key lies in a simple assumption about clause-initial (argument) *wh* words—they look for a functor whose argument grid contains an unresolved dependency of a matching type. Thus, a *wh* nominal looks for a grid with an unresolved N argument, a *wh* PP looks for a grid with an unresolved PP argument, and so on.[1]

---

[1]There is an obvious parallel between this proposal and the idea that *wh* words are operators that must bind a variable. The equivalent of the variable in the proposal I make is the unresolved dependency (an unindexed N symbol) in the verb's grid.

I will henceforth refer to the relationship between a *wh* word and a functor's argument grid as a *wh dependency*, which I will represent with the symbol *WH*. For example:

(1)   N
        <WH>
        |
        who

An opportunity to resolve a *wh* dependency arises under the following conditions.

(2)   An opportunity for the computational system to resolve a *wh* dependency arises when it encounters a functor whose grid includes an unresolved dependency of the appropriate type.

When this happens, both the *wh* dependency and the functor's argument dependency are resolved, as are any agreement dependencies. This is illustrated below for the question *Who knows?*

(3)
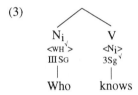

Combination of *who* and *knows* gives the *wh* word an opportunity to resolve its *wh* dependency by association with the verb's unresolved argument dependency, and it simultaneously gives the verb an opportunity to resolve its argument dependency and its agreement dependencies. All dependencies are therefore resolved at the first opportunity, as indicated by the check marks and the copied index in the grid of the verb.

Now consider the sentence *(Guess) what it did?*, in which the *wh* word is unable to combine directly with the verb. The computational system forms this sentence by first combining the *wh* word with the pronoun, as required by the routine outlined at the outset (*Wh* ⊥ X).[2]

---

[2] Although there is no functor-argument relationship between *what* and *it*, the computational system must combine them nonetheless, consistent with its mandate to structure the input as quickly as possible, as discussed in chapter two (p. 21ff). Independent phonological evidence comes from flapping—the 't' at the end of *what* is routinely flapped as *what* combines with *it* in *what it did*. See also the discussion of contraction in chapter eight, section 2.5.

(4)

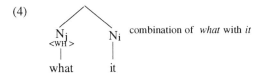

combination of *what* with *it*

Since no dependencies can be resolved at this point, the computational system proceeds to the next step, which involves addition of the verb.

(5)   Step 1: Combination of the verb with the nominal *it*; resolution of the verb's first argument dependency:

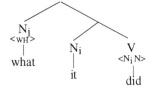

Step 2: Resolution of the *wh* dependency (with the help of downward feature passing) and of the verb's second argument dependency:

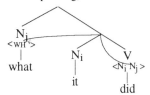

As shown here, the *wh* dependency which has been held in working memory is resolved when the computational system encounters the unresolved nominal argument dependency in the grid of the verb.

The next example illustrates a case in which the *wh* dependency descends into an embedded clause in search of resolution.

(6)   (Guess) who John decided to see.

Step 1: Combination of *who* and the subject nominal:

Step 2: Combination of the matrix verb with the nominal *John*; resolution of the verb's first argument dependency:

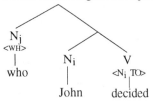

Step 3: Combination of the matrix verb with the infinitival marker *to*; resolution of the verb's second argument dependency:

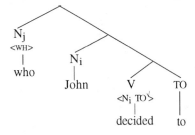

Final steps: Combination of *to* with its verbal argument, *see*; resolution of *see*'s first argument dependency (via 'control'); resolution of the *wh* dependency and of *see*'s second argument dependency:

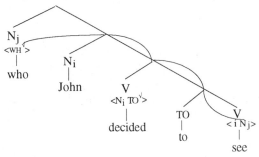

2.2 Some psycholinguistic evidence

Although I will postpone discussion of most psycholinguistic issues until chapter nine, a brief preview at this point will help establish the plausibility of the *wh* dependencies.

It is well known that the difficulty of *wh* constructions of various sorts (relative clauses as well as *wh* questions) increases with the distance between the *wh* word and the point where its dependency is resolved (e.g., Wanner & Maratsos 1978, Gibson 1998, Caplan & Waters 2002; see also chapter nine). In a classic study,

Wanner & Maratsos displayed sentences containing relative clauses on a screen one word a time, interrupting the presentation after the fourth word with a list of names.

(1) a. Subject relative clause:
        The witch [*who* despised sorcerers] frightened little children.
                                    ⇑
                            interruption point

    b. Direct object relative clause:
        The witch [*who* sorcerers despised] frightened little children.
                                     ⇑
                            interruption point

Recall of names and comprehension of the relative clauses were both significantly poorer in the direct object relative clauses than in the subject relatives.

This is just what one would expect if the retention of *wh* dependencies taxes working memory. Because subject relative pronouns occur adjacent to the verb, the *wh* dependency they introduce is resolved immediately, before the interruption point in (1a).[3]

(2)   Subject relative clause:
        The witch [*who* despised sorcerers] frightened little children.
                            ↑   ⇑
                    wh dependency   interruption point
                    is resolved here

In contrast, the *wh* dependency introduced by the object relative pronoun in (1b) is more distant from the verb and its resolution is impeded by the intervening interruption, with negative consequences both for recall of the intruding names and for interpretation of the sentence.

(3)   Direct object relative clause:
        The witch [*who* sorcerers despised] frightened little children.
                                 ⇑   ↑
                    interruption point   *wh* dependency
                                        is resolved here

As with other types of dependencies, the computational system makes every effort to resolve *wh* dependencies at the first opportunity. One sign of this comes from the so-called 'filled gap effect' found in sentences such as (4), where the computational system associates the *wh* word with the grid of *bring* before encountering the verb's real second argument *us* (e.g., Stowe 1986 and chapter nine).

---

[3]In addition to exhibiting the usual *wh* dependency, a relative pronoun such as *who* must also be linked to the nominal modified by the relative clause (here, *witch*). This suggests the presence of a referential dependency of some sort, but this can be set aside for now.

(4)   My brother wants to know [*who* [Ruth will *bring* us home to at
       Christmas]].

Additional evidence for the expeditious resolution of *wh* dependencies comes
from so-called garden path effects, such as the one observed in the following
sentence, from Fodor (1978:434).

(5)   Which books did the teachers read to the children from?

Here the computational system quickly associates the *wh* dependency with *read*,
which is commonly used as a transitive verb and therefore appears to present an
early opportunity to resolve the *wh* dependency. Shortly thereafter, however, it
becomes apparent that *read* is used intransitively in this sentence and that the grid
with which the *wh* word should be associated belongs to the preposition *from*.

The extra burden that *wh* dependencies place on the processor has long been
recognized and has even been used to draw a surprising conclusion. Such
dependencies could not exist, Fodor (1978:471) reasons, 'unless there is some
further influence on language design, over and above the [processor]'—namely a
grammar that favors movement and gaps. But this does not follow.

It is possible that *wh* dependencies exist because pragmatic considerations
provide an inducement to place focused material in a prominent position at the
beginning of the clause. The inducement cannot be overwhelming, of course, as
many languages leave *wh* words 'in situ' (e.g., Chinese, Japanese, Korean, and
Thai). But that does not matter; the inducement to voice consonants intervocalically
is no doubt real too, although not all languages succumb to it.

The point is that once a language accepts the inducement, a computational
routine (*Wh* ⊥ X) develops. This in turn results in a *wh* dependency that the
computational system must resolve in the usual way—as quickly as possible.
Nothing in this account presupposes the existence of a grammar that favors
movement rules and gaps.

3. *WH* ISLAND EFFECTS

There is another way in which the syntax of *wh* questions supposedly calls for a
grammar. In particular, it has long been thought that the formation of *wh* questions
has to be constrained by grammatical principles that block 'extraction' of a *wh* word
from certain types of contexts.

The facts are enormously complex, and the picture is significantly clouded by
pragmatic factors relating to the issue of whether a constituent is topical enough to
be questioned (e.g., Kuno 1987, Deane 1992, Kuno & Takami 1993). Nonetheless, there is clearly a syntactic side to this phenomenon as well. Consider the
following contrast, for example.

(1)   *Wh* word associated with a plain embedded clause:
        What did you ask me [to do with those clothes]?
        |_____↑

(2)   *Wh* word associated with an embedded *wh* clause:
        **What* did you ask me [*which clothes* to do with]?
        |_____↑

The unacceptability of the second of these sentences was initially attributed to the so-called *Wh* Island Condition.

(3)   *The Wh Island Condition:*
        No element can be extracted from a clause that begins with a *wh* word.

Later work derived the *Wh* Island Condition from a more general (and abstract) grammatical principle—initially the Subjacency Condition (e.g., Chomsky 1977:73) and more recently the Minimal Link Condition (Chomsky 1995:295).[4] Our concern is with the deeper question of whether a grammatical constraint is necessary in the first place.

The particular idea that I wish to pursue is that the unacceptability of patterns such as (2) reflects the manner in which the computational system resolves *wh* dependencies in the course of building sentences, not the effects of a grammatical principle.

3.1 How it works

We have already seen that the maintenance of *wh* dependencies that are awaiting resolution places a burden on working memory (section 2). Interestingly, there has been at least one attempt to use this fact to explain *wh* island effects.

Kluender & Kutas (1993:604ff) used event-related potentials (ERPs) to examine the processing of several sentence types, including the following.

(1) a. Do you wonder [if they caught him at it by accident]?
    b. Do you wonder [who they caught _ at it by accident]?

They report a higher amplitude negative-going fluctuation as the word *they* is read in the second sentence than in the first. (Because the wave form is most detectable in the left anterior region of the brain, this phenomenon has been dubbed the 'LAN effect.')

Kluender & Kutas take the negative wave to be a side effect of the effort required to enter the direct object *wh* word in (1b) into working memory. Crucially,

_____

[4]The Subjacency Condition bars movement across more than one 'cyclic node' (NP or IP, for English) in a single step. The Minimal Link Condition requires short moves over long ones.

no such effect is observed in (2), where the *wh* word is a subject and can therefore be immediately associated with the adjacent verb.

(2)   Couldn't you decide [*who* should sing something for Grandma at the family reunion]?

Kluender & Kutas propose that this is the basis for the *wh* island effect. Because maintenance of *wh* dependencies is difficult, they argue, working memory balks at having to deal with more than one *wh* phrase per clause—as it would have to do in *wh* island patterns.

       1st *wh* phrase   2nd *wh* phrase
(3)   *What* did you ask me [*which clothes* to do _ with _]?

(For a different processing-based account of 'islands,' see Marcus 1980 and Berwick & Weinberg 1984, as well as Fodor's 1985 critique.)
    There must be more to it than this, however, since some sentences containing two *wh* dependencies are in fact far more acceptable than others. For instance, (4) sounds much better than (5)—if it is not completely acceptable (e.g., Pesetsky 1982, Richards 1997:40).

(4)   *Which clothes* were you wondering [*what* to do with]?

(5)   *What* were you wondering [*which clothes* to do with]?

How can this be?

Push-down storage

I believe that the answer may lie in how working memory stores information. One commonly mentioned possibility (e.g., Marcus 1980:39, Kempen & Hoenkamp 1987:245) is that working memory makes use of what is often called *push-down storage*—which simply means that the most recently stored element is at the top of the 'memory stack' and therefore more accessible than previously stored elements. Let us consider a concrete case.
    In a sentence such as (6), the *wh* dependency associated with *which clothes* is stored first and is therefore lower in the stack than the *wh* dependency associated with *what*.

                          last stored (top of the stack)
        first stored (bottom of the stack) |
(6)   *Which clothes* were you wondering [**what** to do with]?

This is a felicitous result, since the computational system needs access to the dependency associated with *what* first. As illustrated below, the opportunity to resolve that dependency arises when the verb *do* is encountered.

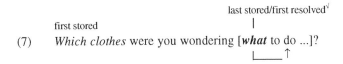

(7)   *Which clothes* were you wondering [***what*** to do ...]?

In contrast, the opportunity to resolve the dependency associated with *which clothes* does not arise until later, with the appearance of the preposition *with*.

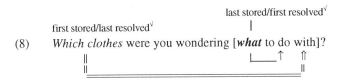

(8)   *Which clothes* were you wondering [***what*** to do with]?

Matters are very different in the case of the unacceptable (5), repeated here as (9).

last stored (top of the stack)
first stored (bottom of the stack) |
(9)   **What* were you wondering [***which clothes*** to do with]?

Here, *what* appears first and is stored lower in the stack than the later-occurring *which clothes*. But this is the reverse of what the computational system needs, since the opportunity to resolve the dependency associated with *what* arises with the appearance of the verb *do*.

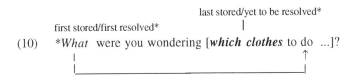

(10)   **What* were you wondering [***which clothes*** to do ...]?

In contrast, the chance to resolve the dependency associated with *which clothes*, which is on top of the stack, does not occur until later, when *with* is encountered.[5]

---

[5]The same effect is achieved in a different way by Fodor's (1978) Nested Dependency Constraint and Pesetsky's (1982) Path Containment Condition.

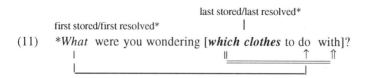

In fact then, the contrast between (8) and (11) can be attributed to the Efficiency Requirement. *Wh* dependencies, like other sorts of dependencies, must be resolved at the first opportunity—which entails their availability at the point where the appropriate functor is encountered. As we have seen, the *wh* dependencies in a sentence such as (8) are arranged in the memory stack in a way that allows each to be resolved at the opportune moment, as demanded by the Efficiency Requirement.[6] This is not the case in (11), where the *wh* dependency associated with *what* is at the bottom of the stack, making it inaccessible at the point where the opportunity to resolve it arises.

3.2 Adjunct *wh* words

The same point can be illustrated by sentences such as (1), in which the second *wh* word is an adjunct.

> adjunct
> ↓
> (1)   *Which tools* did Mary ask [*how* to use]?

As an adjunct, *how* exhibits a dependency on nothing more than a verbal category. Unlike argument *wh* words, it does not seek an argument grid with an unresolved matching dependency. (There would be no point; argument grids do not contain information about adjuncts.)

---

[6]For reasons that are not understood, the cost of *wh* dependencies is higher in a tensed embedded clause (e.g., Chomsky 1986a:37). Even here though, there is a clear asymmetry between patterns in which *wh* dependencies can be resolved in a manner consistent with push-down storage and those in which they cannot. (Sentence (i) is from Kuno & Takami 1993:44; for many similar examples, see McCawley 1981 and Chung & McCloskey 1983.)

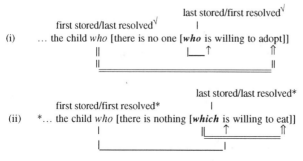

In other respects, however, everything is the same. The computational system proceeds from left to right, holding any *wh* dependencies in push-down storage and seeking to resolve them at the first opportunity. In a sentence such as (1) then, *which tools* is stored first, lower in the stack than *how*. When the verb *use* appears, the *wh* dependency associated with *how* can be immediately resolved, making way for the subsequent immediate resolution of the *wh* dependency associated with *which tools*.

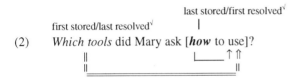

(2)   *Which tools* did Mary ask [*how* to use]?

But now consider (3), in which the order of the *wh* expressions is reversed.

(3)   *When* did Mary ask [*which tools* to use]?

This sentence is acceptable on the 'when-ask' interpretation ('When did Mary make the request?), but not on the 'when-use' interpretation (asking when certain tools are to be used). This can't have anything to do with storage, since nothing prevents the more recently stored *wh* dependency (the one associated with *which tools*) from being resolved first once the verb *use* appears.

Moreover, the same asymmetry shows up when the second *wh* word is an adjunct.

(4)   *When* did Mary ask [*how* to use the tools]?
        ('when-ask,' not 'when-use')

Here again, the 'when-ask' interpretation is fine, but not the 'when-use' interpretation. Why should this be?

The Efficiency Requirement provides a straightforward answer. Because adjuncts such as *when* are seeking a simple verbal category (not a grid with a particular type of unresolved argument dependency), an opportunity to resolve their *wh* dependency arises when the *matrix* verb is encountered. An efficiency driven computational system should therefore resolve the adjunct's *wh* dependency at that point, ruling out its association with the more deeply embedded verb.

A puzzle

But now a new puzzle arises, because of the ambiguity of sentences such as the following.

(5)   Why do you think [John left]?
        ('why-think' & 'why-left' interpretations are both possible)

(6)   When did you say [Mary took the exam]?
        ('when-say' & 'when-take' interpretations are both possible)

(7)   Why do you believe [Jerry went to New York]?
        ('why-believe' & 'why-go' interpretations are both possible)

Not all matrix verbs permit this ambiguity—association of the adjunct with the embedded verb is much less natural in patterns such as the following.

(8)   Why do you insist [that John left]?
        ('why-left' interpretation is marginal)

(9)   When did you reveal [that Jerry went to New York]?
        ('when-go' interpretation is marginal)

For now, I have no explanation for why the adjunct can be associated with the embedded clause in sentences such as (5) to (7). However, a possible clue may come from the fact that two of the matrix verbs in question—*think* and *believe*—are involved in another curious phenomenon. As illustrated below, a negative associated with *think* and *believe* can be interpreted as applying to the embedded clause (e.g., Horn 1978).

(10)   I don't think [Mary failed the exam].
        (implies 'I think Mary didn't fail the exam')

(11)   I don't believe [it will rain].
        (implies 'I believe it won't rain')

Evidently, a word that is syntactically associated with the matrix verb can sometimes be semantically associated with an embedded verb. (Horn suggests that pragmatic inference is involved.) This raises the possibility that the adjunct *why* in a sentence such as *Why do you think John left?* is initially associated with *think* in some way, even on the problematic 'why-left' interpretation.

Haegeman (2003:645) makes a possibly related observation with respect to the 'long fronted' adjunct in sentences such as (12).

(12)   Tomorrow he says that he cannot come.

She notes that such elements behave like topics 'with respect to the *matrix* clause,' so that (12) has roughly the meaning paraphrased in (13).

(13)   About tomorrow, he says that he cannot come.

In the light of these observations, we might explore the possibility that sentences such as *When did you say Mary took the exam* have the meaning paraphrased in (14), with the *wh* word entering into a relation with the matrix verb as well as the embedded verb.

(14)   What was the time *x* such that you said *x* and Mary took the exam at *x*?

No doubt there are other possibilities as well, but I will leave this matter unresolved for now.

4. THE *THAT*-TRACE EFFECT

Perhaps the most mysterious and intriguing of all constraints on extraction is the prohibition against a subject 'gap' in a clause beginning with a complementizer.

(1)   *(Guess) who Mary said [that _ left early].

As (2) illustrates, there is no prohibition against extraction of a subject when no complementizer is present.

(2)   (Guess) who Mary said [_ left early].

Moreover, the presence of a complementizer has no effect on the extractability of elements other than the subject.

(3)   (Guess) who Mary thinks [(that) Sue criticized _].

For the sake of expository convenience, I will refer to this phenomenon as the *that-trace effect*, even though it can be triggered by elements other than *that* (e.g., *whether* and *if*) and even though the system of sentence building adopted here does not employ movement or traces.

(4)   *The that-trace effect:*
       A subject cannot be extracted from a clause beginning with a comple-
       mentizer.

This effect has standardly been attributed to a grammatical principle (typically the Empty Category Principle in Government and Binding theory—e.g., Chomsky 1981:231ff, Rizzi 1990:29ff, Lasnik & Saito 1992:177ff), but I believe it can be traced to processing considerations.

In order to understand the nature of the *that*-trace effect, it is first necessary to examine in more detail the manner in which biclausal sentences are formed.

4.1 The formation of biclausal sentences

Many verbs that take a tensed clause as their second argument allow two options—a bare clause, as in (1), and a clause that is introduced by a complementizer, as in (2). (Some verbs, such as *mutter* and *determine*, permit only the second option; no verb permits only the first option.)

(1)   Bare clausal argument:
         Jerry thinks [*Mary arrived*].

(2)   Clausal argument introduced by a complementizer:
         Jerry thinks [*that Mary arrived*].

The argument grid of the matrix verb in (1) can be stated as follows. (I assume that clauses count as verbal projections; see chapter one, footnote 3.)

(3)   <N V>
          +Finite

At first glance, it might appear that the information summarized here is so sparse that it could incorrectly allow formation of sentences such as *Jerry thinks arrived*, in addition to the acceptable *Jerry thinks Mary arrived*. This is not so—*Jerry thinks arrived* contains a functor (*arrive*) with an unresolved argument dependency and therefore is not a possible sentence for independent reasons.

As the next examples illustrate, matrix verbs differ in terms of the complementizers with which they can occur.

(4) a. Mary muttered [that/*whether Paul left].
    b. Mary wondered [whether/*that Paul left].
    c. Mary knew [that/whether Paul left].

We can account for this straightforwardly if we assume that the complementizers themselves count as the verb's second argument in these cases, as suggested by Baltin (1989) and as depicted below.

(5) a. *mutter:* <N *that*>
    b. *wonder:* <N *whether*>
    c. *know:* <N *that/whether*>

Complementizers in turn are functors that take a finite verbal projection as their argument. (C = complementizer.)

(6) a. *that:* C, <V>
          +Finite

  b. *whether:* C, <V>
             +Finite

A sentence such as *Jerry thinks that Mary arrived* is therefore built as follows.

(7) a. Step 1: Combination of *think* with its first argument:

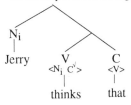

    Step 2: Combination of *think* with *that*; resolution of the verb's dependency on a complementizer argument:

    Step 3: Combination of *that* with the nominal *Mary*; there is no opportunity to resolve any dependencies at this point:

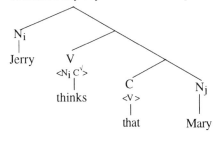

Step 4: Combination of *arrive* with *Mary*; resolution of *arrrive*'s dependency on a nominal argument and of *that*'s dependency on a verbal argument (since *Mary arrived* is a verbal projection):

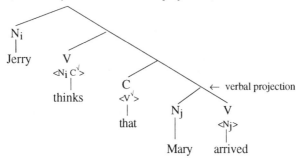

4.2 Back to the *that*-trace effect

Now let us consider the formation of a sentence such as (1), where the verb's second argument is a bare verbal projection with no complementizer.

(1)   (Guess) who Jerry thinks [arrived].

Just before the addition of the embedded verb, this sentence has the form depicted in (2), with both the *wh* dependency and the verb's second argument dependency awaiting resolution.

(2)

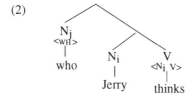

Subsequent combination of *think* with *arrive* resolves the matrix verb's dependency on a verbal argument. Resolution of both the *wh* dependency and the embedded verb's argument dependency takes place immediately thereafter.

(3)

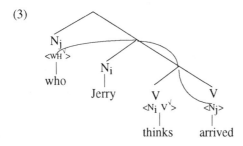

All of this appears straightforward. So what goes wrong when a complementizer is present?

Complementizers again

Sentences that violate the *that*-trace filter constitute one of the great mysteries of contemporary syntactic theory. Although they are clearly aberrant in some way for most speakers (myself included), they are fully acceptable to others (e.g., Sobin 1987, Snyder 2000:580), and they are completely comprehensible to everyone. What is responsible for this?

As I see it, the *that*-trace effect is an efficiency-related phenomenon that arises in speakers who assign a slightly more conservative set of properties to complementizers. So far, we have been assuming that complementizers take a finite verbal projection as their argument.

(4)   *that*: C, <V>
                    +Finite

However, this may not be the most conservative generalization permitted by the facts. Reconsider in this regard the type of structure in which complementizers almost invariably appear in standard English.

(5)

As can be seen here, *that* combines not just with a verbal projection, but with a verbal projection whose first argument dependency has been resolved—in this case by the nominal *Mary*.

If the acquisition device records this information, the argument grid for the complementizer *that* should have the form in (6), with $V^\dagger$ standing for a verb whose first-argument dependency has been resolved (a '*subject-saturated* verb,' for short).

(6)   *that*: <$V^\dagger$>
                    +Finite

Consider now what effect this has on the formation of sentences such as (7).

(7)   *(Guess) who Jerry thinks that arrived.

At the point just after the verb *arrive* is added, the sentence looks like this:

(8)

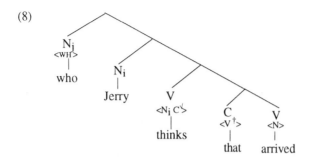

The only way to resolve the argument requirement of the complementizer in this sentence is to first resolve the *wh* dependency, and with it, the first-argument dependency of the embedded verb. This would yield the required subject-saturated verbal projection, namely:

(9)   V
          <N$_j$>
          |
        arrived

But this can't happen—for the reasons discussed above in section 3. Because working memory uses push-down storage, the earlier encountered *wh* dependency cannot be resolved before the more recently encountered dependency associated with *that*.

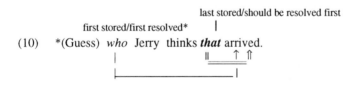

If this is right, then the *that*-trace effect comes down to an efficiency-related timing paradox. The complementizer exhibits a dependency on a subject-saturated verbal projection, but the creation of that verbal projection requires resolution of the *wh* dependency associated with *who*. And this is not possible because of the way push-down storage works—the *wh* dependency is at the bottom of the stack, beneath the dependency associated with the complementizer, and therefore cannot be resolved first.

No such problem arises in the case of 'extraction' of a direct object, as in (11).

(11)   (Guess) *who* Jerry thinks [*that* Mary helped]?

As illustrated in (12), resolution of the *wh* dependency is not necessary to create the subject-saturated verbal projection required by the complementizer since the phrase *Mary helped* already has the required property.

(12)   The sentence just prior to *wh* descent:

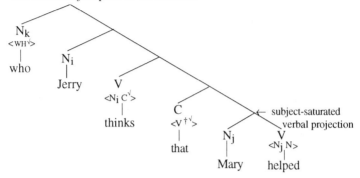

The complementizer can therefore resolve its dependency before resolution of the *wh* dependency, consistent with the workings of push-down storage.

(13)   (Guess) *who* Jerry thinks [*that* Mary helped]?

The asymmetry between subjects and direct objects with respect to the presence of *that* therefore falls out, without reference to a grammatical principle.

English speakers who permit *that*-trace violations

Why then do some speakers of English permit *that*-trace violations? It is possible that, as language learners, they were not conservative enough in formulating the argument grid for complementizers. Instead of requiring that complementizers combine with a subject-saturated verbal category, they permit the argument to be a simple finite verbal projection.

(14)   *that*: <V>
            +Finite

Under these circumstances, both the dependency associated with the complementizer and the dependency associated with the *wh* word can be resolved in a manner consistent with push-down storage.

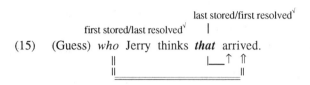

(15)   (Guess) *who* Jerry thinks ***that*** arrived.

As illustrated here, the complementizer's dependency is resolved as soon as the computational system encounters the embedded verb. This is followed by resolution of the *wh* dependency, consistent with its lower position in the memory stack.

Languages that permit *that*-trace violations

There should also be conditions under which there are no *that*-trace effects for *any* speaker. The most obvious example of this arises in languages such as Spanish that allow verb–subject order in embedded clauses.

(16)   Juan piensa [que salió María].
      John thinks that left Maria.
      'John thinks that Maria left.'

As illustrated below, an efficiency driven computational system will routinely combine a complementizer with the embedded verb before the verb resolves its first argument dependency in such languages.

(17)

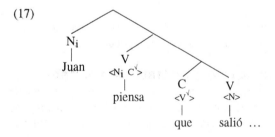

Exposure to such patterns ensures that complementizers will end up requiring just a finite verbal projection as their argument, not a subject-saturated verbal projection. This in turn should ensure the absence of *that*-trace effects—a correct result, as illustrated below for the Spanish equivalent of 'Who does John think that left?'

last stored/first resolved[√]

first stored/last resolved[√] |

(18)   *Quién* piensa Juan [*que* salió]?
         who   thinks Juan that left

As can be seen here, both the *wh* dependency and the complementizer's argument requirement can be resolved in a manner consistent with their position in the memory stack—the complementizer first (because it needs only a verbal projection as its argument) and the *wh* dependency second.

As predicted, this sentence is acceptable in Spanish. Comparable patterns are found in other languages that make frequent use of verb–subject patterns.

(19)   Modenese (Safir 1985:231):
         Che ragas di-t   **che** a chiam-a?
         which boys say-you that it call-Sg
         'Which boys did you say that call?

(20)   Greek (Smith & Tsimpli 1995:96):
         Pjos   ipan [**oti** paretithike]?
         who said-3Pl that resigned-3Sg
         'Who did they say that resigned?'

(21)   Chamorro (Sproat 1984:426):
         Haji na palao'an ti un-tungu' [**na** ginin t-um-átangis]
         who Linker woman not Infl-know that Imperf Infl-cry
         'Which girl didn't you realize that had been crying?

Languages that permit null subjects (i.e., so-called '*pro* drop' languages) also contain many patterns in which a complementizer combines directly with a tensed verb, and they too should not manifest a *that*-trace effect. The hypothesis is difficult to test, since *pro* drop and the occurrence of post-verbal subjects are highly correlated. It is perhaps worth noting, however, that Portuguese, a *pro* drop language with relatively few verb–subject patterns, permits *that*-trace patterns (Safir 1985:238-241). Moreover, Modenese (see (19) above) permits verb–subject patterns but not *pro* drop (ibid.: 231). This suggests that the occurrence of complementizer–verb patterns, regardless of whether they come about by virtue of *pro* drop or verb-subject order, suffices to ensure that there will be no *that*-trace effect. This is just what we expect.

Adjuncts again

A related phenomenon provides further support for the proposed explanation of the *that*-trace effect. As illustrated in (22), English does not permit patterns such as the following, in which the first *wh* word is the subject argument of the embedded verb and the second *wh* word is an adjunct.

(22)   *Who* did you ask [*when* left]?

It is possible that *wh* adjuncts are like complementizers in English—they require combination with a subject-saturated verbal projection. This requirement is straightforwardly satisfied in (23) and in other acceptable sentences containing a *wh* adjunct in a tensed clause.

(23)   Did you ask [*when* John left]?

However, it cannot be satisfied in sentences such as (22), repeated here as (24), in which the *wh* dependency associated with *who* is stored first and therefore is not available when it is needed (i.e., before the attempt to resolve the *wh* dependency associated with *when*).[7]

```
                          last stored/should be resolved first
         first stored             |
(24)     *Who did you ask [when left]?
                             ↑
              requires combination with a verb whose
              first-argument dependency has already been resolved
```

Crucially, though, no such requirement should exist in languages like Spanish, where verb-subject order and the possibilitly of *pro* drop ensure that adjunct *wh* words routinely combine directly with tensed verbs, as in the embedded clause below.

(25)   Me pregunté [*cuándo* partío (Juan)].
       myself ask-1Sg when leave-3Sg (Juan)
       'I asked myself when (John) left.'

And indeed, Spanish sentences containing the same array of *wh* dependencies as (24) are fully acceptable.

(26)   Este es el hombre [*que* me pregunté [*cuándo* partío]].
       This is the man   who myself ask-1Sg when leave-3Sg
       'This is the man who I asked myself when (he) left.'

---

[7]This raises the question of why no English speakers conclude that *wh* adjuncts can combine with just a simple verbal projection, parallel to the case of *that* discussed above, thereby permitting sentences such as (22). The occurrence of relative clause patterns such as *cars that stall* (see next page) may encourage overgeneralization in the case of *that*, but I will leave this question open for now.

Relative clauses

A further advantage of the proposed analysis is that it sheds light on why the *that-*trace effect is neutralized in relative clauses, even in English.

(27)   Cars [that _ stall] are towed away.

The acceptability of these patterns is sometimes treated as an exception (as in Chomsky & Lasnik 1977:451, where the *that-*trace filter is simply stipulated not to apply in relative clauses). In other work, the problem is circumvented by treating *that* in relative clauses as a special type of complementizer (Rizzi 1990:66ff, Lasnik & Saito 1992:179).

The analysis that I propose predicts the acceptability of (27) with no need for special assumptions or adjustments. The key observation is that in contrast to what happens in clauses containing an overt *wh* word, the *wh* dependency in relative clauses that begin with *that* is not overtly expressed. Instead, its presence must be inferred. But when and how does this happen?

The *wh* dependency cannot be inferred until the computational system realizes that it is dealing with a relative clause—which presumably happens right after the complementizer is encountered. (Certainly, no inference can be drawn before this point, as there is nothing about the word *cars* to indicate the presence of a relative clause and of the associated *wh* dependency.)

(28)   Cars [that stall] are towed away.
                        ↑
              wh dependency is inferred here

This is crucial, because it means that the *wh* dependency is encountered *after* the complementizer and is therefore at the top of the working memory stack.

                              last stored
                  first stored |
(29)   Cars [*that WH* stall] are towed away.
                        ↑
              wh dependency

As a result, the *wh* dependency is resolved first. This in turn leads to resolution of the first argument dependency of the verb *stall*, providing the complementizer with a subject-saturated verbal projection to serve as its argument, as required.

                        last stored/first resolved[v]
                  first stored |
(30)   Cars [*that WH* stall] are towed away.
                  ‖   └─↑ ⇑
                  ‖_____‖

Summary

The proposed analysis of the *that*-trace effect shows considerable promise in terms of its ability to account both for the presence of this phenomenon in English and for its absence in various other languages. The crucial factor involves a timing effect— not a grammatical principle.

For reasons discussed earlier, complementizers (and perhaps *wh* adjuncts) in subject–verb languages typically require combination not just with a verbal projection, but with a verbal projection whose first argument dependency has already been resolved. Crucially, however, satisfaction of this requirement is impossible in sentences of the following form, where the dependency associated with the complementizer is stored at the top of the working memory stack and therefore must be dealt with before the verb has a chance to resolve its first argument dependency.

                                            last stored
                 first stored |
(31)   *Who* [subject verb [***complementizer*** verb ...]]
                                                <N...>

No such problem arises in languages with verb-initial word order, where complementizers require no more than combination with a verbal projection and can therefore have their dependency resolved immediately.

For many years the *that*-trace effect has stood as the example *par excellence* of a pure syntactic phenomenon whose properties could only be explained with reference to grammatical principles. The proposed analysis calls this assumption into question.

5. CONCLUSION

The traditional preoccupation with question structures (even esoteric ones) seems justified—there is in fact much to learn about how language works from their investigation.

The key to understanding these patterns lies in the way in which the dependency associated with the sentence-initial *wh* word is resolved. As we have seen, there is reason to think that *wh* dependencies descend through the sentence in search of an argument grid with an unresolved dependency of the appropriate type. The assumption that *wh* dependencies (like all other dependencies) must be resolved at the first opportunity not only fits well with the psycholinguistic facts, it contributes to an account of *wh* island effects and of the *that*-trace effect without reference to grammatical principles.

Admittedly, there are many phenomena and problems about which I have said nothing here,[8] and it is unclear whether or how they will yield to the sort of analysis that I propose. Nonetheless, the success encountered thus far suggests that further extensions may well be feasible, even though I am unable to pursue that possibility here.

The next chapter will take us in a very different direction. The focus there will be on contraction, a phonological phenomenon whose interaction with the computational system offers further insights into how sentences are formed and why they have the particular properties that they do.

---

[8]For example, Dutch permits 'cross-serial' dependencies in which nominals from the bottom of the memory stack are apparently accessed first (e.g., *ik* 'I' is linked to *zag* 'saw', and so on). The following sentence is from Steedman (2000:25).

(i)   ... omdat ik Cecilia Henk de nijlpaarden zag helpen voeren.
          because I Cecilia Henk the hippopotamus saw help feed
          '... because I saw Cecilia help Henk feed the hippopotamus.'

Such patterns are rare, as Steedman notes, but their existence suggests that access to the bottom of the stack is difficult rather than impossible. Presumably, the effort is made only if the computational system is exposed to the right type of sentences and only at very significant processing cost.

Richards (1997) discusses multiple *wh* questions in Bulgarian and other Slavic languages that also seem to require intersecting dependencies.

Chapter 8

The Syntax of Contraction

1. INTRODUCTION

The effects of the computational system are felt beyond a language's morphology, syntax, and semantics. As I will try to show in this chapter, there is also at least one major phonological phenomenon—contraction—whose properties reflect the workings of the computational system.

So far, I have attempted to present my proposals about sentence formation in a way that is neutral between production and comprehension, consistent with the idea that the demands made on working memory during either type of activity are lessened if dependencies are resolved at the first opportunity. Contraction is somewhat different, however. Unlike the resolution of dependencies, it arises only in the course of production. Investigating it therefore permits us to examine the operation of the computational system in a context that is strongly biased toward speaking rather than understanding.

I will focus my discussion on the following seven instances of contraction, all of which are common at least in North American varieties of spoken English.[1]

(1)   Subject + auxiliary/copula:
        They'll (< they will) leave soon.
        He's (<he is) here.

(2)   Semi-auxiliary + *to:*
        They hafta (< have to) go.

(3)   Modal auxiliary + *have:*
        They shoulda (< should have) gone.

(4)   Auxiliary + *not:*
        They don't (< do not) need that.

(5)   *Wh* word + auxiliary:
        Who's (< who is) Mary talking to?

_____

[1] I take no position on whether contraction in these cases is synchronic or diachronic.

(6)   *Want + to:*
        Who do they wanna (< want to) see?
        (but not: *Who do they wanna go?)

(7)   Contraction in *wh* questions:
        Who do you think's (< is) the winner?

A variety of factors seem to determine whether and when contraction is possible. One of them, as we will see in more detail below, is lexical frequency. As Krug (1998:294) observes, almost all of the full forms currently involved in contraction in English come from among the 150 most frequent words in the language.

Moreover, it is well known that certain contractions are subject to grammaticalization, a process that affects both a form's meaning and its grammatical function. An obvious example of this involves items such as *hafta*, *gonna*, and *usta*, which, in addition to being phonologically reduced, have developed a modal and/or aspectual function.

The focus of my discussion will be on the 'syntax' of contraction. The principal point will be that contraction is possible only under particular computational conditions that make eminent sense given the nature of phonological reduction and its place in the overall process of sentence formation.

2. CONTRACTION AND IMMEDIACY

The intuition that I wish to develop is that contraction is most natural where the computational system is able to combine the two elements involved *immediately*. More precisely:

(1)   *Natural Contraction:*
        Contraction of the string XY is most natural when X combines with Y without delay.

This makes good phonetic sense, of course, in that the articulatory processes involved in contraction (assimilation, deletion, vowel reduction, and so forth) are most natural in rapid connected speech. But how precisely should the 'without delay' proviso be interpreted? My proposal is as follows.

(2)   In the pattern ABC, A and B combine without delay if they combine immediately. B and C combine without delay if they combine immediately after the computational system has finished with A and B.

A simple example of the first case involves contraction in patterns such as *He will go*, in which the functor and its first argument contract, giving *He'll go*. Let us turn to this first.

2.1 Subject + auxiliary/copula

Contraction of a subject + auxiliary/copula sequence is extremely common in English, as the following examples help illustrate.

(1) a. She'll stay.
    b. I'm here.
    c. Bob's working hard.
    d. They're ready.

As illustrated in (2), the subject pronoun (A) and the auxiliary or copula (B) combine immediately in accordance with the usual computational practice, thereby creating the conditions for phonological reduction.

(2)   Immediate combination of the subject with the auxiliary verb, creating an opportunity for contraction:

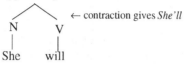

Bybee (2002:124) suggests that contraction in this case violates the 'usual notions of constituent structure,' in that auxiliaries are standardly assumed to form a constituent with the verb to their right, not with the subject. Bybee is right about this of course, but the 'usual notions of constituent structure' to which she refers may well be wrong.

When sentences are formed by an efficiency driven linear computational system, there is in fact a point at which the verb and its subject form a constituent, at least temporarily, as depicted in (2).[2] Crucially, this is also the point at which contraction occurs. Phonological reduction is thus a reflex of combination—a sign that two words have been combined at some point in the course of sentence formation.

Because of the way the computational system works, combinatorial relations themselves are often fleeting, reflecting no more than a transitional step in the sentence formation process. Indeed, in the case at hand, there is good reason to think that the constituent formed by the initial combination of the auxiliary verb and its first argument is quickly 'undone' as the computational system seeks to resolve the verb's second argument dependency. Thus (3a) rather than (3b) reflects the manner in which the computational system completes formation of the sentence *She'll go*.

---

[2]Phillips (2003) independently makes a similar point with respect to a variety of phenomena, including the so-called 'non-constituent coordination' found in sentences such as *[Jerry will] but [Mary won't] stay till the end*. He notes that *Jerry* and *will* form a constituent at the point at which they are initially combined.

(3) a. Right structure: b. Wrong structure:

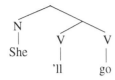

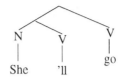

One indication of this comes from the fact that a contracted auxiliary verb can participate in the formation of coordinate structures such as the following.

(4)   She ['ll go] and [may even visit Sally on the way].

This would not be possible if the contracted auxiliary verb and its verbal argument did not form a unit that could be coordinated with the structurally parallel conjunct to its right.

Other factors

Although the computational system defines the conditions under which contraction may occur, it has nothing to say about the particular form yielded by this process. Contemporary English contracts *it is* as *it's*; earlier varieties of English reduced it to *T'is*. British English contracts *I have to* to *I've to*; North American English favors *I hafta*. And so on. As far as I can see, these choices have nothing to do with the operation of the computational system per se.

Moreover, the likelihood that contraction will occur where it is permitted seems to be subject to a variety of extraneous factors, including register, setting, and the like. One particularly important consideration seems to involve the relative frequency with which particular pairs of words combine with each other (e.g., Bybee & Schiebman 1999:576). As Bybee (2002:112) puts it, 'items that are used together fuse together.'

This seems especially apt in the case of subject-auxiliary contraction, as Krug (1998) shows. Drawing on data from the Birmingham corpus of spoken English, Krug found that auxiliary contraction is more likely with a pronoun subject than with a noun subject—an apparent frequency effect, since individual pronouns are far more common in subject position than is any particular noun. (After all, there are only a handful of subject pronouns, but tens of thousands of nouns.)

In addition, there are frequency effects for specific pronoun–auxiliary verb pairs. For example, there are far more instances of *I* plus *am* than of *we* plus *are* in the Birmingham corpus—and a significantly higher contraction rate for the former pattern. A similar asymmetry is found for *I* plus *have* versus *you* and *have*. This is just what one would expect if frequency of combination contributes to contraction.

2.2 Semi-auxiliary + *to*

As we have just seen, subject-auxiliary contraction involves a functor and its first argument, instantiating the first of the scenarios countenanced in our characterization of 'combination without delay,' repeated here.

(1)   In the pattern ABC, A and B combine without delay if they combine immediately. B and C combine without delay if they combine immediately after the computational system has finished with A and B.

The second scenario is instantiated in patterns where contraction affects a functor and its second argument. Common examples of this include the so-called 'semi-auxiliary' verbs illustrated in (2).

(2) a.   They hafta (< have to) do it.
   b.   We've gotta (< got to) finish this.
   c.   You oughtta (< ought to) look at that.
   d.   He's gonna (< going to) leave now.
   e.   They usta (< used to) spend a lot of time here.

Contraction in these patterns takes place under the conditions depicted below. (For the sake of exposition, I omit grids and indices where they are not directly relevant to the point at hand.)

(3)   They have to leave.

     Step 1: Combination of *they* and *have:*[3]

     Step 2: Combination of *have* with *to:*

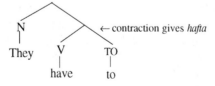

                          ←contraction gives *hafta*

---

[3]As noted above, British English permits contraction at this point, ultimately yielding *They've to leave*. The choice of contracted form here is a matter of convention, not computation.

The key step here is the second one. Immediately after the computational system has finished with *they* and *have* (A and B), it combines *have* and *to* (B and C)—creating the conditions that invite contraction.

At this point, there are two options in terms of how to resolve *to*'s dependency on a verbal argument—the verb *leave* in the example at hand. One possibility is that *leave* combines directly with the phonologically reduced *ta*.

(4)

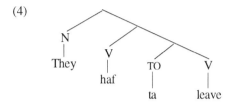

The other possibility is that the contracted form *hafta* is maintained as a constituent.

(5)

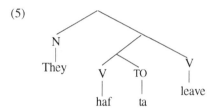

The behavior of *to* in coordination patterns suggests that *have* and *to* have fused, presumably as part of a process of grammaticalization,[4] and that the second structure is the right one. Consider:

(6) a. *They haf [ta leave early] and [to catch the bus downtown].
    b.   They hafta [leave early] and [catch the bus downtown].

The unacceptability of (6a) indicates that *have* and *to* form a unit, as depicted in (5). There is thus no '*to* phrase' in the first half of the sentence and therefore no opportunity for coordination of this type.

Frequency again

As we have already seen, immediate combination is a necessary condition for contraction, but not a sufficient one. This can be seen particularly clearly in the case of *got to*, which permits contraction on its 'obligation' interpretation but not on its 'receive permission' reading.

---

[4]In fact, there seems to be fusion independent of contraction, as shown by the marginal status of sentences such as (i), drawn to my attention by Kevin Gregg.

(i)   ?*They have [to leave early] and [to do the shopping].

(7) a. I got to/gotta stay—I have an appointment.
   b. I got to/*gotta stay—my parents gave me permission.

Similarly, *used to* can be contracted in (8a), where it has the sense of 'habitually,' but not in (8b), where it means 'employed for.'

(8) a. This used to/usta be a broom.
   b. This was used to/*usta sweep the floor.

One factor underlying these contrasts may be frequency of co-occurrence. A survey by Laura Robinson of the 1,100-minute American English corpus of telephone conversations (CALLHOME) revealed the following sharp asymmetries.

TABLE 8.1
Frequency and Contractibility

Item	Contractible?	No. of Instrances
got to ('obligation')	Yes	76
got to ('permission')	No	7
used to ('habitually')	Yes	58
used to ('employed for')	No	0

Once again then, we see evidence for Bybee's aphorism—items that are used together fuse together.

2.3 Modal auxiliary + *have*

Another common contraction pattern arises when a modal auxiliary combines with the auxiliary verb *have*, as in the following examples.

(1) a. Mary shoulda (< should have) waited.
   b. He coulda (< could have) finished earlier.
   c. We woulda (< would have) seen you there.
   d. It mighta (< might have) happened.

Such sentences are formed as follows. (I assume that modals take an uninflected verb as their second argument.)

(2)   Step 1: Combination of the subject and the modal auxiliary:

Step 2: Combination of *should* and *have*, creating the conditions under which reduction to *shoulda* is possible:

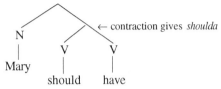

Here too, we have to decide whether the contracted form behaves as a unit with respect to later combinatorial operations. In particular, we must ask whether the subsequent addition of *waited* yields the structure in (3a) or (3b).

(3) a.   *Waited* combines just with *a*, the reduced form of *have:*

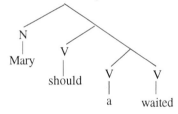

b.   *Waited* combines with *shoulda:*

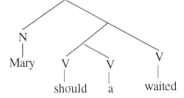

Once again the coordination facts favor the latter structure, in which *should* and *have* form an indivisible unit.

(4) a.   ?*Mary should [a waited] or [have left a note].
    b.   Mary shoulda [waited] or [left a note].

The unacceptability of (4a) is expected if *should* and *have* form a constituent in the first conjunct. Because there is no *have* phrase in the first half of the sentence, there is no opportunity for it to undergo coordination with a *have* phrase in the second conjunct. Selkirk (1984:391) arrives at a similar conclusion based on prosodic considerations.

2.4 Auxiliary + *not*

Consider next the sort of contraction that is common when *not* combines with a preceding auxiliary verb.

(1) a. Mary wouldn't go.
   b. This isn't working.
   c. It hasn't happened yet.
   d. They don't like it.

Strong frequency effects have been observed here. Bybee & Schiebman (1999) report that *do not* is most likely to be contracted in contexts where the two words occur together most frequently, namely after the pronoun *I* and before certain verbs (particularly *know* and *think*).

The more crucial question for us, however, has to do with whether the computational conditions for contraction are met. Consider in this regard the sentence in (1a), whose formation is summarized in (2).

(2)   Mary wouldn't go.

Step 1: Combination of the subject and the auxiliary verb:

Step 2: Addition of the negative, which combines with the auxiliary verb to its left, creating an opportunity for contraction to *wouldn't:*

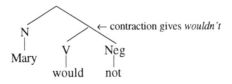

Step 3: Addition of the auxiliary verb's second argument, the uninflected verb *go*:

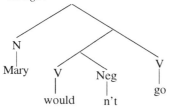

The key step is the second one, in which combination of *would* and *not* creates the conditions necessary for contraction.

Not only does the output of *not* contraction clearly behave like a unit with respect to phenomena such as 'subject–verb inversion' (e.g., *Wouldn't Mary go?*), it can feed into subsequent contraction operations.

(3)   They shouldna (< shouldn't have) gone.

As illustrated below, the contracted form in (3) is produced by immediately combining *shouldn't* with *have*, thereby creating an opportunity for further contraction.

(4)   They shouldna gone.

    a. Contraction of *should* and *not*   b. Contraction of *shouldn't* and *have:*

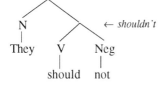 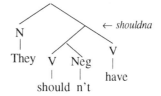

A case that is one step more complex involves *I would not have done it*, which permits the series of contractions illustrated below:

(5) a. Contraction of *I* and *would*:
      I'd

    b. Contraction of *I'd* and *not*:
       I'dn't

    c. Contraction of *I'd'nt* and *have*:
       I'dn'ta

Yet another case, this one involving a lexical verb, is the multiply contracted *I dunno*, illustrated in (6).

(6) a. Contraction of *do* and *not:*   b. Contraction of *don't* and *know:*

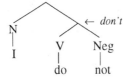

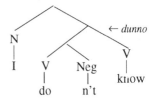

An interesting after-effect of contraction in this case is a subtle shift in meaning: Bybee & Schiebman (1999:587) report that *I dunno* is often used to express speaker uncertainty and to mitigate polite disagreement in conversation.

2.5 *Wh* word + auxiliary

In the course of considering the formation of *wh* questions in chapter seven, I suggested that *wh* words initially combine with the category to their right, even where the two do not enter into a functor–argument relationship (pp. 114-115). A sentence such as (1) is a case in point.

(1)   What will Mary buy?

Here *what* functions as argument of *buy*; it enters into no semantic relation at all with *will*. (I assume that an auxiliary verb combines to the right with both its arguments in question structures; see chapter ten.) Yet, if the proposed computational system is correct, *what* initially combines with *will*, as illustrated below.

(2)   Combination of *what* and *will:*

Combination of the *wh* word with the auxiliary in patterns such as this creates an opportunity for contraction, licensing the phonological reduction exemplified in the following sentences.

(3) a.   What'll Mary buy?
    b.   Who's she helping?
    c.   Who'd you like to talk to?
    d.   Where've you been?
    e.   Why's that thing ticking like that?

Given that contraction presupposes direct and immediate combination of the two elements involved, the phonological reduction manifested here provides independent support for the view that *wh* words do indeed initially combine with the category to their right.

3. *WANT TO* CONTRACTION

As is well known, *want* and *to* commonly contract in patterns such as the following.

(1)   They wanna (< want to) leave.

Want in these patterns is a simple 'control' verb, like *try* or *decide* (see chapter four), with the properties in (2). (As before, an underline is used to mark a lexically designated controller.)

(2)   *want*: V, <N̲ TO>

The formation of the sentence in (1) therefore proceeds as follows.

(3)   They wanna leave.

Step 1: Combination of *they* and *want*:

        N   V
        | |
       They   want

Step 2: Combination of *want* with *to*, creating an opportunity for contraction:

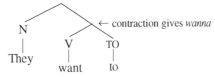

← contraction gives *wanna*

        N
        | V   TO
       They | |
              want to

There is reason to think that *want* and *to* form a unit with respect to subsequent combinatorial operations, so that the final form of the sentence resembles (4).

(4)

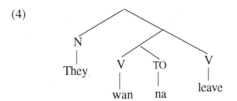

One piece of evidence in support of this conclusion comes from the following contrast, noted by Postal & Pullum (1982:126).

(5) a. *I wan [na dance] and [to sing].
    b. I wanna [dance] and [sing].

As can be seen here, there is evidently no '*to* phrase' that can be coordinated with the second conjunct. This is what we would expect if contraction of *want* and *to* yields an indivisible unit, consistent with the proposal put forward by Pullum (1997).

The infamous contrast

One of the most studied contraction phenomena in all of language involves the contrast illustrated below, first cited by Lakoff (1970:632), who credits Larry Horn with the initial observation.

(6) a. (Guess) who they want to/wanna dismiss.
        (cf. They want to dismiss who.)

    b. (Guess) who they want to/*wanna stay.
        (cf. They want who to stay.)

The commonly held view in the Principles-and-Parameters tradition is that contraction in the second sentence is blocked by the trace of *wh* movement in the embedded subject position.

                                   blocks contraction
                                          ↓
(7)   (Guess) [CP who$_i$ [IP they *want* [CP t$_i$ [IP t$_i$ *to* stay]]]]. (= (6b))

Mysteriously, however, and as the acceptability of (6a) demonstrates, contraction is not blocked by the intermediate trace in the specifier of CP or by PRO—a source of much wonderment over the years (e.g., Jaeggli 1980, Barss 1995, Boeckx 2000).

do not block contraction
↓ ↓

(8) (Guess) [$_{CP}$ who$_i$ [$_{IP}$ they *want* [$_{CP}$ **t**$_i$ [$_{IP}$ PRO *to* dismiss **t**$_i$]]]]. (= (6a))

As I see it, the key to understanding the constraint on *want to* contraction lies elsewhere, in the notion of 'combination without delay' that has proven to be relevant to the other cases of phonological reduction that we have been considering.

(9) In the pattern ABC, A and B combine without delay if they combine immediately. B and C combine without delay if they combine immediately after the computational system has finished with A and B.

Let us begin by considering sentence (6a), in which *want* is once again a simple control verb. The sentence formation process follows the course summarized in (10).

(10) (Guess) who they want to dismiss.

Step 1: Combination of *who* and *they*; there is no opportunity to resolve any dependencies at this point:

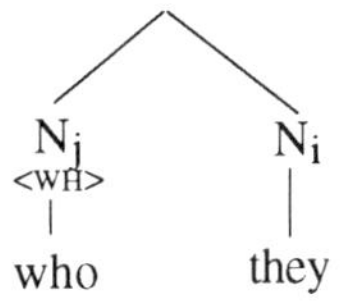

Step 2: Combination of *want* with its first argument, the pronoun *they:*

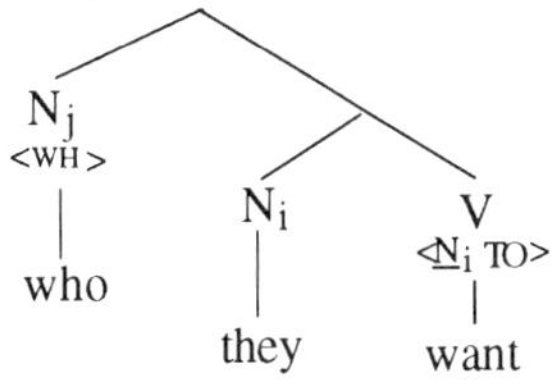

Step 3: Combination of *want* with its second argument, the infinitival marker *to*; contraction of *want* and *to:*

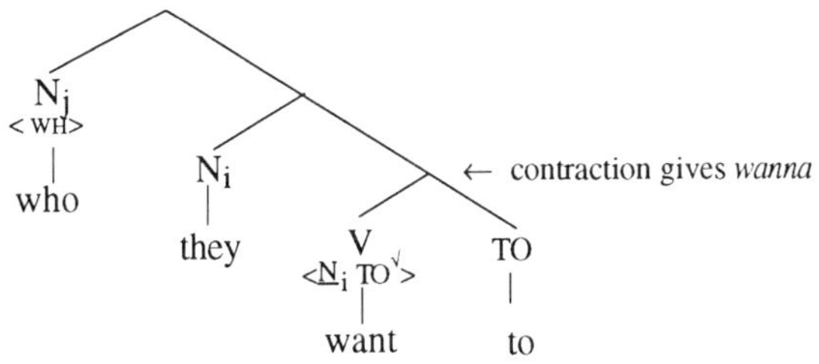

In this pattern, *they* is A, *want* is B and *to* is C. Because the computational system combines *want* with *to* immediately after finishing with *they* and *want* (the preceding step), contraction is allowed. Subsequent operations add the verb *dismiss*, whose argument structure in turn permits resolution of the *wh* dependency.

Matters are very different in the case of (6b), repeated here as (11).

(11)   Who do they want to/*wanna stay?

As can be seen more clearly by considering an affirmative sentence such as (12), *want* takes two nominal arguments in addition to an infinitival argument in this sort of pattern (e.g., Gazdar, Klein, Pullum, & Sag 1985:145). In this, it is just like the 'subject-to-object' raising verbs *expect* and *consider*; see chapter five (p. 81ff).

(12)   They want Mary to stay.
          <N N TO>

This contradicts the view, common in Government and Binding theory, that the second nominal in (12) functions as subject of the embedded verb, as depicted below.

(13)   They want [Mary to stay].

Independent evidence for the view I adopt comes from Postal's (1974:186) observation that a sentential adverb with scope over the matrix clause can appear to the right of the postverbal NP.

(14)   They wanted Mary, *unwisely*, to serve as their president.
          (= 'They unwisely wanted Mary to serve as their president.')

If *Mary* is in the embedded clause, the adverb must be as well, contrary to its interpretation as modifier of *want*. On the other hand, if *Mary* is part of the matrix clause as I propose, *unwisely* can be too, in accord with its semantic function.

Further evidence for the same conclusion comes from the acceptability of the negative polarity item *any* in sentences such as the following.

(15)   I want *none of the money* to go to politicians, [*any* more than you do].
          (cf. *I want some of the money to go to politicians, any more than you do.)

Given that negative polarity items must be licensed by a structurally higher negative in English (chapter two, pp. 18-19) and that the *any* phrase in (15) clearly belongs in the matrix clause, it follows that the postverbal nominal must be in the top clause as well—just as we'd expect if it serves as an argument of *want*.

Now let us consider the implications of this for contraction in the *want to stay* pattern, which is formed in the following manner.

(16)   (Guess) who they want to stay.

Step 1: Combination of *who* and *they*; there is no opportunity to resolve any dependencies at this point:

Step 2: Combination of *want* with its first argument, the pronoun *they*:

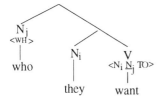

Step 3: Resolution of the *wh* dependency and of *want*'s second argument dependency:

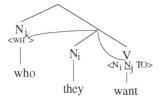

Step 4: Combination of *want* with its third argument, the infinitival marker *to*:

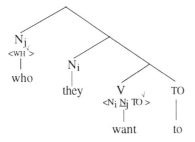

Here, again we can think of *they* as A, *want* as B, and *to* as C. But this time things work out differently, since the computational system does not combine *want* and *to* immediately after it has finished with *they* and *want* (step 2). Instead, as depicted in

step 3, it must resolve the *wh* dependency associated with *want*'s second argument
—the *wh* word *who*. (Recall that the order in which argument dependencies are
resolved is determined by their position in the verb's argument grid.)

This contrasts with the situation found in patterns such as *Who do you wanna
dismiss*, where contraction is permitted. There, as we saw in (10), the
computational system combines *want* with *to* immediately after it is finished with
they and *want*.

There appear to be prosodic correlates of this contrast. Warren, Spear, &
Schafer (2003) report that speakers consistently lengthen *want* in the pattern where
contraction is blocked. In addition, patterns of this type are more likely to manifest
an intermediate prosodic break after *want* than are patterns that permit contraction. It
is not implausible to think that both lengthening of *want* and the appearance of a
prosodic break right after it are reflexes of the time required to resolve the *wh*
dependency—time which ultimately compromises the possibility of contraction.

The difference between the two *want to* patterns thus comes down to the timing
of the contraction operation. Where *want* and *to* combine immediately, contraction
is permitted; where there is a delay, contraction is unnatural.[5] The result is so
inevitable that even very young children seem to be aware of it. Drawing on work
by Thornton (1990), Crain (1991:604) reports that children as young as two
distinguish between the contractible and noncontractible patterns with a high degree
of accuracy.

Two extreme cases

Timing is not sensitive to external factors such as input—it reflects the internal
operation of the computational system. For this reason, we expect the constraint on
contraction to manifest itself even in the absence of instruction or extensive
experience.

The early emergence of the contrast between the two *want to* patterns in very
young children is one indication of this. Additional evidence comes from the status
of the contrast in British English, in which *want to* contraction is not found at all.

---

[5]Pullum (1997:95 & 97) observes that *want to* contraction is also blocked in patterns such as the
following.

(i)   I don't want [[to do nothing] to be the response of this administration].

(ii)   You have to really WANT [to be an effective over-consumer].
       (with the interpretation '... in order to be an effective over-consumer')

(iii) I want, to be precise, a bright red 1962 MGA roadster.

There are a number of reasons why this might be so. For one thing, there is a prosodic break
between *want* and *to* in these patterns, perhaps reflecting the fact that *to* is not an argument of
want—it is part of the subject argument of the embedded clause in (i) and it occurs at the
beginning of a modifier clause in (ii) and (iii). This brings to mind the contrast between the two
cases of *used to* mentioned on p. 144, with contraction prohibited in the less frequent adjunct
pattern (*The broom was used to sweep the floor*).

Bailes (2000) studied the sensitivity of six speakers of British English to this phenomenon. After first establishing that the speakers did not contract *want* and *to* in their own speech (and presumably were not exposed to *want to* contraction in the speech of others in their community), Bailes elicited their judgments of (written) sentences such as the following.

(17) a. What do you wanna eat?
     b. *Who do you wanna eat the chips?

He found a sharp contrast between the two cases—his subjects accepted the first pattern 83% of the time, but never accepted the second pattern. This is just what one would expect if the contrast reflects a timing phenomenon intrinsic to the operation of the computational system.

At the other extreme, there may be speakers of American English for whom *want to* contraction escapes computational constraints altogether. Pullum (1997) mentions the existence of 'liberal dialects' in which contraction is permitted even in sentences such as *Who do you want to stay?*, where computational considerations rule it out for most speakers. For now at least, I concur with his suggestion that *want to* contraction in these cases is subject only to the condition that the two elements be part of the same phonological phrase when they combine with each other—a condition of no relevance to our understanding of the computational system.

4. COPULA CONTRACTION IN *WH* QUESTIONS

Finally, let us consider the sort of contraction found in question structures such as the following, in which the copula contracts and cliticizes to the verb in the higher clause. (The subject of the embedded clause is of course *who*.)

(1)   (Guess) who they think's (< is) here.

This sentence is formed in the manner depicted below.

(2)   Step 1: Combination of *who* and *they*; there is no opportunity to resolve any
        dependencies at this point:

Step 2: Combination of *think* with its first argument, the pronoun *they:*

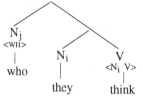

Step 3: Combination of *think* with *is*, immediately followed by contraction:

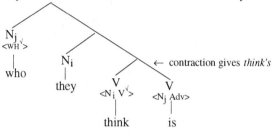

← contraction gives *think's*

Step 4: Resolution of the *wh* dependency and of the copula's first argument dependency:

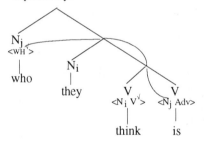

Step 5: Combination of the copula with its second argument:

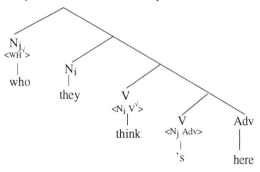

The vital step here is of course the third one, in which *think* combines without delay with *is*—satisfying the computational condition for contraction. Contraction would have been blocked if the computational system had to resolve the *wh* dependency right after combination of *they* and *think*, since this would have created a delay in the combination of *think* and *is*. But there is no such delay, since the mechanics of push-down storage dictate that dependency requirements of the more recently encountered verb *think* must be resolved before those of the more distant *wh* word.

(3)   (Guess) *who* they *think* is here.

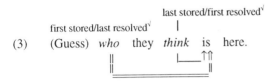

But now consider the acceptability of copula + negative contraction in patterns such as the following.

(4)   Who did you think isn't ready for the exam?

If the *wh* dependency is resolved immediately after combination of *think* with *is* (step 4 above), why doesn't this create a delay that blocks contraction of *is* and *not*?

The answer may be that *isn't* is not formed by contraction in Modern English; rather, it stands as a separate lexical item. This fits well with Zwicky & Pullum's (1983) conclusion that *n't* in contemporary English is an inflectional suffix, not a contracted clitic.

A prohibition against copula contraction
As is well known, reduction of *be* is impossible in patterns such as the following, from Selkirk (1984:401).

(5)   *The water's bad and the air's _ too.
        (cf. The water is bad and the air is too.)

This phenomenon was originally attributed to a syntactic prohibition against contraction before a 'deletion site' (e.g., King 1970, Lakoff 1970, Kaisse 1983)—notice that the adjective *bad* has been deleted in the second conjunct of (5).[6] However, this does not seem to be general enough, as contraction can be blocked even when there is no immediately following deletion site. Consider in this regard the following pattern, in which the copula has been contracted.

---

[6]A second constraint, not discussed here, involves the category of the phrase to the left of the copula. See Kaisse (1983) for extensive discussion.

(6)   John's to leave tonight.
        (cf. John is to leave tonight.)

The key observation involves the unacceptability of this sort of contraction in the second conjunct of sentences such as (7).

(7)   *Mary's to leave tonight, and John's to _ as well.
        (cf. ?Mary is to leave tonight, and John is to _ as well.)

Notice that the copula cannot be contracted in the second conjunct, even though it does not occur immediately in front of a deletion site.

Another contrast illustrating the same point is exemplified in (8). (The contracted *I've to* form, although apparently more natural in British English than in American English, is common. A Google search of the Internet in March of 2004 by Laura Robinson revealed 43,500 instances of it. A search by Mark Messer for *they've to* turned up 1500 examples.)

(8) a.   They've to go now, and I've to go in a few minutes.
    b.   *They've to go now, and I've to _ in a few minutes.
         (cf. They've to go now, and I have to _ in a few minutes.)

Once again contraction of the verb—this time *have*—is blocked despite the fact that it is not followed by a deletion site.

In sum then, whatever the right constraint on copula contraction turns out to be, it is unlikely to involve the presence of an immediately following deletion site, contrary to the commonly held view. My suspicion at this point is that the required constraint is primarily prosodic in character, as suggested by Selkirk (1984:402) and Anderson & Lightfoot (2002:25ff), among others.

5. CONCLUSION

The syntax of contraction is best understood in terms of computational timing. In particular, reduction of X and Y is most natural when the computational system combines them without delay—a natural requirement given that the articulatory processes involved in contraction are most natural in rapid speech, as noted at the outset.

As we have seen, the immediacy condition is crucial not only to licensing phonological reduction in several major contraction patterns in English (e.g., subject + auxiliary, *wh* word + auxiliary, auxiliary + *have*, semi-auxiliary + *to*), it also offers revealing insights into puzzling contrasts involving *want to* contraction and copula contraction in *wh* questions. In these phenomena we find additional support both for the general view of the computational system put forward here and for the details of how it works—in a linear manner, combining words at the first opportunity.

As first mentioned in chapter one, the ultimate goal of the ideas that I have been pursuing is to reduce the theory of sentence structure to the theory of sentence processing. My strategy to this point has been to outline a linear computational system that shows enough promise in terms of its treatment of the traditional problems of syntactic theory to make this attempt worthwhile. There is always more that could be done, of course, but it is perhaps not wise to ignore the other side of the story any longer. The time has come to explore the prospects of the reductionist program from a processing perspective. I turn to this matter in chapter nine.

Chapter 9

Syntax and Processing

1. INTRODUCTION

Thus far, I have deliberately focused my attention on various classic phenomena of syntactic theory—sentence structure, coreference, control, agreement, extraction, and contraction. My goal has been to show that an efficiency driven linear computational system can provide revealing insights into the nature of these phenomena. Indeed on these grounds alone, there is much to recommend this view of syntax.

However, as noted at the outset, the approach we are exploring is motivated by more than just the traditional concerns of syntactic theory. It also aims to subsume the theory of sentence structure under the theory of sentence processing. In terms of the metaphor suggested in chapter one, we have rejected the idea of architects and blueprints. Instead we take an utterance's edifice to be the work of carpenters who plan as they build, constrained only by the conceptual-symbolic materials (words and morphemes) with which they work and the need to finish the job as quickly and efficiently as possible.

From these simple assumptions much follows, as we have seen. Not only do we derive syntactic representations with a binary branching design and a subject–object asymmetry, we are able to account for the defining properties of many important syntactic phenomena, ranging from pronoun interpretation and control to agreement and contraction.

But this is not enough. If the ideas that I have put forward are right and if the computational system that builds sentences is just a processor, then claims about how it operates must be supported by more than just data about the acceptability of particular forms and interpretations. Psycholinguistic evidence from the study of how sentences are processed in real time must also be brought into play. (No such requirement holds for traditional grammatical theory of course—it makes claims about what structure must look like, not how it is built.) Let us consider in more detail precisely what is at stake here.

2. WHAT IS AT STAKE

It is important to be clear from the outset about what has to be established on the psycholinguistic side. My principal claim is that the theory of sentence structure can and should be subsumed under the theory of sentence processing. This does *not* mean that the theory of sentence structure and the theory of sentence processing are one and the same thing.

The domain of the theory of sentence processing extends far beyond the questions of form and interpretation that constitute the focus of syntactic theory. Among the issues that research into sentence processing must address are the following (for a general review and discussion, see Frazier 1998, Fodor & Inoue 1998, Sturt & Crocker 1998, Hagoort, Brown, & Osterhout 1999, Crocker 1999, Pickering 1999, Garrett 2000, and Townsend & Bever 2001):

- Is there a single processor for both encoding and decoding, or are there two separate processors?
- Is parsing during listening qualitatively different from parsing during reading?
- Is a sentence initially assigned a structure based solely on syntactic considerations, or are all relevant sources of information (semantic, lexical, contextual, pragmatic) brought to bear from the outset?
- What is the role of lexical frequency in parsing?
- Can the parser look ahead?
- Are different potential analyses for a sentence computed in parallel (and perhaps ranked in terms of likelihood), or does the processor compute just one analysis at a time, with backtracking when it errs?
- Why do some languages (e.g., Spanish) prefer to associate the relative clause in phrases like *the daughter of the colonel [who was standing on the balcony]* with the first noun (so-called 'high attachment') whereas other languages (e.g., English) apparently exhibit no such preference.
- How does the processor recover from mistakes, such as those associated with garden paths?

These are all important matters, but they are independent of the particular claim that I have put forward with regards to syntax.

The emergentist theory makes a two-fold claim. First, grammar in the traditional sense is unnecessary. And, second, the computational system proposed to deal with the phenomena discussed in the first chapters of this book is just an efficiency driven linear processor. That is, it builds sentences from left to right one word at a time, resolving dependencies at the first opportunity so as to ease the burden on working memory.

Linearity and efficiency could be implemented in different ways—by separate processors for encoding and decoding or by a single shared processor, by a processor that could look ahead or by one that couldn't, by a processor that is sensitive to lexical frequency or by one that isn't, and so on. My claim requires only that there be evidence that dependencies are resolved at the first opportunity in the course of processing. Nothing more than this is needed, and nothing less will suffice.

Moreover, there is no reason at all to think that predictions relating to linearity and efficiency must distinguish the sort of processor that I propose from the sort of processors associated with more traditional approaches to language. As we will see below, there is a general consensus that processors try to get things done as quickly as possible. A computational system (such as mine) that consists just of a processor could therefore end up making the *same* predictions about the rapid resolution of dependencies as a computational system that incorporates both a grammar *and* a processor.

The point is not that a 'stand-alone' processor works better than one that is linked to a grammar. The point is that a grammar is unnecessary, and that the processor that takes its place works the way that it does because it is driven to resolve dependencies at the first opportunity. The preceding chapters have dealt with the question of whether the key properties of a language's syntax can be explained without reference to a grammar. Our job here is to determine whether dependencies are resolved in the predicted manner in the course of sentence processing.

There is a very substantial literature on processing, far too much to review and interpret thoroughly in the space of a single chapter. However, I believe that enough of a beginning can be made to demonstrate the essential correctness of the central thesis that I wish to establish—the computational system for language is just an efficiency driven linear processor whose properties are best understood in terms of its task, which is to build sentences one word at a time from left to right under significant time constraints.

Let us begin by considering the resolution of argument dependencies.

3. RESOLVING ARGUMENT DEPENDENCIES

A defining feature of work on sentence processing is the assumption that sentences are formed one word at a time from left to right. As observed by Frazier (1987:561), there is a consensus that 'perceivers incorporate each word of an input into a constituent structure representation of the sentence, roughly as each item is encountered' (see also Frazier 1998:126, Hagoort, Brown, & Osterhout 1999:275, and Pickering 1999:124, among others).

There is a great deal of empirical support for this assumption, much of it coming from two sources—the detection of syntactic anomalies and the processing of so-called garden paths. Let us consider each in turn.

3.1 The detection of syntactic anomalies

Very early evidence for the view that sentences are formed as their component words are encountered comes from pioneering work by Marslen-Wilson (1975) in the shadowing paradigm (in which subjects repeat speech as they hear it). Marslen-Wilson found that syntactic anomalies such as the use of *already* in the second sentence below could be detected and spontaneously corrected within 250 milliseconds of being encountered—a clear illustration of 'the speed and precison with which sructural information can be utilized' (p. 227).

(1)   He thinks she won't get the letter. He's afraid he forgot to put a stamp on the *already* before he went to post it.

More recent techniques, including the study of event-related potentials (the positive and negative voltage fluctuations that occur during sentence processing), point toward the same conclusion. For instance, Osterhout and Holcomb (1993) report that a positive-going voltage spike is triggered within 50 to 300 milliseconds after the word *to* in (2) and after the word *was* in (3) when subjects listen to these sentences.

(2)   *The broker persuaded *to* sell the stock.

(3)   *The broker hoped to sell the stock *was* sent to jail.

Similarly, McKinnon & Osterhout (1996) report an almost immediate positive-going spike after the word *that* when sentences such as (4) are read.

(4)   *The man seems *that* it is likely to win.

Such rapid responses to ill-formedness suggest that an attempt (unsuccessful in these cases) is made to resolve dependencies as individual words are encountered—which is why missteps are detected so quickly.

Additional evidence for the same conclusion comes from the study of eye movements during reading. Ni, Fodor, Crain, & Shankweiler (1998) report that regressive eye movements occur immediately upon encountering the word *eating* in the following sentence.

(5)   *It seems that cats won't usually *eating* the food we put on the porch.

Here again, such rapid detection of the error would not be possible if the sentence was not being constructed as its parts are encountered.

3.2 Garden path effects

The classic evidence for the functioning of the parser comes from so-called *garden path effects*—the feeling of having hit a dead end in the course of processing particular types of sentences. These intuitions are supported by experimental evidence from a variety of sources, including eye movements during reading, response times on self-paced reading tasks, electrophysiological activity in the brain, and even the amount of time it takes to give acceptability judgments.

A simple illustration of a garden path effect comes from the contrast in the way the sentences in (1) are read, in the absence of clues from prosody or punctuation. (This example and those in (2) and (3) are from Frazier & Clifton 1996:10-11; the figures in parentheses indicate the mean decision times, in milliseconds, for grammaticality judgments.)

(1) a. Though George kept on reading the story Sue bothered him. (1160 ms.)
   b. Though George kept on reading the story still bothered him. (1545 ms.)

A processing problem arises in (1b), where the noun phrase *the story* is initially misattached to the optionally transitive verb *read*. The processor must subsequently backtrack and reanalyze *the story* as subject of the second clause.

A garden path effect also underlies the contrast between the following two sentences.

(2) a. Mary kissed John and his brother when she left. (1065 ms.)
   b. Mary kissed John and his brother started to laugh. (1667 ms.)

A moderate processing problem arises in the second of these sentences, where there is a tendency to incorrectly associate the string *and his brother* with the first clause.

Yet another garden path effect is discernible in the contrast illustrated in (3).

(3) a. The teacher told the children the ghost story that she knew would frighten them. (1359 ms.)
   b. The teacher told the children the ghost story had frightened that it wasn't true. (3150 ms.)

Readers typically misanalyze *the ghost story* as third argument of the verb *tell* in (3b). In fact, of course, it should be part of a relative clause modifying *children*.

Frazier & Clifton (1996:8) suggest that garden path effects reflect the operation of a general processing principle, which they paraphrase as follows (see also Frazier 1987:564).[1]

(4)   Choose the first available analysis.

Other work offers principles similar in spirit. Frazier (1987:583) suggests that the processor adopts as its overarching strategy a simple guideline—'Structure the input as soon as possible.' Mazuka & Lust (1990:166) require that the processor utilize information as soon as it becomes available. And Inoue & Fodor (1994:35)

---

[1]This principle subsumes two earlier processing strategies—Late Closure (if grammatically permissible, attach new items into the most recently postulated clause or phrase) and Minimal Attachment (postulate the fewest number of nodes possible). See, for example, Frazier (1987).

propose a 'general least effort principle,' which they call 'Minimal Everything.' (See also Frazier 1998:127 on this point.)

These ideas fit well with the processing contrasts exemplified in (1) to (3). In each case of a garden path effect, the processor encounters a dead end because of its haste to incorporate new material into the sentence by associating it with an already available element. In (1b), the noun phrase *the story* is misattached because the processor seeks to immediately resolve the possible theme argument dependency associated with the just encountered verb *read*. In (2b), *and his brother* is treated as part of the previously posited second argument of *kiss*. In (3b), *the ghost story* is initially misanalyzed in a way that allows it to function as third argument of the already available verb *tell*. And so on.

All of this is very much in keeping with the spirit of the proposals that I have put forward. The sorts of missteps associated with garden paths are just what one would expect of an efficiency driven processor that has to deal with complex material under severe time constraints. As Frazier & Clifton (1996:21) observe, the operation of the processor reflects 'universally present memory and time pressures resulting from the properties of human short-term memory.' These pressures promote the resolution of argument dependencies at the first opportunity, leading to the pitfalls associated with the processing of garden path sentences.

3.3 Processing and the lexicon

There is a complication in all of this, but it does not jeopardize the central claim that is at stake here—namely that the processor resolves argument dependencies in a way that maximizes efficiency. The complication has to do with the precise manner in which the processing system makes use of information from 'external sources' such as the lexicon, context, knowledge of the world, and so forth. (Bever, Sanz, & Townsend 1998:278 refer to this as the 'central problem' of language processing research.)

There are two basic positions on this issue. One view, put forward by Frazier & Clifton (1996) and Ferreira & Clifton (1986) among others, is that the processor is essentially autonomous. At least in its preliminary analysis of the input, it does not attend to information about the relative frequency of particular uses of a word or to potentially disambiguating contextual information.

The second view, represented by MacDonald, Pearlmutter, & Seidenberg (1994:682) and MacDonald (1999), is that syntactic processing is governed by the same sorts of factors that are relevant to simple lexical processing, including frequency effects and contextual information.

There is no doubt that lexical factors influence processing in some way. For example, a lexical effect is clearly discernible in the following pair of sentences from Hagoort, Brown, & Osterhout (1999:278).

(1)   The teacher sees the boy and the girl sees the teacher.

(2)   The teacher buys the ticket and the girl sees the teacher.

There is a noticeable tendency to initially treat *the girl* as part of a coordinate NP in (1), but not in (2), where the semantic properties of *buy* make this interpretation unlikely.

But how and when do semantic considerations intervene? One possibility, favored by Frazier & Clifton (1996:13), is that an autonomous syntactic parser provides an initial analysis of sentence structure, which can subsequently be assessed and revised by other processing modules that are sensitive to factors such as frequency and context. MacDonald, Pearlmutter, & Seidenberg (1994:695ff) dispute this suggestion, arguing that there is no independent evidence for a distinct second stage in parsing that exploits contextual and lexical information in the way proposed by Frazier and her colleagues.

The issues here are obviously difficult and may remain contentious for some time—as Bever, Sanz, & Townsend (1998:278) sagely observe, 'the damn thing is probably more complex than our models will allow.' Crucially, though, the complexity has to do with how and when the processor identifies and classifies argument dependencies. This is very different from the question of when dependencies, once identified, are resolved. There seems to be no controversy on the latter question—the processor seeks to resolve argument dependencies at the first opportunity. This is the crucial point for establishing the psycholinguistic plausibility of the computational system that I have proposed.

4. RESOLVING REFERENTIAL DEPENDENCIES

Referential dependencies too should be resolved at the first opportunity. Two such types of dependencies were dealt with in some detail in earlier chapters—one introduced by pronouns and the other by infinitival verbs, as illustrated in (1) and (2), respectively.

(1)   The reflexive pronoun *himself* introduces a referential dependency (represented by the index *x*), which is immediately resolved by the index of *Harvey* in the grid of *admire:*

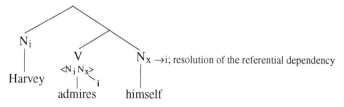

(2)   The infinitival verb *leave* projects its subject argument as a referential
       dependency, which is immediately resolved by the index of *Mary* in the grid
       of *decide:*

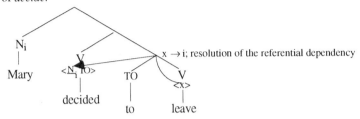

If the theory of syntactic computation proposed here is right, there should be
processing evidence that referential dependencies are resolved without delay. Let us
consider each type of referential dependency in turn.

4.1 Pronoun interpretation

Nicol & Swinney (1989) make use of a cross-modal priming task to investigate the
processing of reflexive and plain pronouns in English. Experiments of this type call
for subjects to indicate whether they recognize probe words that are flashed on a
screen at various points as they listen to sentences. Some of the probe words are
semantically related to words in the stimulus sentence while others are not. (For
example, the probe word *hospital* might be used for a sentence that contained the
word *doctor*.) The key assumption, validated in previous work, is that subjects
make quicker decisions about probe words that are semantically related to words
that have been recently activated.

Now, if referential dependencies are in fact interpreted at the first opportunity
(immediately, in most cases), exposure to a pronoun should trigger immediate
reactivation of its antecedent. This in turn should create a priming effect that
shortens the response time for a semantically related probe word that is presented
right after the pronoun. Sample sentences from the Nicol & Swinney study are
given in (1) and (2), with the probe point marked by †.

(1)   Test sentence involving a reflexive pronoun:
       The boxer told the skier that the doctor for the team would blame himself †
       for the recent injury.

(2)   Test sentence involving a plain pronoun:
       The boxer told the skier that the doctor for the team would blame him †
       for the recent injury.

On the assumption that pronouns are interpreted at the first opportunity, as
required by the Efficiency Requirement, the reflexive pronoun in (1) should
reactivate *the doctor for the team* (its antecedent). This in turn should result in a

shorter reaction time for a semantically related probe word such as *hospital* that is presented right after the reflexive is heard.

(3)   The boxer told the skier that the doctor for the team would blame *himself* ...

                                                                             ↑

                                             should reactivate *doctor*,
                                             its antecedent

By the same reasoning, the plain pronoun in (2) could reactivate *the boxer* and/or *the skier*, which are possible antecedents, but not *the doctor*. This in turn should lead to shorter response times for semantically related probes such as *fight* (for *boxer*) and *snow* (for *skier*).

(4)   The boxer told the skier that the doctor for the team would blame *him* ...

                                                                      ↑

                                                should reactivate *boxer* and *skier*,
                                             its potential antecedents

Nicol & Swinney's results bore out these predictions. Probe words that were semantically related to *doctor* had shorter reaction times after *himself* than after *him*. In contrast, probe words that were semantically related to *boxer* or *skier* had shorter reaction times after *him* than after *himself*.

Further evidence for the immediate resolution of referential dependencies introduced by reflexive pronouns comes from a study by Sturt (2003), who recorded subjects' eye movements as they were reading sentences such as the following.

(5) a. Jonathan was pretty worried at the City Hospital. He remembered that the surgeon had pricked *himself* with a used syringe needle. There should be an investigation soon.

    b. Jonathan was pretty worried at the City Hospital. He remembered that the surgeon had pricked *herself* with a used syringe needle. There should be an investigation soon.

The key prediction was that if referential dependencies are resolved at the first opportunity, processing difficulties should arise as soon as the reflexive pronoun is encountered in patterns such as (5b), but not (5a). That is because the gender of the reflexive pronoun in (5b) does not match the stereotypical gender (masculine) of *the surgeon*, the NP which the computational system selects as its antecedent.

(6)   He$_i$ remembered that [*the surgeon*$_j$ had pricked *herself* ...]

                                    <N$_j$ N$_x$>

                                       ↓

                                j $\Rightarrow$ apparent gender mismatch

Sturt reports that both first-fixation and first-pass reading times for the reflexive pronoun were faster when the pronoun's gender matched the stereotypical gender of the antecedent, as in (5a), than when it did not, as in (5b). This is just the sort of contrast that one would expect if resolution of the referential dependency introduced by the reflexive pronoun takes place immediately.

In many sentences, interpretation of both reflexive pronouns and plain pronouns is fast and simple. The computational system can immediately resolve the referential dependency introduced by the reflexive pronoun, and the pragmatic system has easy access to the antecedent(s) required to determine the reference of the plain pronoun.[2] (Sentences such as (3) and (4) above appear to work this way.)

Matters are not always so straightforward though, especially in the case of plain pronouns, which are commonly used in multi-sentence discourses where more than one potential antecedent can be in focus. This is known to create difficulties for the processor (Piñango, Burkhardt, Brun, & Avrutin 2001, Sekerina, Stromswold, & Hestvik 2004:147). One indication of this comes from Sekerina at al's study of the interpretation of sentences such as the following.

(7)   Context:
       In these pictures, you see a box, a man, and a box. The boy has placed the box on the ground.
   a. Reflexive pronoun pattern:
       Which picture shows that *boy has placed the box behind himself?*

   b. Plain pronoun pattern:
       Which picture shows that *boy has placed the box behind him?*

By tracking the subjects' gaze as they scanned the relevant pictures, Sekerina et al. were able to determine how long it took them to arrive at an interpretation for each pronoun. They found a significantly longer reaction time for plain pronouns, leading them to conclude that 'processing of reflexives, where the interpretation is obtained within the clause via syntactic mechanisms alone, is less costly than that of referentially ambiguous pronouns' (p. 147).

Eye-tracking studies during reading reveal other complications associated with the interpretation of plain pronouns. As Garrod, Freudenthal, & Boyle (1994) note, for instance, it takes longer to interpret pronouns that refer to a distant antecedent than to a more recently mentioned one. In addition, reading time increases when the antecedent is non-topicalized versus topicalized.

Another indication of the difficulty of processing pronouns in discourse situations comes from an experiment by Greene, McKoon, & Ratcliff (1992). The authors investigated the interpretation of pronouns in written passages such as the following, which were presented on a screen one word at a time.

---

[2]Based on a review of the early literature, Sanford & Garrod (1989) conclude that an attempt to interpret plain pronouns is initiated immediately upon encountering them.

(8)   Mary and John were doing the dishes after dinner. One of them was washing while the other dried. Mary accidentally scratched John with a knife and then she dropped it on the counter.

Generally, exposure to a pronoun reduces the amount of time it takes to respond to queries about the prior occurrence of its antecedent, so that a question about whether the word *Mary* has appeared might receive a quicker response if asked after the coreferential pronoun *she* than before it. However, no such effect was observed in this case, leading Greene and his colleagues to suggest that speakers do not always immediately identify the referent of a plain pronoun when the discourse includes multiple participants (see also Oakhill & Garnham 1989).

In fact, as Sanford & Sturt (2002:382) note, there are cases in which the full specification of the referent of a pronoun is not even possible.

(9)   Mary bought a brand new Hitachi radio. It was in Selfridge's window. Later, when Joan saw it, she too decided it would be a good purchase.

This passage is perfectly comprehensible even though it is unclear whether Mary bought the particular radio in the window or just a radio of the same type, and even less clear what precisely the various instances of *it* refer to.

Such results and observations are compatible with the view of pronoun interpretation put forward in chapter three. Only reflexive pronouns are interpreted by the computational system, and only they require resolution of their referential dependency at the first opportunity as a matter of procedural necessity. The referential dependencies introduced by plain pronouns are the responsibility of the pragmatic system, which operates in an environment where instant decisions are not always feasible or strategically appropriate.

Summarizing then, the evidence from the processing literature supports the conclusion that reflexive pronouns are interpreted by the computational system as quickly as possible (immediately, in the cases we have been considering). This in turn lends support to the analysis of pronoun interpretation proposed in chapter three, according to which the syntax of coreference is reduced to the requirement that referential dependencies be resolved at the first opportunity in the course of sentence formation.

4.2 Control

Nicol & Swinney (1989) have used cross-modal priming to investigate the processing of control patterns, with the idea that PRO should reactivate its antecedent. Unfortunately, the relevance of their study to our concerns is limited by their choice of points (marked here by †) at which to probe for reactivation effects.

(1)   The actress invited the dentist from the new medical center
        to † go to the par†ty at the † mayor's † house.†

Nicol & Swinney chose as their crucial probe point the position right after the
infinitival marker *to*, which they take to be to the immediate right of PRO—the null
pronoun that represents unexpressed subject arguments in Government and Binding
theory.

(2)   The actress invited the dentist from the new medical center
        [PRO to † go to the par†ty at the † mayor's † house].†
                ↑
             first probe point

Crucially though, Nicol & Swinney found no reactivation effect for the probe point
after *to*.

   Although potentially problematic for PRO-based theories of control, this result
is expected on the analysis of control that I have put forward. This is because a
probe point after *to* is too early—it precedes the verb, which is the earliest point at
which the missing argument can be detected and identified in the theory I propose.
(Recall that missing arguments are expressed as referential dependencies in the
verb's argument grid, not as null pronouns.)

(3)   The actress invited the dentist from the new medical center
        [to † go to the par†ty at the † mayor's † house].†
          <x>
           ↑
        earliest point at which the missing
        argument could be activated

   Interestingly, there *was* a reactivation effect for the third probe point (after *at
the*). This is a plausible result from our perspective. Although it does not fall
immediately after the verb, this probe point at least occurs in a position where the
effects of resolving a referential dependency in the verb's argument grid might still
be felt.[3]

   A similar result is reported by McElree & Bever (1989), who investigated the
contrast between the following two types of sentences, among others.

(4) a. Control pattern (missing subject assumed to be PRO):
        The stern judge who met with the defense adamantly refused
        [PRO to argue about the appeal].

---

[3]No significant reactivation effect was associated with the second probe point. This is somewhat
puzzling, since it occurs after the verb. However, the fact that it falls *inside* a word may be relevant
here.

b. Non-control pattern:
The stern judge who met with the defense flatly rejected
the arguments for an appeal.

The sentences were presented on a computer screen one phrase at a time, with a
probe word (*stern* in the case of the above examples) making its appearance at one
of the positions marked by †. The subject's task was simply to indicate whether the
probe word had appeared previously in the sentence.

(5) a. The stern judge who met with the defense adamantly refused
[PRO to † argue about the appeal].†

b. The stern judge who met with the defense flatly rejected
the † arguments for an appeal.†

Because the unexpressed subject argument in (5a) is coreferential with *the stern
judge*, readers were predicted to be quicker and more accurate in responding to the
probe *stern* in that sentence than in (5b), which does not involve a control relation.
This turned out to be right. Interestingly, however, McElree & Bever report no
facilitation effect at the first probe position in (5a), although there was one at the
second position.

This is just what we would expect if unexpressed subject arguments are
represented as referential dependencies in the grid of the infinitival verb. On this
view, McElree & Bever's first probe position occurs too soon to trigger a
reactivation effect, as illustrated below.

(6)   The stern judge who met with the defense adamantly refused
[to † argue about the appeal].†
↑
<x>
earliest point at which the missing
argument could be activated

If there is to be a reactivation effect at all, it should be at the second probe
position—which is precisely where it was found.

An even more promising study from our perspective was carried out for
Spanish by Demestre, Meltzer, García-Albea, & Vigil (1999). The crucial patterns
are as follows.

(7) a. Pedro ha aconsejado a María [ser más *educada/*educado* con los
Peter has advised   to Maria to.be more polite-Fem/Masc with the
trabajadores].
employees
'Peter has advised Maria to be more polite with the employees.'

b. María ha aconsejado a Pedro [ser más *educado/*educada* con los
Maria has advised   to Peter to.be more polite-Masc/Fem with the
trabajadores].
employees
'Maria has advised Peter to be more polite with the employees.'

The key factor here involves the choice of gender on the adjective *educado/educada* 'polite,' which is determined by the referent of the understood subject of the infinitival verb *ser* 'be'—María in (7a) and Pedro in (7b). (*Aconsejar* 'advise' is an object control verb, just like its English counterpart.)

Reasoning that a gender error should be perceived immediately if the understood subject argument of *ser* 'be' is computed right away, Demestre et al. set out to investigate this matter by measuring event-related brain potentials. (As already noted, ERPs are sensitive to various linguistic phenomena, including agreement mismatches.)

Working with 96 test items and fourteen subjects, Demestre et al. found a significant wave form difference between the acceptable and unacceptable patterns, with the gender mismatch triggering a negative-going voltage wave right after the adjective. As the authors note, gender agreement errors could not have been identified this quickly if the computational system had not already interpreted the understood subject of the infinitival verb.

(8)   Pedro$_i$ ha aconsejado a María$_j$ [ser más *educado* ...]

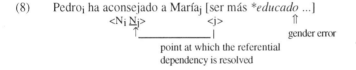

This is exactly what one would expect if the referential dependencies involved in control patterns are resolved at the first opportunity, as demanded by the Efficiency Requirement.

Once again then, we find in the psycholinguistic literature support for our analysis of a syntactic phenomenon—the referential dependencies involved in control patterns really do seem to be resolved at the first opportunity.

A puzzle in raising constructions

There is a potential complication, however. Work by Thomas Bever and his colleagues (e.g., Bever, Sanz, & Townsend 1998) has uncovered a difference between control and raising structures such as the following. (For the sake of exposition, I use the traditional PRO/trace notation in this one case.)

(9) a. Control pattern:
        [The stubborn shopkeepers] hoped [PRO to † be happy].†

    b. Raising pattern:
        [The stubborn shopkeepers] seemed [*t* to † be happy].†

The key finding is that subjects respond more quickly at the second probe point in the raising pattern than in the control pattern, leading Bever to conclude that traces prime for their antecedent more strongly than PRO. (PRO seemed to have little if any priming effect in these experiments; not surprisingly, neither PRO nor trace has a priming effect at the preverbal probe point.)

This is a very interesting result, but it does not necessarily support the traditional view that control patterns and raising patterns are formed in different ways, with a null pronoun in the former case and a trace in the latter, contrary to the analysis proposed in chapter five.

Recall from chapter five that I take the two structures to be alike in one respect and different in another. They are alike in that the first argument of the embedded verb is expressed as a referential dependency that is resolved at the first opportunity by an index in the grid of the matrix verb. On the other hand, they differ with respect to the lexical properties of the matrix verb. In particular, whereas control verbs such as *hope* assign a thematic role to their first argument, raising verbs such as *seem* do not.

(10) a. *hope*: <N̲ TO>
                ag

     b. *seem*: <N̲ TO>   '

This in turn means that the thematic role of the matrix subject in raising patterns is determined by virtue of its link to the first-argument dependency of the embedded verb. Thus *Harry* in (11) is perceived to be an agent by virtue of its association with the first argument of the embedded verb.

(11)   Harry$_i$ seemed [to work hard].

This extra relationship, which is found only in raising patterns, may well be responsible for the asymmetry in priming effects, as McElree & Bever (1989:30) themselves suggest.

5. RESOLVING AGREEMENT DEPENDENCIES

As explained in chapter six, the syntax of agreement can be reduced to the requirement that agreement dependencies be resolved at the first opportunity. Efficiency, not grammar, provides the best account of the morphosyntactic facts.

The psycholinguistic evidence also points toward the rapid resolution of agreement dependencies. One such piece of evidence comes from electrophysiological activity in the brain in response to agreement mismatches such as the following.

(1)   *The elected officials hopes to succeed.

In a study of event-related potentials, Osterhout & Mobley (1995) had subjects read sentences such as the one above and then judge their acceptability. They found that the agreement mismatch triggered an almost immediate positive spike in electrical activity that peaked about 500 milliseconds after the violation—the usual response to syntactic anomalies on this sort of task. A similar finding is reported by Coulson, King, & Kutas (1998).[4]

This is exactly what one would expect if the computational system we have proposed is at work. As explained in chapter six, the resolution of agreement dependencies proceeds in a wholly procedural manner. An attempt to resolve these dependencies is required as soon as the computational system encounters an argument carrying person and number features. In the case at hand, this leads to a mismatch and failure to resolve the agreement dependencies with sufficient dispatch—a fact that is reflected in the brain's electrophysiological response.

By the same reasoning, we would *not* expect a spike after the verb in sentences such as those below, even though the verb's features do not find a match in the subject.

(2) a.   There is glass on the floor.
   b.   There are glasses on the floor.

That is because, on the account I have put forward, the expletive carries no features and therefore does not provide the computational system with an opportunity to resolve the verb's agreement dependencies. To my knowledge, ERP techniques have not yet been used to investigate the processing of such sentences.

A different sort of agreement mismatch provides supporting evidence for our conclusion that the referential dependencies introduced by reflexive pronouns are resolved at the first opportunity. The key sentences are as follows.

---

[4]Although Coulson et al. concur that the positive spike reflects the presence of an agreement anomaly, they suggest that this effect is observed after exposure to unexpected stimuli in general, not just syntactic anomalies. Phillips, Kazanina, & Abada (2004) suggest that the positive spike is a reflection of the higher-than-usual processing cost that anomalies create.

(3) a.   *The hungry guests helped himself.
    b.   *The successful woman congratulated himself.

Here too Osterhout & Mobley report a positive spike in electrical activity almost immediately upon exposure to the agreement anomaly. This is consistent with the view that the computational system immediately tries to resolve the referential dependency introduced by the pronoun.[5]

6. RESOLVING *WH* DEPENDENCIES

The defining property of an English *wh* construction is that a clause-initial *wh* word seeks out a sentence-internal functor. In the case of argument *wh* words, this dependency is resolved by a process of downward feature-passing that descends through the sentence in search of a functor with an unresolved dependency on a nominal argument. For example:

(1)

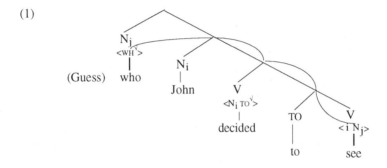

If the analysis proposed in chapter seven is correct, then *wh* dependencies—like all dependencies—must be resolved at the first opportunity. There is ample psycholinguistic evidence that the processing of *wh* constructions proceeds in precisely this way.

As noted in chapter seven, early evidence for the prompt resolution of *wh* dependencies came from Fodor's (1978) observation of a garden path effect in sentences such as the following.

(2)   Which book did the teacher read to the students from?

---

[5]Another line of research, not directly relevant here, involves the processing of sentences such as the following (e.g., Pearlmutter, Garnsey, & Bock 1999).

(i) [The key to the cabinets] was rusty from many years of use.

The number mismatch between *cabinets* and the adjacent verb causes some processing difficulty, but not as much as a mismatch between *key* and the verb.

Here, listeners initially link the *wh* phrase to the optionally transitive verb *read*, creating a dead end from which they must retreat when the preposition is encountered at the end of the sentence. De Vincenzi (1991) attributes this effect to the Minimal Chain Principle, which compels the processor to posit the shortest possible 'chain' between a *wh* word and the associated trace (see also Crain & Fodor 1985). I interpret the facts slightly differently: the processor is seeking to resolve the *wh* dependency at the first opportunity, and the apparently transitive *read* seems to offer that opportunity.

A similar conclusion can be drawn from an experiment by Stowe (1986) that made use of a self-paced reading task in which words were presented one at a time on a computer screen. After subjects read each word, they had to press a button to call for the next word—which made it possible for the experimenter to keep track of their reading time for each item. Among the contrasts investigated by Stowe was the pair of sentence types illustrated in (3).

(3) a.   Declarative sentence:
         My brother wanted to know [if Ruth will bring us home to Mom at Christmas].

   b.   *Wh* question:
         My brother wanted to know [who Ruth will bring us home to at Christmas].

Confirming earlier work by Crain & Fodor (1985), Stowe found a significantly longer reading time for *us* in the second sentence than in the first. She takes this to indicate that the processor seeks to link the *wh* word to a functor as quickly as possible, which leads it in its haste to initially misinterpret *who* as the direct object argument of *bring*. The subsequent appearance of *us* creates a 'filled gap effect,' forcing the processor to revise its initial hypothesis and to restructure the sentence—hence the increase in reading time.

Evidence of a different sort for the prompt resolution of *wh* dependencies comes from the use of ERPs to determine at what point speakers perceive the anomaly in the second of the following two sentences.

(4) a.   The businessman knew [which customer the secretary called _ at home].

   b.   *The businessman knew [which article the secretary called _ at home].

If *wh* dependencies are resolved at the first opportunity, the anomaly in (4b) should be discerned right after the verb *call*—the point at which the feature-passing operation links the verb to the semantically incompatible *wh* phrase in our system. Working with visually presented materials, Garnsey, Tanenhaus, & Chapman (1989) uncovered a significant difference in the wave forms of the two sentences right after the verb *call*—suggesting that this is the point at which the feature-passing operation links the *wh* argument to the verb, just as we predict.

Additional evidence for the same conclusion comes from experimental work involving the cross-modal priming paradigm (see p. 167). The key sentence type is illustrated in (5).[6] As before, † marks the point at which the experimenters checked for reactivation effects.

(5)   The policeman saw the boy [who the crowd at the party † accused † of the crime].

Swinney, Ford, Frauenfelder, & Bresnan (1988) report that there is a reactivation effect for *boy* at the second probe point, resulting in a shorter reaction time to a semantically related word (e.g., *youngster*) here than in the preverbal position. This is just what we expect, since the position of the second probe corresponds to the exact place where the feature-passing operation links the *wh* dependency to the argument grid of the verb *accuse*.

(6)   The policeman$_i$ saw the boy$_j$ [who$_j$ [the crowd at the party]$_k$ accused ...].
         | $<N_k\ N_j>$
         |_____↑

Long-distance feature passing

As noted in chapter seven, the feature-passing operation can descend into the sentence as deeply as necessary to resolve the *wh* dependency introduced by a *wh* word. If the computational system responsible for carrying out this operation is just a processor, then we expect the difficulty of the sentence to increase with the depth of the descent into the sentence.[7]

One piece of evidence in support of this conclusion comes from the fact, first noted in chapter seven, that subject *wh* dependencies are easier to process than their lengthier direct object counterparts (e.g., Wanner & Maratsos 1978, Gibson 1998, Caplan & Waters 2002).

(7) a.   Subject relative clause:
          The witnesses [*who* misled the investigators] ...
                                ↑
                         wh dependency
                         is resolved here

     b.   Direct object relative clause:
          The witnesses [*who* the investigators misled] ...
                                                    ↑
                                            wh dependency
                                            is resolved here

---

[6]Swinney et al. use *that* instead of *who* in their test sentences.

[7]However, as Gibson (1998:4ff) notes, there is no agreement on precisely how the depth of a dependency should be calculated—is the processor sensitive to the number of intervening words, the number of intervening syntactic nodes, or some other measure? See also Hagoort, Brown, & Osterhout (1999:276) and O'Grady, Lee, & Choo (2003).

Contrasts in more complex sentences illustrate the same point. For instance, Frazier & Clifton (1989) investigated the processing of sentences such as the following with the help of a self-paced reading task.

(8) a. One clause, early gap:
        What did the cautious young man whisper _ to his fiancée during the movie last night?

    b. One clause, late gap:
        What did the cautious young man whisper to his fiancée about _ during the movie last night?

    c. Two clauses, early gap in embedded clause:
        What did you think [the man whispered _ to his fiancée during the movie last night]?

    d. Two clauses, late gap in embedded clause:
        What did you think [the man whispered to his fiancée about _ during the movie last night]?

Their results revealed slower reading times for late gaps versus early gaps and for two-clause sentences versus one-clause sentences. This suggests that the cost of feature passing increases with the distance that must be traversed, as expected.

Further support for the view that *wh* dependencies must be maintained (at significant cost to working memory) comes from an ERP study conducted by Phillips, Kazanina, & Abada (2004). They report that the negativity effect associated with the storage of a *wh* dependency (see chapter seven, p. 119) is maintained throughout the full length of even the long *wh* dependency found in sentences such as (9).

(9)   The lieutenant knew *which accomplice* [the detective hoped [that the shrewd witness would recognize _ in the lineup]].

It is perhaps worth mentioning at this point that the study of reading times offers circumstantial evidence that an unresolved *wh* dependency is reactivated at the beginning of a new clause. The key observation, from Gibson & Warren (2004), is that reading time on the embedded verb (*please*) is shorter in (10) than in (11).

(10)   *Wh* dependency extending across a clause boundary:
        The manager *who* [the consultants claimed [that the new proposal had pleased _]] will hire five workers tomorrow.

(11)   *Wh* dependency within a clause:
        The manager *who* [the consultant's claim about the new proposal had
        pleased _] will hire five workers tomorrow.

Given that the *wh* dependency is equally long in the two sentences and that the most
salient structural difference between the two patterns is the presence of an internal
clause boundary in (10), Gibson & Warren infer that the *wh* filler is reactivated at
this particular point.
        Still to be answered though is the question of why the reactivation should occur
at clause boundaries. The grammatical interpretation, of course, is that there is an
intermediate trace in the specifier position of CP.

(12)   The manager *who* [the consultants claimed [CP *t* [IP that the new proposal
        had pleased _]]] will hire five workers tomorrow.

A more promising possibility from the perspective I adopt is that the reassessment
of unresolved dependencies is called for at clause boundaries simply because
constituents of this type make up a natural unit of processing.

Adjunct *wh* words

So far, our review of the psycholinguistic literature has focused exclusively on
argument *wh* words, but the analysis outlined in chapter seven also makes
predictions about adjunct *wh* words such as *when*, *why*, and *how*. As noted there
(p. 122ff), words of this type exhibit a dependency on a verbal category, without
regard for its argument grid. As a result, the first opportunity to resolve the *wh*
dependency introduced by the adjunct in sentences such as those in (13) should
arise when the matrix verb is encountered.

(13) a. Why did you infer [that John left]?
        ('why-infer' interpretation is strongly preferred)

     b. When did you reveal [that Jerry went to New York]?
        ('when-reveal' interpretation is strongly preferred)

Intuitions about the meaning of these sentences bear out this prediction, as does the
psycholinguistic evidence.
        Frazier & Clifton (1996:137ff) investigated the processing of sentences such as
the following in a variety of contexts, some supporting the matrix 'when-inform'
interpretation, some supporting the embedded 'when-cured' interpretation, and
some supporting both.

(14)   When [did Dr. Tanen inform Sam [that he was cured]]?

They found significantly shorter reading times for sentences with the matrix interpretation, both in contexts that support this interpretation and in contexts that support both interpretations equally. Although the occasional association of the *wh* word with the embedded verb remains problematic (see chapter seven, pp. 123-124), these findings do suggest an overarching preference for the interpretation formed by the shorter downward feature passing operation—as one would expect in an efficiency driven system.

7. CONCLUSION

From the outset, the key point of this book has simply been that an efficiency driven linear computational system, not a grammar, offers the best hope of understanding why sentences have the particular properties that they do. Whereas previous chapters have sought to develop this thesis through the analysis of syntactic phenomena ranging from coreference to extraction, this chapter has focused on processing-related properties of the proposed computational system. Its commitment to linearity (building structure one word at a time) and to quickness (resolving dependencies at the first opportunity) is central to its explanatory success, but the postulation of these properties cannot be vindicated by the study of facts about acceptability and interpretation alone. Ultimately, psycholinguistic data from the investigation of real-time sentence processing must be brought into play. Put simply, we need evidence that sentences are built from left to right one word at a time in a way that seeks to resolve dependencies at the first opportunity.

There can be no easy verification of a prediction as far-reaching as this. The literature, which we have only sampled here, is complex. Various important issues (such as the role of the lexicon, of extralinguistic knowledge, of frequency effects, and so on) are unsettled. And, of course, many phenomena remain to be studied at all. Yet, there is strong evidence from many different sources for the key idea— sentences do seem to be built from left to right in real time, and dependencies do seem to be resolved as quickly as possible.

Many questions about the character of the sentence-building system remain open, however. Although I have formulated the Efficiency Requirement in linguistic terms for the sake of concreteness ('Resolve *dependencies* at the first opportunity'), its actual mandate is simply to ease the burden on working memory—presumably a desideratum of any cognitive system. As MacDonald, Pearlmutter, & Seidenberg (1994:700) observe, the processing mechanisms for language 'seem to reflect general properties of memory, perception and learning, properties that are involved in nonlinguistic domains' as well. This raises the possibility that the sentence processor is not a special-purpose device, although nothing turns on this here.

The possibility of subsuming syntax under *any* theory of processing has typically been treated dismissively, when it is not entirely ignored, both in the literature on syntactic theory and in the literature on sentence processing. Indeed,

Newmeyer (1998:152) accurately summarizes the consensus on the subject when he concludes that it is 'hopeless to think that one can derive grammatical principles from parsing principles.'

For the most part, research on syntactic theory and research on processing have proceeded independently, but with each endeavor acknowledging the legitimacy of the other. Thus, on the one hand, work on the theory of sentence structure typically sets the problem of sentence processing to the side, assuming only that the grammar is accessed in some ill-defined way in the course of speech production and comprehension (e.g., Chomsky 1995:170, Newmeyer 1998:105-06, Crocker 1999). And on the other hand, most work on sentence processing assumes without question that the processor depends on and interacts with grammatical rules and principles from the theory of sentence structure (e.g., Fodor 1989:177ff, Frazier & Clifton 1996:9 & 25, Frazier 1998:126).

I take the view that this sort of dual approach is fundamentally misguided. There is no need for two separate systems. A single efficiency driven linear computational system offers the best way to engage the classic problems confronting both the theory of sentence structure and the theory of sentence processing.

If this is right, then there is much that needs to be rethought, including long-standing assumptions about how language is acquired. I address this issue in a preliminary way in chapter ten.

Chapter 10

Language Acquisition

1. INTRODUCTION

Of all the mysteries confronting linguistic theory, none has proven more difficult or contentious than the question of how language is acquired. In a way, this is puzzling since so much is 'out in the open'—children acquire language based on experience that we can directly observe, and we have easy access to their immature utterances and errors. Yet, very fundamental questions remain unanswered, the most controversial of which has to do with how much is learned and how much is inborn.

No one doubts that a great deal of language is learned from experience—a language's vocabulary and morphology are obvious examples. Moreover, it seems likely that learning is facilitated in at least some cases by parental feedback to phenomena such as semantic overextensions (calling a horse a dog), morphological overregularization (saying *goed* for *went*), lapses of politeness (underuse of *please*), and so forth (e.g., Saxton 1997, Saxton, Kulscar, Marshall, & Rupra 1998). The controversy lies elsewhere—in more abstract properties of language, especially its syntax.

As I have acknowledged throughout this book, the syntax of human language exhibits a number of remarkable properties—sentence structure has a binary organization, subjects are structurally more prominent than direct objects, reflexive pronouns seemingly require local c-commanding antecedents, verbal agreement is triggered by subjects rather than direct objects, contraction is blocked in certain cases, a subject cannot be extracted from a clause that begins with a complementizer, certain types of *wh* clauses prohibit extraction whereas others don't, and so forth.

The presence of such properties in language after language calls out for explanation, as does the fact that these properties are acquired without apparent effort by children who have trouble learning that the past tense of *eat* is *ate* rather than *eated*.

The puzzle that these facts present has long been interpreted as evidence for an innate Universal Grammar.[1] Chomsky (1977:65) puts it this way:

---

[1]What precisely it means for a principle to be 'innate' is not entirely clear. For the sake of exposition, I will follow Samuels (2004) in taking an innate principle to be one that cannot be acquired by cognitive/psychological processes.

Suppose we find that a particular language has the property P... Suppose, furthermore, that P is sufficiently abstract and evidence bearing on it sufficiently sparse and contrived so that it is implausible to suppose that all speakers, or perhaps any speakers, might have been trained or taught to observe P by induction from experience. Then it is plausible to postulate that P is a property of [inborn Universal Grammar].

The situation that Chomsky describes is often referred to as the 'logical problem of language acquisition'—how can children come to know things for which there is inadequate evidence in experience? The answer that he proposes, of course, is that an innate Universal Grammar provides the necessary bridge.

The standard response of those opposed to Universal Grammar is to argue that the burden of acquiring language can be borne by various learning strategies— sensitivity to statistical tendencies in the input, responsiveness to feedback from caregivers, item-by-item learning, conservatism, competition among alternatives, and so on. (MacWhinney 2004 develops this idea in considerable detail.)

I do not believe that this will be enough. For many phenomena in language, including those considered in the preceding chapters, the facts are simply too complex, the input too sparse, mastery too rapid, and errors too infrequent. Induction from experience is not the answer.

At the same time of course, I do not agree with the idea that Universal Grammar is needed to account for how language is acquired, any more than I believe that it is needed to account for why language has the particular properties that it does. As I see it, the burden for explaining both phenomena is borne entirely by the computational system (i.e., the processor), whose efficiency driven character defines how language works for speakers of all ages. Let us consider this matter in more detail with the help of a concrete example.

2. THE STRUCTURE DEPENDENCE PUZZLE

A phenomenon that has proven useful over the years for illustrating the advantages of a UG-based approach to language acquisition involves a set of simple facts involving the formation of *yes–no* questions in English. Indeed, the facts are so intriguing that they have been, as Levine (2002:326) notes, 'incessantly repeated in the literature' since they were first brought forward by Chomsky (1975:30ff). And Chomsky's analysis quickly became a 'parade case of an innate constraint,' as one of its leading advocates (Crain 1991:602) put it.

The starting point for Chomsky's observation is that the sorts of simple *yes-no* questions that abound in children's experience, namely patterns such as (1), provide insufficient information about the nature of the 'rule' that places the verb at the beginning of the sentence.

(1)   Is Mary ready?
       (cf. Mary is ready.)

That is because such sentences are consistent with two very different generalizations, one that makes reference to structure (the 'structure-dependent' rule) and one that doesn't (e.g., Crain & Nakayama 1987:525-526).

(2) a. The structure-dependent generalization:
         In questions, the verb in the main clause moves to the beginning of the sentence.

    b. The non-structure-dependent generalization:
         In questions, the first verb moves to the beginning of the sentence.

A language learner cannot figure out which of these generalizations is right by looking at sentences in which there is only one clause and only one verb. In such sentences, fronting the verb in the main clause gives exactly the same result as fronting the first verb.

(3)   Mary is ready.
            ↑
       first verb;
       verb in main clause

The crucial test case involves how we question a sentence such as (4), in which the first verb is not in the main clause.

(4)   People [who are rich] are happy too.
                   ↑   ↑
            first verb   verb in main clause

Here the two generalizations part ways, as (5) shows.

(5) a. The fronted item is the verb from the main clause (structure-dependent generalization):
         Are [people who are rich] _ happy too?

    b. The fronted item is the first verb (non-structure-dependent generalization):
         *Are [people who _ rich] are happy too?

As the unacceptability of (5b) shows, only the structure-dependent generalization gives the right result.

2.1 The case for UG

So how do children figure out how inversion works, the proponent of UG asks. The standard answer (e.g., Pullum & Scholz 2002:17) is that there are only two possibilities—either the relevant principle (the Minimal Link Condition in recent UG accounts) is given in advance as part of a genetically endowed Universal Grammar, or it must be acquired through trial and error based on experience.

Chomsky dismisses the idea of learning from experience in this case by appeal to the 'argument from poverty of stimulus' (e.g., Chomsky 1980b:34). In order to *learn* that the inversion rule acts on the verb in the main clause rather than the first verb in the sentence, children need to encounter sentences in which the verb in the main clause is not also the first verb in the sentence, as just noted. But, Chomsky (1980a:40) argues, sentences of this sort are vanishingly rare. In fact, he suggests, 'a person could go through much or all of his life without ever having been exposed to [such sentences].' Hence, he concludes, the learner has to rely on UG to formulate the inversion rule correctly.

This in turn entails that the development of inversion should be more or less error-free in the relevant respects. Crain & Nakayama (1987) tested this hypothesis with the help of an elicited production task. Thirty children aged 3;2 to 5;11 were given prompts such as the following.

(1)   Ask Jabba if the boy [who is watching Mickey] is happy.
                               ↑   ↑
                          first verb   *verb in main clause*

By seeing whether children responded by saying (2a) or (2b), Crain & Nakayama were able to determine which inversion rule was being used.

(2) a. The structure-dependent response:
        Is [the boy who is watching Mickey] _ happy?

    b. The non-structure-dependent response:
        *Is [the boy who _ watching Mickey] is happy?

No errors of the type in (2b) occurred, leading Crain and Nakayama to conclude that children's hypotheses about question formation are indeed constrained by UG.

2.2 The case for learning

Sampson (1989) and Pullum (1996) adopt a different approach, suggesting that the input actually *does* contain sentences that permit structure dependence to be inferred from experience, contrary to what Chomsky contends. Among the examples offered by Pullum from a corpus of written English are the following:

(1) a. *Is* [what I *am* doing] _ in the shareholder's best interests?
    (cf. [What I *am* doing] *is* in the shareholder's best interests.)

        ↑   ↑
    first verb   verb in main clause is fronted

  b. *Is* [the boy who *was* hitting you] _ still here?
    (cf. The boy [who *was* hitting you] *is* still here.)

  c. *Could* [anyone who *is* interested] _ see me later?
    (cf. Anyone [who *is* interested] *could* see me later.)

  d. *Will* [the owner of the bicycle that *is* chained to the gate] _ come to my office?
    (cf. The owner of the bicycle [that *is* chained to the gate] *will* come to my office.)

Notice that in each of these sentences a verb from the main clause undergoes 'inversion' even though it is not the first verb in the corresponding affirmative sentence—just the evidence needed to correctly formulate the inversion rule.

Pullum suggests that such sentences are relatively frequent, constituting perhaps 1% of the interrogative patterns and more than 10% of the *yes–no* questions in at least certain types of discourse. Might the input perhaps not be as impoverished as Chomsky thought?

Evidently, Chomsky was wrong in his belief that one could spend *one's entire life* without ever encountering question patterns in which the inverted verb was not the first verb in the corresponding affirmative sentence. But there is still a problem with Pullum's observation—none of his data came from speech to *children*. (His examples are from the *Wall Street Journal*, including conversations quoted there.)

This is crucial, as the point is not just that adults get inversion right, but that very young children also do (recall the Crain & Nakayama experiment). Yet Mac-Whinney (2004) reports that the sorts of sentences exemplified in (1) occur only about once in every *three million* utterances in speech directed toward children.

This means that the average child would hear an example of the key sentence type approximately once every three years (assuming exposure to about a million utterances a year—see Pullum & Scholz 2002). It is therefore highly unlikely that *all* children learning English are exposed to such sentences in sufficient number to explain how they avoid *ever* making mistakes.

MacWhinney suggests a different sort of input-based solution. The key sentence type, he proposes, consists of *where* questions such as (2), in which the fronted copula corresponds to the verb in the main clause rather than the first verb in the sentence. (See also Pullum & Scholz 2002.)

(2)   Where *is* [the other dolly [that *was* in here]]?
       (cf. [The other dolly [that *was* in here] *is* where?])
                                    ↑   ↑
                              first verb   *verb in main clause is fronted*

Because such patterns are apparently more frequent than those in (1) in speech to children, MacWhinney's proposal seems to revive the case for learning. But matters may not be so straightforward.

This whole debate avoids a more fundamental question. In particular, does anyone actually believe that a child who was not exposed to sentences such as (2) would be incapable of figuring out how inversion works in *yes–no* questions? My intuition, for what it is worth, is that even a child who was somehow prevented from hearing such sentences would still not think that monstrosities such as (3) are possible in English.

(3)   *Is [the boy who _ watching Mickey] is happy?

But why not? Why have *no* errors involving 'structure dependence' ever been observed in naturalistic speech, and why did Crain & Nakayama (1987) elicit none in their experiment either? This clearly calls for an explanation.

So, on the one hand, I side with Chomsky and other proponents of UG in agreeing that trial-and-error learning from experience is not the answer. On the other hand, I don't think that an inborn grammatical system is the answer either. There is, I believe, another possibility that needs to be considered.

2.3 Inversion without grammar

We begin by asking the familiar question—what if there were no grammar, just an efficiency driven linear processor that resolved dependencies at the first opportunity permitted by a word's lexical properties?

The key lexical property in the case of inversion patterns involves the direction in which copula and auxiliary verbs look for their first argument. In statement patterns, they search to the left, just as thematic verbs do (e.g., *Grass is green*, *They are happy*). In *yes–no* questions, in contrast, they look to the right (*Is grass green?*, *Are they happy?*). The copula *be* therefore has the (learned) properties summarized in (1). (For the sake of illustration, I assume that *be*'s second argument is an adjective; in fact, of course, categories of other types can serve in this capacity as well.)

(1)   *be*: V, <N A>
              ← → (statement)
              → → (question)

With this in mind, let us reconsider the contrast relevant to the structure dependence puzzle.

(2) a. Inversion affects the verb in the main clause:
     Are [people who are rich] happy too?

   b. Inversion affects the first verb:
     *Are [people who rich] are happy too?

The formation of (2a) is straightforward. To begin, *are* combines to the right with its first argument (*people who are rich*).[2]

(3)

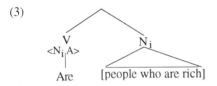

In the next step, *are* combines with its second argument, the adjective *happy*, exactly parallel to what happens in simple question structures such as *Is grass green?*[3]

---

[2] I simplify here for the sake of exposition. In fact, of course, the formation of this sentence proceeds in a strictly word-by-word fashion, as follows.

(i)

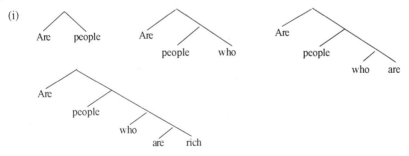

[3] This does not look like an ordinary syntactic structure, but remember that representations are simply a record of the sentence's computational history (see chapter two, p. 17ff)—first, *are* combines with a nominal to its right, then it combines with an adjective to its right.

(i)

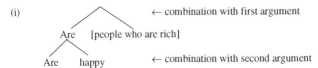

(4)

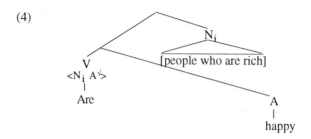

Now consider the case of (2b), in which the 'wrong' copula appears at the beginning of the sentence. At least two things go awry when the computational system attempts to form this sentence. First, the verb's first argument (*people who rich*) is ill-formed, presumably because predicative adjectives do not permit *wh* arguments.

(5)

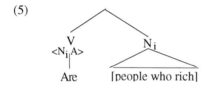

Second, the computational system is unable to find an adjective to serve as the verb's second argument. (*Happy* serves as argument of the second *are*, not the first one.)

(6)

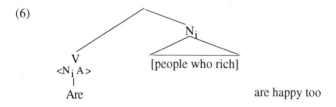

In other words, the sentence simply cannot be formed, given the properties of the lexical items involved and the way the computational system works. This, presumably, is an important part of the reason why utterances of this type are not heard in the speech of children—or anyone else for that matter.

In sum, there is no need for an innate grammatical principle, or for a learned grammatical principle either. The facts simply follow from the way in which the computational system goes about resolving the rightward-looking dependencies introduced by copula and auxiliary verbs in question structures.

3. WHAT SPEAKERS OF A LANGUAGE 'KNOW'

In discussing the phenomena that make up the core of a language's syntax, I have been careful throughout this book not to use words like 'knowledge' or 'principles.' Syntax is an instance of procedural cognition—an operating system that is built into the structure of the brain itself (see also Searle 2002:33).

If users of a language 'know' anything, it is simply the properties of lexical items. For instance, speakers of English know that a copula verb takes a nominal argument and an adjectival argument (for example), and that it looks to the right for both its arguments in *yes–no* questions. As we saw in the preceding section, the rest just follows from the way in which the computational system goes about building sentences—one word at a time, from left to right, resolving dependencies at the first opportunity.

A similar point holds for the interpretation of reflexive pronouns. Although the facts are extraordinarily intricate, speakers of English need know only one thing, namely that anaphors introduce a referential dependency. Given the way the computational system works (i.e., efficiently), such dependencies must be resolved at the first opportunity. This in turn has a wide range of effects, ensuring (for instance) that the reflexive pronoun in a sentence such as (1) takes *Sue's sister* as its antecedent.

(1)   Mary$_i$ thinks [that [Sue's$_j$ sister]$_k$ overestimates herself$_x$]].
$$<N_k \ N_x>$$
$$\downarrow$$
$$k$$

The standard analysis proposes that the interpretation of reflexive pronouns is subject to Principle A, a grammatical constraint requiring a local, c-commanding antecedent. But this is an illusion. The sentence has the interpretation that it does because the index of *Sue's sister* in the grid of the verb *overestimate* offers the first opportunity to resolve the pronoun's referential dependency. The computational system reacts accordingly; there is no need for a grammatical constraint.

The same goes for agreement, which appears to be constrained by a grammatical principle that favors subjects as agreement triggers. Once again, this is an illusion. Speakers of English need know only that inflected forms have particular lexical properties—for example, verbs with the *-s* suffix carry a third person singular agreement dependency. The computational system does the rest.

As we saw in chapter six, the resolution of agreement dependencies at the first opportunity ensures that the verb will agree with its 'subject' in simple sentences such as (2).

(2)   Mary speaks two languages.

And, equally importantly, it ensures that the verb will agree with a different nominal in other cases, including the first conjunct of the coordinate phrase in (3).

(3)   There is [*a man* and two women] at the front door.

There is nothing to learn here, other than the featural properties of particular inflectional forms. The choice of agreement trigger simply reflects the exigencies of efficient processing.

Or consider contraction. As we saw in chapter eight, the notorious contrast illustrated in (4) follows from a simple fact about the timing of combinatorial operations.

(4) a.   Who do they$_i$ want to (> wanna) see?
            <$\underline{N_i}$ TO>

   b.   Who$_j$ do they$_i$ want to (> *wanna) go?
            <N$_i$ $\underline{N_j}$ TO>

In particular, *want* can combine with *to* right after combining with *they* in the first pattern, but not in the second one, where it must first resolve the *wh* dependency associated with *who*.

(5)   Who$_j$ do they$_i$ want ...
            | <N$_i$ $\underline{N_j}$ TO>
            |_____↑

Here again, there is nothing to learn. The contrast simply follows from the operation of the computational system and the nature of contraction, which involves phonological processes that work best in rapid connected speech.

My position on the acquisition of these phenomena is an unusual one, as it rejects both types of traditional explanation for how the properties of complex patterns emerge. On the one hand, I deny that constraints on inversion, coreference, agreement, contraction, and other syntactic phenomena are entirely learned from experience. In fact, I believe that learning is out of the question in these cases, for the usual reasons. The complexity of the facts, the limited availability of relevant experience, the speed of acquisition, and the general absence of mistakes all belie trial-and-error learning.

On the other hand, I also reject the idea that the properties of core syntactic phenomena are given by an innate Universal Grammar. As noted at the outset, my view is that Universal Grammar is not needed to account for how language is acquired, any more than it is needed to account for why language has the particular properties that it does. In each case, the burden of explanation falls on the processor—the efficiency driven linear computational system that has been the focus of this book.

4. THE EMERGENCE OF ROUTINES

In the view I have put forward, the key properties of a language's syntax reflect a neurophysiologically motivated drive for efficiency in the interests of minimizing the burden on working memory. This leaves little room for syntactic development in the conventional sense. There is no Universal Grammar that has to mature, contrary to what Radford (1990), Wexler (1998), and others have proposed. And there are no parameters to be set, contrary to the even more widely held view (e.g., Lightfoot 1991, Fodor 1994, and countless others). Instead, learning consists largely of the emergence of computational routines—the operations and sequences of operations that are required to form and/or interpret particular sentences.

Some of the routines and subroutines from earlier chapters are informally restated in the following table. The left-hand column paraphrases the routines, and the right-hand column summarizes their apparent 'grammatical' consequences.

TABLE 10.1
Computational Routines and Their Consequences

Routine	Consequences
Looking to the left for a verb's first argument and to the right for its second argument	SVO word order; subjects structurally higher than direct objects
Looking to the right for a verb's first argument in *yes-no* questions	'Structure-dependent' patterns of inversion
Resolving the referential dependency introduced by reflexive pronouns at the first opportunity	Local, c-commanding antecedents for most reflexive pronouns
Resolving the referential dependency expressing an infinitival verb's covert subject at the first opportunity	C-commanding controllers in the next highest clause
Resolving agreement dependencies at the first opportunity	Subject agreement in most sentence types
Resolving *wh* dependencies at the first opportunity in a manner consistent with push-down storage	*Wh* island effects and *that*-trace effects
Permitting contraction only when the elements involved combine with each other without delay	Prohibition against *want to* contraction in certain patterns

How do computational routines become established in the course of language acquisition? The answer appears simple, at least in principle: computational routines emerge as particular operations or sequences of operations are executed over and over again. In the words of Anderson (1993:18), they 'gather strength as they prove useful' (see also Lieberman 2000:35 and Townsend & Bever 2001:175).

Evidence for this can be found among various of the phenomena considered in previous chapters. Let us consider a series of cases in turn.

4.1 Wholly efficiency driven routines

Some computational routines are direct implementations of the Efficiency Requirement; they do no more than resolve a dependency at the first opportunity. Although the lexical items that trigger such routines have to be learned, the routines themselves 'come for free.' Their emergence should therefore be rapid and more or less errorless. The computational routine for resolving the referential dependencies introduced by reflexive pronouns is a case in point.

As explained in detail in chapter three, the computational system seeks to resolve referential dependencies at the first opportunity—immediately, if possible. This should therefore be the response of first resort when a referential dependency is encountered in sentences such as *Mary hurt herself*, and there should be little if any room for error once the relevant lexical items themselves have been acquired.

This seems right. Bloom, Barss, Nicol, & Conway (1994) examined the use of first person pronouns in three children over a three-year period, beginning when they were two years old. Erroneous uses of reflexive *myself* were extremely rare, occurring in just 0.3% of the sentences containing a first person pronoun.

Another example illustrating the same point involves the resolution of agreement dependencies. As explained in chapter six, the resolution of these dependencies by features of the subject nominal is mandated by efficiency considerations in most sentences. Agreement with the subject should therefore be the first resort pursued by the computational system, once the verb's agreement features have been identified. Here again, there is no room for error—we shouldn't find instances of object agreement in English, for instance.

This too seems right. Although very young children frequently omit tensed verbs (especially copulas and auxiliaries, as in *Me there*) and employ an uninflected verb where an inflected form is called for *(She like me)*, agreement mismatches (e.g., *I likes her*) are extremely rare (Rice & Wexler 1996, Borer & Rohrbacher 2002:137).

4.2 Partially efficiency driven routines

Not all computational routines are shaped solely by efficiency considerations, of course. The form of many routines is determined jointly by considerations of efficiency and by the stipulative properties of the items to which they apply. The routine that builds transitive sentences is a case in point. The version of this routine that is used in SVO languages such as English looks to the left for the verb's first argument and to the right for its second argument ($N_1 \perp V$; $V \perp N_2$). In principle though, a transitive verb could just as easily look to the right for both its arguments, as happens in VSO languages, or to the left for both arguments, as happens in SOV languages.

The developmental facts suggest that such routines are mastered gradually, over a period of months, as they are repeatedly implemented in the course of interpreting and (eventually) forming transitive sentences such as *Mary likes dogs*, *Harry eats spinach*, and so forth. Routines are thus 'usage-based,' to use Tomasello's (2003) term.

When children in the one- and two-word stage try to interpret transitive sentences under conditions where they have to rely on syntactic clues alone, they often make mistakes. For example, when asked to use toys to act out the meaning of sentences like *The truck bumped the car*, they frequently respond by making the car bump the truck (de Villiers & de Villiers 1973, Slobin & Bever 1982, Thal & Flores 2001). Comparable results have been reported by Hirsh-Pasek & Golinkoff (1996:99ff) on preferential looking tasks.[4]

Indeed, there is reason to think that the computational routine for transitive clauses may be reliably triggered only by familiar lexical items in the early stages of language acquisition. Akhtar & Tomasello (1997) taught two- and three-year-old children novel verbs by demonstrating actions (such as one toy animal pushing another one down into a chute) and then saying, 'Do you see that? That's called *blicking*.' The children were then asked to 'Make Cookie Monster blick Big Bird.'

Although the children could carry out the right type of action, they did poorly on identifying the correct agent prior to age three and a half. This led Akhtar & Tomasello to conclude that younger children are uncertain where to look (left or right) for the verb's agent argument with unfamiliar verbs.

If this is correct, it suggests that the computational routine for transitive clauses may begin as a word-based procedure for specific familiar lexical items (*eat, kiss, push*, etc.) and gradually be extended and generalized to the transitive verb category. Tomasello (1995) develops an idea along these lines in some detail, suggesting that 'constructions' (for me, computational routines) are initially organized around individual verbs. Goldberg (1999) offers a similar idea, proposing, for example, that the transitive construction originates in the use of high-frequency verbs such as *do, make, get, eat*, and *hold*.

In any case, it is clear that the computational routine used for transitive clauses goes on to play a significant role in the processing of English sentences. As Townsend & Bever (2001:175) note, 'almost every instance of English clauses and most sentences have the superficial form N V ((N) N),' making it 'the most

---

[4]This experimental paradigm presents children with two pictures (say, one of a truck pushing a car and one of a car pushing a truck) and then tracks which picture they look at as they listen to the sentence *The car is pushing the truck*.

strongly confirmed abstract pattern' in the language. Indeed, Townsend & Bever argue that this routine (*template* in their terms) has a major role to play in explaining the relative difficulty of passives, direct object relative clauses, and other constructions that do not comply with it (pp. 193–194).

(1)   Sentence types that do not comply with the NVN template:
     a.   Passive:
        The cat is being chased by the dog.

     b.   Direct object relative clause:
        The reporter [*who the senator attacked*] admitted the error.

In addition, they suggest, the dominance of the routine contributes to various garden path effects (p. 247ff).

(2)   Garden paths created by following the NVN template:
     a.   *The editor played the tape* agreed the story was a big one.
     b.   *The reporter saw the woman* was not very calm.
     c.   When *men hunt the birds* typically scatter.

Other routines are perhaps less central, but each has a contribution to make. A verb's agreement dependencies come to be resolved immediately after combination with a feature-bearing argument, verbs of motion look to the right for a prepositional argument, prepositions combine with a nominal argument to the right, copulas and auxiliaries look rightward for their first argument in *yes–no* questions, and so on. As these and other routines are strengthened, the morphosyntactic phenomena that they subtend become increasingly familiar, paving the way for the seemingly effortless production and comprehension of speech that is a hallmark of language use.

5. DEVELOPMENT AND COMPUTATIONAL SPACE

Processing makes demands on working memory to support both the temporary storage of information and the execution of various operations (e.g., Kemmerer 1999:321). Put more concretely, the formation and interpretation of sentences requires *computational space*—that is, a network of activated neurons in working memory. As one would expect, the precise amount of space required appears to be dependent, in part at least, on the type of sentence being processed. Just, Carpenter, & Keller (1996) report that increased sentential complexity results in the recruitment of more neural tissue in each of a network of cortical areas; see also Sakai, Hashimoto, & Homae (2001).

    Are the necessary resources available to language learners from the outset? Might an initial shortfall in computational resources be responsible for the developmental profile associated with language acquisition? There are at least two sorts of evidence that suggest that changes in working memory capacity are tied to linguistic development.

First, it is known that working memory capacity increases along with speech rate during the period from age 4 to 10 (e.g., Hulme & Tordoff 1989, Lieberman 2000:113). This is suggestive, since the increases take place as children's ability to deal with complex sentences is also growing.

Another way to approach the question is to ask what happens to adults when their working memory capacity is compromised. For instance, it is frequently suggested in the literature on language loss that the syntactic deficits associated with agrammatic aphasia arise from stress on processing resources, especially working memory (e.g., Linebarger et al. 1983a, 1983b, Caplan & Hildebrandt 1988, Just & Carpenter 1992, Kolk & Weijts 1996, Just, Carpenter, & Keller 1996, Zurif 1998, Caplan & Waters 1999, Dick, Bates, Wulfeck, Utman, Dronkers, & Gernsbacher 2001:120). Indeed, it has even been observed that the lesion sites associated with receptive agrammatism overlap with the regions supporting working memory—for example, Hickok (2000) and Stowe (2000); see Smith & Jonides (1997) for a review.

This raises the possibility that agrammatic aphasia might provide a sort of baseline for assessing the developmental deficits that arise in the course of language acquisition. In particular, if certain types of developmental errors are due to an initial shortage of computational space, comparable difficulties should occur in agrammatic aphasia, where working memory resources also appear to be compromised.

In fact, there are intriguing parallels between language acquisition and language loss. I will focus here on two phenomena whose properties I have already discussed in some detail—the resolution of referential dependencies in the case of pronouns and the resolution of *wh* dependencies in the case of relative clauses.

5.1 Pronominal coreference

As we have seen, the interpretation of reflexive pronouns is a prototypical case of computational efficiency—the referential dependency is often resolved not just at the first opportunity, but *immediately*, by an index present in the grid of the verb with which the pronoun combines.

But what of plain pronouns such as *him* and *her*? As we saw in chapter three, plain pronouns introduce referential dependencies that the computational system cannot promptly resolve. That is why they can look for their interpretation to a distant NP in the same sentence, why they can be linked to an antecedent in a previous sentence, and why they can even be used deictically to refer to a previously unnamed individual or entity.

(1) a. Distant antecedent:
   *Dave*ᵢ believes [that Mary$_j$ admires him$_j$/*himself$_j$].

   b. Antecedent in a preceding sentence:
   *Mary*ᵢ arrived yesterday. I saw her$_i$ at the library this morning.

   c. Deictic use (pointing):
   Hey, look at him.

These facts suggest that reflexive pronouns might be easier to interpret than plain pronouns, all other things being equal. We have already seen that there is psycholinguistic evidence for this (e.g., Piñango et al. 2001, Sekerina et al. 2004; see chapter nine). Interestingly, evidence from language acquisition and from language loss points toward the same conclusion.

First language acquisition

Language learners manifest an initial difficulty interpreting plain pronouns in certain types of contexts. Especially relevant for us is the finding that pre-school children have trouble with pronouns in patterns such as (2), mistakenly linking them to the nearer antecedent about 50% of the time. In contrast, they correctly interpret reflexive pronouns in these constructions more than 90% of the time (Read & Hare 1979, Otsu 1981, Jakubowicz 1984, Solan 1987, Chien & Wexler 1990, Kaufman 1994).

(2)   Dave believes [that John admires him/himself].

In Chien & Wexler's (1990) study, for instance, 177 children aged two and a half to seven participated in a truth value judgment task, in which they had to respond to queries such as the following with regard to the pictures in Figure 10.1.

(3)   This is Mama Bear; this is Goldilocks.
      Is Mama Bear touching her?

Figure 10.1. Sample pictures from Chien & Wexler (1990). Reprinted with permission.

Chien and Wexler report that children younger than six did poorly on this task. They responded 'yes' to the query 'Is Mama Bear touching her?' more than half the time for the picture on the right, interpreting the plain pronoun *her* as if it were the reflexive pronoun *herself.*

This pattern of errors—difficulty with plain pronouns, but not reflexives—is just what we would expect if the resources made available by working memory are initially limited. Reflexive pronouns are interpreted correctly, since this involves nothing more than the immediate resolution of their referential dependency, which is desirable in any case. However, the same forces that facilitate the interpretation of reflexive pronouns work against plain pronouns, encouraging immediate resolution of their referential dependency too, rather than recourse to the pragmatic system for additional processing.

Agrammatism

Grodzinsky, Wexler, Chien, Marakovitz, & Solomon (1993) report that the eight agrammatics they tested had no trouble interpreting the reflexive pronoun in patterns such as (4a), but that they performed at a chance level on the definite pronoun in (4b), often interpreting it as coreferential with the subject.[5] (Early evidence for the same conclusion comes from Caplan & Hildebrandt 1988:199ff, who report a similar result on an act-out task that they conducted with three seriously impaired agrammatics. See also Grodzinsky 1990.)

(4) a.   Is Mama Bear touching herself?
    b.   Is Mama Bear touching her?

As Grodzinsky et al. note (pp. 408-09), this is exactly the pattern of results observed by Chien & Wexler (1990) for children. And, I propose, it has exactly the same explanation. In both cases, working memory considerations encourage the computational system to immediately resolve the referential dependency introduced by the pronoun. There is no reason to think that children and agrammatics can't distinguish between reflexive pronouns and plain pronouns; they just lack the resources needed to consistently implement the distinction.

5.2 Relative clauses

Consider next the contrast between a subject relative clause such as (1a) and a direct object relative clause such as (1b).

(1) a.   Subject relative clause:
       the girl [who helped the boy]

---

[5] I deliberately set aside the question of what happens when the pronoun has a quantified antecedent such as *everyone*. Chien & Wexler report superior performance on these patterns, but others have reported the opposite result (Grimshaw & Rosen 1990:212, Kaufman 1994:186, McKee 1992:47, van der Lily & Stollwork 1997); see O'Grady (1997:236) for a review.

b. Direct object relative clause:
   the girl [who the boy helped]

A defining feature of these constructions is that a clause-initial relative pronoun introduces a *wh* dependency that must be resolved by contact with an argument grid containing a matching argument dependency (see chapter seven).

Subject and direct object relative clauses differ from each other in an interesting way in terms of how quickly the *wh* dependency is resolved. In subject relative clauses, resolution is all but instantaneous, since the *wh* word immediately combines with a verb in search of its first argument.

(2)   Subject relative clause:
      the girl [who helped the boy] ...
                        ↑
                wh dependency
                is resolved here

However, matters are somewhat more challenging in the case of direct object relative clauses, where the *wh* dependency cannot be resolved until after the verb combines with its first argument (*the boy*).

(3)   Direct object relative clause:
      the girl [who the boy helped] ...
                        ↑   ↑
                     first   *wh* dependency
                   argument is resolved here

In cases where the processor's working memory resources are compromised, we would therefore expect a difference in the difficulty of the two patterns to show up. This seems to be right.

First language acquisition

There is reason to think that children learning English as a first language find subject relative clauses easier than their direct object counterparts, once an important confounding factor is taken into account. That factor involves the long-standing practice of testing children's comprehension of relative clauses by considering patterns such as the following, in which the relative clause is embedded within a matrix clause.

(4) a.   Subject relative clause modifying a subject head (SS type):
         The dog [who _ bumped the pig] pushed the lion.

    b.   Direct object relative clause modifying a subject head (SO type):
         The dog [who the pig bumped _] pushed the lion.

   c. Subject relative clause modifying a direct object head (OS type):
      The dog pushed the lion [who _ bumped the pig].

   d. Direct object relative clause modifying a direct object head (OO type):
      The dog pushed the lion [who the pig bumped _].

Such sentences simultaneously test children's understanding of two properties of relative clauses. On the one hand, they call for an understanding of the internal structure of the relative clause itself. (Is it a subject relative clause or a direct object relative clause?) On the other hand, they require an understanding of the relationship of the relative clause to the rest of the sentence. (Where does the relative clause begin and end? Does it modify the subject or the direct object?)

    The key issue for us has to do just with the first property—that is, with children's ability to resolve the *wh* dependency by associating it with the appropriate position (subject or direct object) in the verb's grid. With this in mind, I reanalyzed comprehension data first collected from children aged 3;0 to 5;6 by Tavakolian (1978). As reported in O'Grady (1997:179), this reanalysis uncovered a strong preference for subject relative clauses. The following data are for relative clauses that modify a subject (the SS and SO types).

TABLE 10.2
Correct Interpretation of the *Wh* Dependency

Subject Wh *Dependency*	*Direct Object* Wh *Dependency*
91%	45%

In other words, children found it easier to deal with subject *wh* dependencies, which are resolved immediately, than with direct object *wh* dependencies, where there is a delay. This is exactly what we would expect if the computational system for language is initially underpowered and therefore encounters difficulties with operations that extend across longer distances.[6]

Agrammatism

A parallel preference for subject relatives is well documented in the literature on agrammatism. For instance, Caramazza & Zurif (1976) report that an agrammatic patient they studied had serious difficulty in a picture-matching comprehension task involving reversible direct object relative clauses such as (5).

(5)   The man [who the woman is hugging _] is happy.

---

[6]Limitations on working memory capacity need not be all bad, however. Based on an intriguing piece of computer modeling, Elman (1993) argues that they may actually facilitate language acquisition by initially reducing the complexitiy of the input.

This result was subsequently replicated in five additional subjects by Sherman & Schweickert (1989). A wider-ranging investigation was undertaken by Grodzinsky (1989), who used a picture-matching task to assess the interpretation of the following patterns by four agrammatic patients.

(6)   SS pattern:
       The boy [who _ is pushing the man] is young.

       SO pattern:
       The man [who the boy is pushing _] is bold.

       OS pattern:
       Point to the man [who _ is pushing the boy].

       OO pattern:
       Point to the boy [who the man is pushing _].

Grodzinsky reports that the agrammatic patients did better on both types of subject gap relatives (i.e., the SS and OS patterns) compared to the two types of direct object relatives.[7]

Interestingly, a parallel pattern of deficits has been noted for patients with Parkinson's disease, a degenerative neurological disorder (Grossman, Carvell, Stern, Gollomp, & Hurtig 1992). Of particular interest here is Kemmerer's (1999) suggestion that Parkinson's involves a reduction in the working memory resources available for sentence processing. This is just what we would expect, given the linguistic deficits.

In sum, an important parallel in the interpretation of relative clause structures emerges from the study of first language acquisition and agrammatism. In both cases, subject *wh* dependencies appear to be easier to deal with than direct object *wh* dependencies. In fact, Caplan & Waters (2002:71) report that 'no amount of practice ... seems to be able to make object-relative sentences as easy to process as subject-relative sentences;' see also Just & Varma (2002:56). This is exactly what we would expect if limitations on computational space impinge on the processor's ability to carry out the computations required for the resolution of *wh* dependencies.

Second language acquisition

The effect of shortages in computational space may also be felt in the case of second language acquisition. For instance, it is well known that second language learners find direct object relatives more difficult than subject relatives (see Hamilton 1994 and O'Grady 2003 for a review), and there are indications that plain pronouns are

---

[7]However, Caplan & Futter (1986) report no preference for the OS pattern over the OO pattern in an act-out task that they conducted with a single agrammatic patient.

harder to interpret than reflexives pronouns (see once again O'Grady 2003 for a review).

Might working memory deficits impede second language development as well, at least initially? Possibly. There is evidence—although not yet totally clear-cut—that success in second language acquisition correlates in some way with working memory capacity (e.g., Gathercole & Thorn 1998, Miyake & Friedman 1998, Ellis 2001, Robinson 2002). This matter is explored in slightly more detail in O'Grady (2003), but clearly deserves a great deal more attention.

6. PROPERTY AND TRANSITION THEORIES

As observed by Gregg (1996), drawing on a distinction proposed by Cummins (1983), an adequate account of language acquisition must offer two sorts of explanation. On the one hand, it must include a *property theory* that explains the properties of language and how they are acquired, given the familiar limitations on input and experience. On the other hand, it must offer a *transition theory* that explains how language learners are able to move through the acquisition process, escaping from the errors and missteps that are characteristic of early development.

The proposal that I have outlined offers the beginnings of both a property theory and a transition theory. Let us briefly consider each in turn.

6.1 The property theory

The emergentist thesis that I have developed acknowledges that there is an intellectually interesting learnability problem—significant properties of language cannot be learned. Rather, they must be attributed to the operation of an inborn computational system (a processor) that is driven by the need to resolve dependencies at the first opportunity, thereby reducing the burden on working memory. Fundamental constraints on structure building, coreference, control, agreement, extraction, and contraction then follow as a matter of computational necessity.

But the computational system does more than just account for why language has the particular properties that it does. It also defines a de facto 'initial state' for language learning by encouraging the acquisition of patterns in which dependencies are resolved immediately—the ideal situation from the point of view of working memory. This creates the illusion of innate linguistic predispositions—reflexive pronouns are correctly interpreted from the outset, control constructions are quickly mastered, children have little or no trouble understanding subject relative clauses, the constraints on contraction and extraction are in place from the beginning, and so on. In fact though, these are all simple side-effects of efficiency, as we have seen over and over again.

Departures from this initial state must be possible of course. After all, English permits direct object relatives, in which the *wh* dependency cannot be resolved immediately (although it is of course still resolved at the first opportunity). Japanese allows sentences in which an apparent reflexive pronoun can have a distant antecedent (see p. 50). And so on.

But if I'm right, children should be very cautious about such things—they should be willing to use these sorts of patterns only after exposure to the appropriate input. In fact, it has been known for some time that when it comes to syntax, children are very conservative learners. As Pinker (1994:282) puts it, 'a well-designed child, when faced with several choices in how far to generalize, should, in general, be conservative: start with the smallest hypothesis about language that is consistent with what parents say, then expand it outward as the evidence requires' (see also Berwick 1985:37, Slobin 1985:1199, and O'Grady 1997:326).

From a learnability perspective, conservatism is a good strategy. Overgeneralizations in syntax are perilous and potentially difficult to correct (e.g., Baker 1979, Pinker 1989:5ff, O'Grady 1997:282ff). Caution is clearly the best policy, but how does a two-year-old child know this?

It has been suggested that children's conservatism in the course of language acquisition follows from an innate learning principle, such as the Subset Principle of Wexler & Manzini (1987:61). However, a property theory based on an efficiency driven computational system offers a different explanation for why conservatism makes sense—departures from the initial state increase the burden on working memory. They therefore take place only in response to clear indications from the input that they are needed.

Interestingly, there appears to be no parallel conservatism in the lexicon, where overgeneralization is common (e.g., *eated* for *ate*, or *goed* for *went*). Crucially though, there is no reason to think that overgeneralized word forms place a greater demand on working memory than their irregular counterparts. In the absence of this deterrent, overgeneralization occurs, resulting in the familiar errors.

In sum then, the structure of the computational system contributes to our understanding of several important puzzles relevant to language acquisition. Why do languages have the particular properties that they do? Why are some of these properties manifested from the earliest stages of language acquisition? How do children avoid the pitfalls associated with overgeneralization? As we have just seen, the property theory that I propose gives essentially the same answer to all three questions—because the computational system used to produce and understand sentences seeks to minimize the burden on working memory.

6.2 The transition theory

What about development, including errors that are characteristic of the early use of the computational system, such as mistakes in the interpretation of plain pronouns and direct object relative clauses?

The transition theory that I envision does not posit 'stages' of acquisition, at least not in the sense of discrete developmental periods in which particular modules of language are missing or particular parameters are mis-set. Rather, it holds that development takes place as the computational system succeeds in its competition with other cognitive functions for processing space.

This in turn leads to an improvement in its capacity to deal with more demanding phenomena, including those that do not permit immediate resolution of dependencies, as in the case of plain pronouns and direct object relative clauses. Further development takes place as computational routines are strengthened and automatized at different rates—the less demanding and more frequent routines first (e.g., those involving reflexives pronouns and subject relatives), and the more demanding and less frequent ones later.[8]

Once we consider first (and second) language acquisition alongside language loss and note the parallels among them, the case for the processing account becomes even stronger. True, we could say that a particular module of Universal Grammar matures late in the case of first language acquisition, that it is mysteriously no longer accessible to adults learning a second language, and that it is especially susceptible to damage in the case of aphasia. But this ignores two sets of facts. First, the structures that are compromised in the case of language acquisition and language loss appear to be those that make greater demands on working memory (e.g., direct object relatives versus subject relatives). And second, the study of agrammatism provides independent evidence that the sorts of deficits we have been considering can be linked to the part of the brain associated with working memory for language.

The precise extent to which working memory is compromised and the rate at which deficits are remedied can be expected to vary from individual to individual. This is true not only for language loss, where every patient exhibits a unique pattern of cell damage and recovery (e.g., Caplan & Hildebrandt 1988:299), but also for language acquisition, where differences in rate of development are widely attested both for a first language (e.g., Bates, Bretherton, & Snyder 1988) and for second languages (Larsen-Freeman & Long 1991:167).

Such differences notwithstanding, the net effects of shortages in computational space should have predictable consequences for language acquisition and language loss, resulting in the *relative* difficulty of certain structures with respect to others. Resolving a dependency at the first opportunity is always better than postponing it, and resolving a dependency immediately is best of all. Thus, all other things being equal, reflexive pronouns will be easier to interpret than plain pronouns, subject relatives will be easier than direct object relatives, and so on. Herein lies the

---

[8]It is difficult to tease apart the effects of computational demands and frequency, since the less demanding patterns tend also to be more frequent (e.g., St. John & Gernsbacher 1999, Dick, Bates, Wulfeck, et al. 2001, Townsend & Bever 2001:372). Nonetheless, in at least one crucial case, computational complexity appears to be the decisive factor. As noted above, direct object relative clauses remain harder to process than subject relatives no matter how often they are heard (Caplan & Waters 2002:71).

foundation of the theory of development suggested by the computational approach to language that I have proposed.

7. CONCLUSION

Although all children growing up under normal circumstances are exposed to the language(s) of their community, there are no doubt vast differences in the form and content of the particular utterances they hear. Some parents employ shorter sentences than others, some parents ask their children more questions than others, some parents use more pronouns than others, no two parents use exactly the same set of lexical items, and so forth (e.g., Snow & Ferguson 1977, Gallaway & Richards 1994).

In addition, there are significant disparities between the information available to children and the type of linguistic system they end up with. Experience provides little direct information about prohibitions on extraction and contraction, for example. Linguists are able to identify the constraints to which these phenomena are subject only by considering the unacceptability of various sorts of complex sentences that do not occur in anyone's speech. (That's what all those asterisked sentences are about in chapter seven.)

But this avenue of inquiry is obviously not open to children. They do not request acceptability judgments, and (fortunately for them) they do not reason about data in the way professional linguists do. They don't have to.

So long as children are exposed to words (nouns, verbs, pronouns) with the familiar lexical properties and arranged in the appropriate order (e.g., SVO, adjectives before nouns, prepositions before noun phrases), success is guaranteed. By adhering to a simple guideline—reduce the burden on working memory—their computational system will produce a syntax appropriate for the language at hand, including constraints on coreference, control, extraction, and contraction for which there is no direct evidence in experience.

In fact, success is ensured even in the face of differences in how well the brains of individual language learners work. As is frequently noted, language acquisition is successful across huge ranges in IQ (e.g., Curtiss 1988). Computing may be easier for some brains than for others, but the *relative* ease of particular computational options stays the same, and it is always best to resolve dependencies at the first opportunity. The right choices will be made by any brain with a computational system sensitive to the burden on working memory, regardless of how 'smart' it is.

By way of conclusion, it is perhaps worth bringing a fairly obvious point to the fore, namely that our understanding of how language acquisition works is heavily dependent on our understanding of how language works. It is no accident that proponents of abstract formal grammars find themselves committed to the view that an innate Universal Grammar is needed to account for how language is learned.

And it is likewise no accident that the rejection of this view is associated with an entirely different theory of how sentences are formed and interpreted.

The evaluation of these (and other) alternatives will therefore require close attention both to the properties of language and to the manner in which those properties emerge in the course of linguistic development. If the view put forward here is right, the best approach to both types of phenomena will be centered around the operation of an efficiency driven computational system.

Chapter 11

Concluding Remarks

1. THE EMERGENTIST THESIS

The theory that I have been describing is emergentist in the sense outlined at the outset. That is, it seeks to attribute the defining properties of language to more basic nonlinguistic forces, particularly efficiency-related processing considerations.

The emergentist approach to language calls for a fundamental reassessment of the status of syntactic rules and representations, but it does not abandon the symbol-oriented study of cognition, as some connectionist approaches do. To the contrary, the efficient computation of symbols is responsible for many core features of language, including the design of sentence structure, the interpretation of reflexive pronouns, control in infinitival clauses, the operation of agreement, and constraints on extraction and contraction, among other things.

My idea is that the form and interpretation of sentences reflect the general conditions under which information processing takes place, with an emphasis on the rapid integration of symbols into a larger representation as a way to minimize the burden on working memory. From this, many new possibilities have opened up, offering unsuspected insights into the workings of language.

If the leading idea of this book is right, the heart of language consists of a computational system with two jobs to do. On the one hand, it must further the agenda of the conceptual system by combining words in ways that convey the countless notions, relations, and contrasts that languages seek to express. On the other hand, it must manage the processing and storage costs that arise in dealing with multifaceted temporally sequenced representations.

The computational system appears to adopt a simple solution to both problems. On the one hand, it makes use of elementary Combine and Resolve operations to bring together words and satisfy their dependencies. On the other hand, it seeks to carry out these operations with a minimum of delay, consistently acting at the first opportunity so as to ease the burden on working memory.

As words are combined and their dependencies resolved, a sentence with a particular internal organization emerges. In accordance with long-standing views, its constituents are oganized into a binary-branching hierarchical structure, with the subject higher than the direct object—but not because of an innate 'blueprint.' A sentence's design is just a reflection of its formation by a computational system that is driven to combine functors with their arguments one at a time, from left to right, at the first opportunity.

The emergentist approach offers an even more radical account of the classic constraints of syntactic theory. As explained in chapters three through eight, the defining properties of many core syntactic phenomena appear to follow straight-forwardly from the requirement that dependencies be resolved at the first opportunity. These include the familiar constraints on pronoun interpretation, control, raising, agreement, extraction, and even contraction—phenomena whose study has been at the center of research into syntax since the 1960s.

2. THE VIABILITY ISSUE

Does it really work? The honest answer, of course, has to be no. It's an open secret that when it comes to language nothing really 'works.' As Chomsky (2002:127) observes with respect to the Minimalist Program, 'if you want to know what seems to refute the strong minimalist thesis, the answer is just about everything you can think of or pick at random from a corpus of material.' Problems and counter-examples are everywhere; the language always wins. That's just the way things are.

But the situation is not entirely bleak either. In fact, the emergentist approach stands up rather well under the weight of the difficult phenomena that I have tried to analyze in this book. Certainly, its coverage of the facts (its descriptive adequacy) is within the range considered acceptable for more familiar grammar based ap-proaches; in places, it may even be better.

On the other hand, in English alone there are hundreds of phenomena about which I have said nothing, including such standard puzzles as passivization, quantifier scope, and parasitic gaps. And if we venture beyond English, there are tens of thousands. I have made some preliminary proposals concerning Korean, and a number of papers on this topic can be found at my Website, http://www.ling.hawaii.edu/faculty/ogrady/. But this is no more than a start, and the empirical challenges are of course daunting, as usual.

Many linguistic phenomena will no doubt appear to be incompatible with the emergentist approach—just as coreference, control, and agreement in English once seemed to be. And, in principle, it is perfectly possible that although the syntax of coreference follows from the operation of an efficiency driven processor, the properties of quantifier scope (for instance) can only be explained in terms of an autonomous Universal Grammar.

The key point for now though is that the particular facts on which this book focuses involve prototypical *grammatical* phenomena. Indeed, by virtue of their complexity, their resistance to pragmatic explanation, and their occurrence in much the same form in a wide variety of languages, they are central to the case for the grammar-oriented study of language. Success in explaining them in terms of an efficiency driven linear processor is therefore potentially very telling, even though countless other phenomena await their turn to challenge the emergentist thesis. At some point (although not yet), the tide turns and the burden of proof shifts.

2.1 Beyond description

In the end of course, theories are only partly about accounting for facts. As Chomsky (2002:102) notes, science calls for a 'dedication to finding understanding, not just coverage.'

What the emergentist approach offers is a new way to confront the two major empirical challenges of linguistics—descriptive adequacy (what are the properties of language?) and explanatory adequacy (how can languages with those properties be learned?). In both cases, the answer lies with the computational system (i.e., the processor), whose efficiency driven character determines how language works and underwrites its acquisition. There is no innate grammatical blueprint, no Universal Grammar that imposes abstract constraints on the form of sentence structure. Sentences have the properties that they do because of the way they are built, not because of an *a priori* design.

It is important to acknowledge of course that the proposed processor, like the grammar it replaces, is something of an abstraction. As Chater & Christiansen (1999:235) observe, 'the brain can be viewed as consisting of a very large number of simple processors, neurons, which are densely interconnected into a complex network.' Whether the networks of neurons involved in the processing of sentences are organized in ways that make it reasonable to talk about task-specific 'sentence processor' does not matter for now. The key claim of this book is simply that the brain processes sentences in certain ways (linearly, efficiently, and so forth), not that there has to be a single identifiable processing mechanism in a particular place in the brain.

Working memory is central to all of this, but even it may not exist in the form traditionally imagined. As noted briefly in chapter one (p. 6), what we think of as working memory may just be the ability of a network of neurons to support a wave of activation (e.g., MacDonald & Christiansen 2002). This too does not matter for now. Efficiency retains its explanatory function even if its effect is to ease the burden on a neural network rather than on a working memory module.

Regardless of how these issues are resolved, there is a fundamental shift in perspective here that needs to be made precise: I am not proposing a processing based theory of Universal Grammar; I am proposing that the notion of Universal Grammar should be dispensed with in favor of an efficiency driven linear processor.

Universal Grammar is not just the name for the cognitive system that defines the essential properties of human language, regardless of the nature of those properties. It is a theory of *grammatical* structure—and a very interesting theory at that. Rightly or wrongly, my proposal takes such a theory to be unnecessary once the proper theory of processing is in place.

From a methodological perspective, it makes sense for an explanatory theory of language to start with a processor. Unlike a grammar, a processor is conceptually necessary—cognition and perception would be impossible without a device to analyze information as it is received by the sensory systems.

Moreover, there is no disagreement over the explanatory potential of processing based theories, even among proponents of grammar based approaches to language. As Chomsky (2001:5) notes, 'insofar as properties of [language] can be accounted for in terms of [an interface condition] and general properties of computational efficiency and the like, they have a principled explanation.'[1] Ideas along these lines have in fact been pursued for many years, and there is a sizable literature devoted to processing explanations for specific syntactic phenomena, as noted in chapter one.

The real question is whether we need anything more. Janet Dean Fodor (1978:470) puts it this way:

> ...there *must* be psychological mechanisms for speaking and understanding, and simplicity considerations thus put the burden of proof on anyone who would claim that there is more than this. To defend the more traditional view, what is needed is some sign of life from the postulated mental grammar.

Are there such signs of life, or is it possible to get along without a grammar?

As traditionally construed, grammar has played a central role in discharging two vital responsibilities in syntactic analysis—distinguishing possible sentences from impossible ones, and characterizing differences among languages. Let us consider each in turn.

2.2 Capturing acceptability

I have no argument with the idea that linguistic theory is responsible for explaining why some utterances are acceptable and others are not. I have made frequent reference to contrasts in acceptability throughout this book, and I believe that the basis for these contrasts lies in a simple fact—words impose requirements that must be satisfied in a computationally expedient manner. When this does not happen, the result is an unacceptable utterance.

A variety of things can go wrong. Perhaps a dependency is not resolved, either because there is no argument or because the argument is in the wrong place.

(1) a. Missing argument:
         *Arrived.

   b. Argument in the wrong place (for a leftward-looking functor):
       *Arrived John.

---

[1]As Newmeyer (2003:588) notes, however, the Minimalist Program has not met with great success in achieving this objective. See chapter one, p. 13.

Maybe an agreement dependency cannot be resolved at the first opportunity, as when a verb with a singular agreement feature has a plural noun phrase as its first argument.

(2)   *The men sees the girl.

Perhaps a reflexive pronoun looks too far for its antecedent, bypassing a closer index-bearing nominal.

(3)   *John$_i$ thinks that [Jerry$_j$ discussed himself$_i$].

None of these things happen in acceptable sentences.

Over time, the illusion of rules emerges. As we saw in earlier chapters, the sequences of computational operations needed to produce and understand the sentences of a language develop through repeated use into routines. Once strengthened to the point where they are more or less fixed, these routines have the de facto effect of defining a set of acceptable sentences. Because there is a routine that looks to the left for the verb's first argument, subject-verb word order is licensed. Because there is a routine that resolves agreement dependencies at the first opportunity, agreement with the subject becomes the strategy of first resort. Because referential dependencies are resolved without delay, a reflexive pronoun will have a local antecedent. And so forth.

This gives a result similar in its consequences to having grammatical constraints. What we traditionally think of as a grammar then, is just a processor that has been become set in its ways.

Could computational routines really be just grammatical rules under another name? No. As noted in chapter one, computational routines correspond to real-time *processes*, while rules describe *patterns* of elements (Jackendoff 2002:57). Or to put it another way, again following Jackendoff (ibid.:31), rules say what the structure is, whereas routines say how it is built—two very different things.

Might a full account of language require *both* rules and routines? This is conceivable, of course, but if it is true, then rules must do something more than restate facts about language that follow from the operation of the computational system/processor. As I have repeatedly stated, it is my contention that the computational system, once properly characterized, completely subsumes the function of traditional grammar (including Universal Grammar). There are thus no rules in the traditional sense.

It is important to recognize once again that proponents of the grammar based approach to language are making more than just a terminological proposal. They are not simply suggesting that the term *grammar* be used for whatever system happens to determine why some sentences of a language are acceptable and others are not.

Rather, they are claiming that a system of a particular sort is responsible for those contrasts and that that system incorporates a set of linguistic rules and principles defining the abstract formal properties of sentence structure. I claim that there are no such rules and principles. Sentences have the properties that they do because of the way they are built—one step at a time, by an efficiency driven linear processor that eventually becomes fixed on particular routines.

2.3 Differences among languages

If a general efficiency driven computational system is responsible for determining how language works, then why aren't all languages the same?

Pritchett (1992:3) insists that there can be no account of cross-linguistic variation without a grammar. If the theory of language processing is universal, he suggests, a theory of grammar is necessary to account for why languages differ in the ways that they do.

I don't believe that this is right. The relevant universal component of the theory of processing is simply the requirement that dependencies be resolved at the first opportunity (more abstractly, that the burden on working memory be reduced). Languages cannot differ on this point, but they can differ in terms of the properties of lexical items and the dependencies that they introduce.

Perhaps, for example, a particular language will have no morphemes that introduce agreement dependencies. In that case, there will be no agreement—a common state of affairs (Thai, for instance). Or perhaps a language will have morphemes that introduce two sets of agreement dependencies, as Swahili does, leading to agreement with the verb's first and second arguments.

Maybe a language will use one form for referential dependencies that are immediately resolved by the computational system and a different form for referential dependencies that are passed to the pragmatic system for resolution there, as English does with its contrast between *himself* and *him*. Or perhaps it will have a 'double-duty' pronoun like Japanese *zibun* that can introduce either type of referential dependency (see chapter three, p. 50).

Perhaps a language will have a computational routine that places a *wh* word at the beginning of the clause, in recognition of its focal character.

(1)   (Tell me) [*what* you bought].

Under these circumstances, a *wh* dependency will arise which the computational system will then have to resolve, with the various consequences explored in chapter seven (e.g., *wh* island and *that*-trace effects). On the other hand, a language may leave its *wh* words 'in situ,' as Mandarin does, avoiding *wh* dependencies.

(2)   Ni   mai le *sheme* (ne)?
        you buy Perf what   Ques
        'What did you buy?'

So far, so good. But there is still the major puzzle of how these sorts of typological differences interact with the processing considerations that seem so central to the computational system that we have been investigating throughout this book.

Processing and typology

The role of processing in explaining language typology has been discussed insightfully and extensively by Hawkins (1999), whose perspective closely resembles mine in many respects.

Hawkins's position is that grammatical conventions are simply 'frozen processing preferences' (p. 280) and that cross-linguistic variation is best understood in terms of processing as well. A simple example involving relative clauses will help illustrate the basic point.

English and Malagasy differ with respect to the type of relative clause patterns that they permit. As the following examples from Keenan & Comrie (1977:70) illustrate, Malagasy allows only subject relative clauses, whereas English allows both subject relatives and direct object relatives.

(3) a. Relativization of the subject:
    ny mpianatra [izay nahita ny vehivavy _]
    the student   that saw   the woman
    'the student who saw the woman'

   b. Relativization of the direct object:
    *ny vehivavy [izay nahita _ ny mpianatra]
    the woman   that saw   the student
    'the woman who the student saw'

The contrast is real and important. How can it be accommodated?

In languages that permit both subject relatives and object relatives, there is strong evidence that the latter makes greater demands on the processor because of the longer wait for an opportunity to resolve the *wh* dependency (see chapter seven, pp. 116-117). Crucially, as Hawkins notes (1999:266), there is also impressive typological evidence that as the difficulty of processing a particular pattern increases, the likelihood that it will occur in the languages of the world declines. Or, put another way, the greater the demands that a particular pattern makes on the processor, the less likely that languages will develop a computational routine for dealing with it.

This in turn explains the familiar implicational facts. Fewer languages permit direct object relatives than subject relatives, because the former pattern is computationally more demanding. And any language that permits direct object relatives must also have subject relatives—if the 'harder' pattern is possible, then so is the comparable 'easier' one.

I think that Hawkins is exactly right about this and that there is no need for grammatical principles in the traditional sense to deal with crosslinguistic variation. Languages differ in terms of the dependencies they allow—as noted above, some languages have agreement dependencies and some don't. Some languages have *wh* dependencies and some don't. And, as we have just seen with respect to relative clauses, languages differ in terms of whether they are willing to 'pay' for the computational routines needed to resolve dependencies in particular patterns (with the proviso that if a more costly routine is permitted, a less costly one must be allowed as well).

Beyond this though, languages are indeed fundamentally alike. The overarching strategy for managing dependencies—resolution without delay—is the same, as is the efficiency driven character of the linear processor that carries out this mandate on whatever dependencies it encounters.

Beyond processing

As noted in chapter one, emergentism is committed to the view that the properties of language are best understood in terms of more basic nonlinguistic forces. The need to minimize the burden on working memory is one of those forces, and I have tried to make the case that it is the key to understanding the nature and functioning of the computational system for language.

But the computational system is just one component of the language faculty, and its role is that of a subordinate. It does not get to 'decide' whether a particular language has *wh* dependencies, for example. It determines that they are costly, but it cannot decide whether they are worth the price. Its job is simply to resolve whatever dependencies it encounters at the first opportunity.

From a purely computational perspective, it might make sense for languages to have no *wh* dependencies and therefore to permit only in situ *wh* questions. But the fact is that many languages, English included, are willing to 'pay the price' to have clause-initial *wh* words, presumably for reasons that are functionally motivated in their own right. It makes sense to place focused material early in the sentence (Givón 1990:800), and it makes sense to indicate a sentence's modality at the outset.

Similarly, many languages are willing to absorb the cost of agreement dependencies, presumably because agreement offers a generally reliable coding strategy for tracking the relationship between a functor and at least one of its arguments (Keenan 1976, Croft 1991:24-25).

If this is right, then competing forces determine the full form of a language. The computational system is designed to minimize the burden on working memory, but in the end it has to play the hand that it is dealt. And the hand is not always perfect—languages do things with word order and with morphology that are motivated by considerations other than sympathy for working memory.[2]

One way to think about the tension between processing factors and other forces is to adopt the leading idea of *optimality theory*—language reflects the interaction of 'soft' constraints, whose precise effect is determined by their relative ranking with respect to each other in particular languages. Thus, one might say, the value of having focused words at the beginning of the sentence wins out over the desirability of minimizing the burden on working memory in the case of English *wh* questions, whereas the reverse ranking is manifested in Mandarin.

This has some promise, but caution is in order. Although it makes sense on the emergentist perspective that I have adopted to think that the relative impact of particular functional *forces* can vary from language to language, I am reluctant to adopt the more common practice of positing actual discrete *constraints* (let alone innate constraints) whose ranking is determined in the course of language learning.

Indeed, in some cases, the constraints that are posited in work on optimality theory turn out to be nothing more than principles of classic Universal Grammar.

(4)   A trace is governed. (Grimshaw 1997:374)

(5)   Pronouns must be A-free in their binding domain. (Fischer 2004:485)

In other (more palatable) versions of optimality theory, the constraints require an independent functional motivation (e.g., Bresnan & Aissen 2002).

(6)   Subject/Agent > Subject/Patient (Aissen 1999:683)
       (An agent subject is more natural than a patient subject.)

(7)   Subject/X > Subject/x (Aissen ibid.:684)
       (A discourse prominent subject is more natural than a subject that is not
       discourse prominent.)

Here too though, my view is that constraints per se do not exist. They offer a convenient way to state generalizations, but the content of those generalizations should follow from something more basic. The constraints themselves should not be part of the actual theory of language.

The Efficiency Requirement works that way. It provides a helpful generalization, but has no ontological status of its own. Its content ('Resolve dependencies at the first opportunity') follows from the need to minimize the burden on working memory which, in turn, reflects a fact about the electrophysiology of the brain—neuronal activation is difficult to sustain.

---

[2]Remember that this does not mean that the computational system is inefficient. The 'decision' to have or not have *wh* dependencies is made 'off-line.' The computational system always resolves whatever dependencies it encounters at the first opportunity.

In sum, forces other than efficiency are clearly at work in language. Their presence is felt in the existence of agreement dependencies and *wh* dependencies, among other places. If the emergentist perspective is right, they too should be essentially nonlinguistic in character, reflecting deeper facts about cognition and perception, if not processing. Unfortunately, the precise character of these forces remains to be determined, as does the nature of their interaction with each other.

3. A FINAL WORD

The metaphor that has guided and shaped the leading idea of this book evokes an image of design and construction. When it comes to language, I have suggested, there are no architects or blueprints, just carpenters. The properties of sentences emerge from the processes that permit their construction, not from rules that constrain their form.

In a sense, this idea involves a quite minor departure from more conventional work in linguistics. I have, for instance, adopted an entirely standard view of the lexicon, and there is nothing radical in the idea that there are combinatorial operations that seek to satisfy lexical requirements—every approach to language proposes this in one form or another. The suggestion that those operations apply in a linear manner is less common of course, but certainly not unprecedented, as I noted in chapter one.

Moreover, there is a long tradition within syntax, especially in the Minimalist Program and its predecessors, that seeks to understand syntactic constraints in terms of notions such as locality and economy that invite a possible processing based interpretation, even though care has always been taken to distinguish the grammar from the processor (e.g., Chomsky 1995:167).

It may turn out, then, that the particular idea that I have outlined is just a small step beyond what traditional approaches propose. The consequences of this step are significant though, both for how we see the language faculty and for how we think about phenomena such as language acquisition. There is a fundamental shift in the burden of explanation from an autonomous grammatical system to a processor whose properties seem largely to follow from the nature of working memory.

Nobel laureate Steven Weinberg (2000:86-87) had this to say about explanation:

> To qualify as an explanation, a fundamental theory has to be simple—not necessarily a few short equations, but equations that are based on a simple physical principle, in the way that the equations of general relativity are based on the principle that gravitation is an effect of the curvature of space-time. And the theory also has to be compelling—it has to give us the feeling that it could scarcely be different from what it is.

Does the theory I have put forward meet these criteria? There certainly appears to be a simple physical principle—for electrophysiological reasons, the maintenance of neuronal activation is costly. This in turn places a high value on operations that minimize the burden on working memory, creating effects that are felt throughout a language's syntax.

But could the theory scarcely be different? It is too early to say, obviously. There is much to recommend the ideas we have been considering, I think, but there is also good reason for caution. Errors have no doubt been made in the formulation of particular analyses, and many important phenomena are yet to be analyzed at all. Nonetheless, enough progress has perhaps been made to justify further pursuit of this type of inquiry.

References

Adger, David & Josep Quer. 2001. The syntax and semantics of unselected embedded questions. *Language* 77, 107–133.

Aissen, Judith. 1999. Markedness and subject choice in optimality theory. *Natural Language and Linguistic Theory* 17, 673–711.

Akhtar, Nameera & Michael Tomasello. 1997. Young children's productivity with word order and verb morphology. *Developmental Psychology* 33, 952–966.

Anderson, John R. 1993. *Rules of the mind.* Mahwah, NJ: Erlbaum.

Anderson, Stephen & David Lightfoot. 2002. *The language organ: Linguistics as cognitive psychology.* New York: Cambridge University Press.

Andrews, Avery. 1982. The representation of case in Modern Icelandic. In J. Bresnan (ed.), *The mental representation of grammatical relations,* pp. 427–503. Cambridge, MA: MIT Press.

Aoun, Joseph, Elabbas Benmamoun, & Dominique Sportiche. 1999. Further remarks on first conjunct agreement. *Linguistic Inquiry* 30, 669–681.

Authier, J.-Marc. 1991. V-governed expletives, Case theory, and the Projection Principle. *Linguistic Inquiry* 22, 721-740.

Bach, Emmon. 1982. Purpose clauses and control. In P. Jacobsen & G. Pullum (eds.), *The nature of syntactic representation,* pp. 35–57. Dordrecht: Reidel.

Bach, Emmon & Barbara Partee. 1980. Anaphora and semantic structure. In J. Kreiman & A. Ojeda (eds.), *Papers from the parasession on pronouns and anaphora,* pp. 1–28. Chicago: Chicago Linguistic Society.

Bailes, Gregg. 2000. *Wanna* contraction in a British English environment. M.A. thesis. Department of Linguistics and English Language, University of Durham.

Baker, C. Lee. 1979. Syntactic theory and the projection problem. *Linguistic Inquiry* 10, 533–582.

Baltin, Mark. 1989. Heads and projections. In M. Baltin & A. Kroch (eds.), *Alternative conceptions of phrase structure,* pp. 1–16. Chicago: University of Chicago Press.

Barss, Andrew. 1995. Extraction and contraction. *Linguistic Inquiry* 26, 681-694.

Barss, Andrew & Howard Lasnik. 1986. A note on anaphora and double objects. *Linguistic Inquiry* 17, 347–354.

Bates, Elizabeth, Inge Bretherton, & Lynn Snyder. 1988. *From first words to grammar: Individual differences and dissociable mechanisms.* New York: Cambridge University Press.

Bates, Elizabeth & Judith Goodman. 1999. On the emergence of grammar from the lexicon. In B. MacWhinney (ed.), *The emergence of language,* pp. 29–79, Mahwah, NJ: Erlbaum.

Berwick, Robert. 1985. *The acquisition of syntactic knowledge.* Cambridge, MA: MIT Press.

Berwick, Robert & Amy Weinberg. 1984. *The grammatical basis of linguistic performance: Language use and acquisition.* Cambridge, MA: MIT Press.

Bever, Thomas, Montserrat Sanz, & David Townsend. 1998. The emperor's psycholinguistics. *Journal of Psycholinguistic Research* 27, 261–284.

Bloom, Paul, Andrew Barss, Janet Nicol, & Laura Conway. 1994. Children's knowledge of binding and coreference: Evidence from spontaneous speech. *Language* 70, 53–71.

Boeckx, Cedric. 2000. A note on contraction. *Linguistic Inquiry* 31, 357-366.

Boeckx, Cedric & Norbert Hornstein. 2003. Reply to "Control is not movement." *Linguistic Inquiry* 34, 269–280.

Boeckx, Cedric & Norbert Hornstein. 2004. Movement under control. *Linguistic Inquiry* 35, 431–452.

Bolinger, Dwight. 1952. *Linear modification.* Publications of the Modern Lan-guage Association 647, 1117–1144.

Booth, James, Brian MacWhinney, & Yasuaki Harasaki. 2000. Developmental differences in visual and auditory processing of complex sentences. *Child Development* 71, 981–1003.

Borer, Hagit & Bernhard Rohrbacher. 2002. Minding the absent: Arguments for the Full Competence Hypothesis. *Language Acquisition* 10, 123–175.

Bresnan, Joan. 1982. Control and complementation. In J. Bresnan (ed.), *The mental representation of grammatical relations*, pp. 282–390. Cambridge, MA: MIT Press.

Bresnan, Joan & Judith Aissen. 2002. Optimality and functionality: Objections and refutations. *Natural Language and Linguistic Theory* 20, 81–95.

Bybee, Joan. 2002. Sequentiality as the basis of constituent structure. In T. Givón & B. Malle (eds.), *The evolution of language out of pre-language*, pp. 109–134. Philadelphia: John Benjamins.

Bybee, Joan & Joanne Scheibman. 1999. The effect of usage on degree of constituency: The reduction of *don't* in American English. *Linguistics* 37, 575–596.

Caplan, David & Christine Futter. 1986. Assignment of thematic roles to nouns in sentence comprehension by an agrammatic patient. *Brain and Language* 27, 117–134.

Caplan, David & Nancy Hildebrandt. 1988. *Disorders of syntactic comprehension*. Cambridge, MA: MIT Press.

Caplan, David & Gloria Waters. 1999. Verbal working memory and sentence comprehension. *Behavioral and Brain Sciences* 22, 77–126.

Caplan, David & Gloria Waters. 2001. Working memory and syntactic processing in sentence comprehension. *Cognitive Studies* 8, 10–24.

Caplan, David & Gloria Waters. 2002. Working memory and connectionist models of parsing: A reply to MacDonald and Christiansen (2002). *Psychological Review* 109.1, 66–74.

Caramazza, Alfonso & Edgar Zurif. 1976. Dissociation of algorithmic and heuristic processes in sentence comprehension: Evidence from aphasia. *Brain and Language* 3, 572–582.

Carpenter, Patricia, Akira Miyake, and Marcel Just. 1994. Working memory constraints in comprehension: Evidence from individual differences, aphasia, and aging. *Handbook of psycholinguistics*, pp. 1075–1122. San Diego: Academic Press.

Chater, Nick & Morten Christiansen. 1999. Connectionism and natural language processing. In S. Garrod & M. Pickering (eds.) *Language processing*, pp. 233–279. East Sussex, UK: Psychology Press.

Chien, Yu-Chin & Kenneth Wexler. 1990. Children's knowledge of locality conditions in binding as evidence for the modularity of syntax and pragmatics. *Language Acquisition* 1, 225–295.

Chomsky, Noam. 1975. *Reflections on language*. New York: Pantheon.

Chomsky, Noam. 1977. On wh movement. In P. Culicover, T. Wasow, & A. Akmajian (eds.), *Formal syntax*, pp. 71–132. New York: Academic Press.

Chomsky, Noam. 1980a. On cognitive structures: A reply to Piaget. In M. Piattelli-Palmarini (ed.), *Language and learning: The debate between Jean Piaget and Noam Chomsky*, pp. 35–52. Cambridge, MA: Harvard University Press.

Chomsky, Noam. 1980b. *Rules and representations*. New York: Columbia University Press.

Chomsky, Noam. 1981. *Lectures on government and binding*. Dordrecht: Foris.

Chomsky, Noam. 1986a. *Barriers*. Cambridge, MA: MIT Press.

Chomsky, Noam. 1986b. *Knowledge of language*. New York: Praeger.

Chomsky, Noam 1995. *The minimalist program*. Cambridge, MA: MIT Press.

Chomsky, Noam. 2001. Beyond explanatory adequacy. *MIT Occasional Papers in Linguistics*. Number 20, 1–28.

Chomsky, Noam. 2002. *On nature and language*. New York: Cambridge Univer-sity Press.

Chomsky, Noam & Howard Lasnik. 1977. Filters and control. *Linguistic Inquiry* 8, 425–504.

Chomsky, Noam & Howard Lasnik. 1995. The theory of principles and parameters. In N. Chomsky, *The minimalist program*, pp. 13-127. Cambridge, MA: MIT Press.

Christiansen, Morten & Nick Chater. 2001. Connectionist psycholinguistics: Capturing the empirical data. *Trends in Cognitive Science* 5, 82–88.

Chung, Sandra & James McCloskey. 1983. On the interpretation of certain island facts in GPSG. *Linguistic Inquiry* 14, 704–713.

Collins, Chris. 2001. Eliminating labels. *MIT Occasional Papers in Linguistics*. Number 20, 1-25.

Corbett, Greville. 1983. Resolution rules: Agreement in person, number and gender. In G. Gazdar, E. Klein, & G. Pullum (eds.), *Order, control, and constituency*, pp. 175–206. Dordrecht: Foris.

Costa, João. 1997. On the behavior of adverbs in sentence-final context. *The Linguistic Review* 14, 43–68.

Coulson, Seanna, Jonathan King, & Marta Kutas. 1998. Expect the unexpected: Event-related brain response to morphosyntactic violations. *Language and Cognitive Processes* 13, 21–58.

Cowart, Wayne. 1991. Mental representations of conjoined noun phrases. Ms., Language Sciences Laboratory, University of Southern Maine.

Crain, Stephen. 1991. Language acquisition in the absence of experience. *Behavioral and Brain Sciences* 14, 597–650.

Crain, Stephen & Janet Dean Fodor. 1985. How can grammars help processors? In D. Dowty, L. Kartunnen, & A. Zwicky (eds.), *Natural language parsing: Psychological, computational and theoretical perspectives*. Cambridge University Press.

Crain, Stephen & Mineharu Nakayama. 1987. Structure dependence in grammar formation. *Language* 63, 522–543.

Crocker, Matthew. 1999. Mechanisms for sentence processing. In S. Garrod & M. Pickering (eds.), *Language processing*, pp. 191–232. East Sussex, UK: Psychology Press.

Croft, William. 1991. *Syntactic categories and grammatical relations: The cognitive organization of information*. Chicago: University of Chicago Press.

Croft, William. 2001. *Radical construction grammar: Syntactic theory in typol-ogical perspective*. New York: Oxford University Press.

Croft, William. 2003. *Typology and universals*. Second edition. Cambridge, UK: Cambridge University Press.

Culicover, Peter & Ray Jackendoff. 2001. Control is not movement. *Linguistic Inquiry* 32, 493–512.

Cummins, Robert. 1983. *The nature of psychological explanation*. Cambridge, MA: MIT Press.

Curtiss, Susan. 1988. Abnormal language acquisition and the modularity of language. In F. Newmeyer (ed.), *Linguistics: The Cambridge survey. Vol. 2*, pp. 96–116. New York: Cambridge University Press.

Dalrymple, Mary. 2001. *Lexical functional grammar. (Syntax and Semantics 24)* San Diego: Academic Press.

Dalrymple, Mary & Ronald Kaplan. 2000. Feature indeterminacy and feature resolution. *Language* 76, 759–798.

de Villiers, Jill & Peter de Villiers. 1973. Development of the use of word order in comprehension. *Journal of Psycholinguistic Research* 2, 331–341.

De Vincenzi, Marica. 1991. *Syntactic parsing strategies in Italian*. Dordrecht: Kluwer.

De Vincenzi, Marica. 1996. Syntactic analysis in sentence comprehension: Effects of dependency types and grammatical constraints. *Journal of Psycholinguistics Research* 25, 117–133.

Deacon, Terrence. 1997. *The symbolic species: The co-evolution of language and the brain*. New York: Norton.

Deane, Paul. 1992. *Grammar in mind and brain: Explorations in cognitive syntax*. New York: Mouton de Gruyter.

Deevy, Patricia. 1998. A processing account of partial agreement effects. Paper presented at the annual meeting of the Linguistic Society of America.

Demestre, Josep, Sheila Meltzer, José García-Albea, & Andreu Vigil. 1999. Identifying the null subject: Evidence from event-related brain potentials. *Journal of Psycholinguistics Research* 28, 293–312.

Dick, Frederic, Elizabeth Bates, Beverly Wulfeck, Jennifer Utman, Nina Dronkers, & Morton Gernsbacher. 2001. Language deficits, localization and grammar: Evidence for a distributive model of language breakdown in aphasics and normals. *Psychological Review* 108, 759–788.

Dixon, R.M.W. 1977. Semantic neutralization for semantic reasons. *Linguistic Inquiry* 8, 599–602.

Edelman, Gerald. 1992. *Bright air, brilliant fire: On the matter of the mind*. New York: Basic.

Ellis, Nick. 2001. Memory for language. In P. Robinson (ed.), *Cognition and second language instruction*, pp. 33–68. New York: Cambridge University Press.

Elman, Jeffrey. 1993. Learning and development in neural networks: The importance of starting small. *Cognition* 48, 71-99.

Elman, Jeffrey. 1999. The emergence of language: A conspiracy theory. In B. MacWhinney (ed.), *The emergence of language*, pp. 1–27, Mahwah, NJ: Erlbaum.

Elman, Jeffrey. 2004. An alternative view of the mental lexicon. *Trends in Cognitive Sciences* 8, 301–306.

Elman, Jeffrey, Elizabeth Bates, Mark Johnson, Annette Karmiloff-Smith, Domenico Parisi, & Kim Plunkett. 1996. *Rethinking innateness: A connectionist perspective on development.* Cambridge, MA: MIT Press.

Ferreira, Fernanda & Charles Clifton, Jr. 1986. The independence of syntactic processing. *Journal of Memory and Language* 25, 348-368.

Fischer, Silke. 2004. Optimal binding. *Natural Language and Linguistic Theory* 22, 481–526.

Fodor, Janet Dean. 1978. Parsing strategies and constraints on transformations. *Linguistic Inquiry* 9, 427–473.

Fodor, Janet Dean. 1985. Deterministic parsing and subjacency. *Language and Cognitive Processes* 1, 3–42.

Fodor, Janet Dean. 1989. Empty categories in sentence processing. *Language and Cognitive Processes* 4, 155–209.

Fodor, Janet Dean. 1994. How to obey the Subset Principle: Binding and locality. In B. Lust, G. Hermon, & J. Kornfilt (eds.), *Syntactic theory and first language acquisition: Cross-linguistic perspectives. Vol. 2: Binding, dependencies, and learnability*, pp. 429–451. Mahwah, NJ: Erlbaum.

Fodor, Janet Dean & Atsu Inoue. 1998. Attach anyway. In J. D. Fodor & F. Ferreira (eds.), *Reanalysis in sentence processing*, pp. 101–141. Dordrecht: Kluwer.

Frazier, Lyn. 1987. Sentence processing: A tutorial review. In M. Coltheart (ed.), *Attention and performance XII: The psychology of reading*, pp. 559–586. Hillsdale, NJ.

Frazier, Lyn. 1998. Getting there (slowly). *Journal of Psycholinguistic Research* 27, 123–146.

Frazier, Lyn & Charles Clifton. 1989. Successive cyclicity in the grammar and the parser. *Language and Cognitive Processes* 4, 93–126.

Frazier, Lyn & Charles Clifton. 1996. *Construal.* Cambridge, MA: MIT Press.

Fries, Charles. 1952. *The structure of English: An introduction to the construction of English sentences.* New York: Harcourt, Brace, & Co.

Gallaway, Clare & Brian Richards (eds.). 1994. *Input and interaction in language acquisition.* New York: Cambridge University Press.

Garnsey, Susan, Michael Tanenhaus, & Robert Chapman. 1989. Evoked potentials and the study of sentence comprehension. *Journal of Psycholinguistics Research* 18, 51–60.

Garrett, Merrill. 2000. Remarks on the architecture of language processing systems. In Y. Grodzinsky, L. Shapiro, & D. Swinney (eds.), *Language and the brain: Representation and processing*, pp. 31–69. San Diego: Academic Press.

Garrod, Simon & Anthony Sanford. 1994. Resolving sentences in a discourse context: How discourse representation affects language understanding. In M. Gernsbacher (ed.), *Handbook of psycholinguistics*, pp. 675-698. San Diego: Academic Press.

Garrod, Simon, Daniel Freudenthal, & Elizabeth Boyle. 1994. The role of different types of anaphor in the on-line resolution of sentences in a discourse. *Journal of Memory and Language* 33, 39–68.

Gathercole, Susan, & A.S.C. Thorn. 1998. Phonological short term memory and foreign language learning. In A. Healy & L. Bourne (eds.), *Foreign language learning: Psycholinguistic studies on training and retention*, pp. 141–158. Mahwah, NJ: Erlbaum.

Gazdar, Gerald, Ewan Klein, Geoffrey Pullum, & Ivan Sag. 1985. *Generalized phrase structure grammar.* Oxford, UK: Blackwell.

Gibson, Edward. 1998. Linguistic complexity: Locality of syntactic dependencies. *Cognition* 68, 1–76.

Gibson, Edward & Tessa Warren. 2004. Reading-time evidence for intermediate linguistic structure in long-distance dependencies. *Syntax* 7, 55-78.

Givón, Talmy. 1979. From discourse to syntax: Grammar as a processing strategy. In T. Givón (ed.), *Discourse and syntax. (Syntax and Semantics 12)*, pp. 81–112. New York: Academic Press.

Givón, Talmy. 1990. *Syntax: A functional typological introduction. Volume II.* Philadelphia: John Benjamins.

Gleason, H. A. 1955. *An introduction to descriptive linguistics.* New York: Holt & Co.

Goldberg, Adele. 1995. *Constructions: A construction grammar approach to argu-ment structure.* Chicago: University of Chicago Press.

Goldberg, Adele. 1999. The emergence of the semantics of argument structure constructions. In B. MacWhinney (ed.), *The emergence of language*, pp. 197–212. Mahwah, NJ: Erlbaum.

Gordon, Peter, Barbara Grosz, & Laura Gillion. 1993. Pronouns, names, and the centering of attention in discourse. *Cognitive Science* 17, 311–347.

Gordon, Peter & Randall Hendrick. 1997. Intuitive knowledge of linguistic co-reference. *Cognition* 62, 325–370.

Gordon, Peter & Randall Hendrick. 1998. The representation and processing of coreference in discourse. *Cognitive Science* 22, 389–424.

Greene, Steven, Gail McKoon, & Roger Ratcliff. 1992. Pronoun resolution and discourse models. *Journal of Experimental Psychology: Learning, Memory and Cognition* 18, 266–283.

Gregg, Kevin. 1996. The logical and developmental problems of second language acquisition. In W. Ritchie & T. Bhatia (eds.), *Handbook of second language acquisition*, pp. 49–81. San Diego: Academic.

Gregory, Michelle, William Raymond, Alan Bell, Eric Fosler-Lussier, & Daniel Jurafsky. 1999. The effects of collocational strength and construal predictability in lexical production. *Chicago Linguistic Society 35: The panels*, 151–166.

Grimshaw, Jane. 1990. *Argument structure.* Cambridge, MA: MIT Press.

Grimshaw, Jane. 1997. Projections, heads, and optimality. *Linguistic Inquiry* 28, 373–422.

Grimshaw, Jane & Sarah Rosen. 1990. Knowledge and obedience: The developmental status of binding theory. *Linguistic Inquiry* 21, 187–222.

Grodzinsky, Yosef. 1989. Agrammatic comprehension of relative clauses. *Brain and Language* 37, 430–499.

Grodzinsky, Yosef. 1990. *Theoretical perspectives on language deficits.* Cam-bridge, MA: MIT Press.

Grodzinsky, Yosef, Kenneth Wexler, Yu-Chin Chien, Susan Marakovitz, & Julie Solomon. 1993. The breakdown of binding relations. *Brain and Language* 45, 396–422.

Grossman, Murray, Susan Carvell, Matthew Stern, Stephen Gollomp, & Howard Hurtig. 1992. Sentence comprehension in Parkinson's disease: The role of attention and memory. *Brain and Language* 42, 347–384.

Haegeman, Liliane. 1994. *Introduction to government and binding theory.* Second edition. Cambridge, MA: Blackwell.

Haegeman, Liliane. 2003. Notes on long adverbial fronting in English and the left periphery. *Linguistic Inquiry* 34, 640–649.

Hagoort, Peter, Colin Brown, & Lee Osterhout. 1999. The neurocognition of syntactic processing. In C. Brown & P. Hagoort (eds.), *The neurocognition of language*, pp. 273–307. New York: Oxford University Press.

Hamilton, Robert. 1994. Is implicational generalization unidirectional and maximal? Evidence from relativization instruction in a second language. *Language Learning* 44, 123–157.

Hauser, Marc, Noam Chomsky, & W. Tecumseh Fitch. 2002. The faculty of language: What is it, who has it, and how did it evolve? *Science* 298, 1569–1579.

Hausser, Roland. 2001. *Foundations of computational linguistics: Human-computer communication in natural language.* 2nd ed. Berlin: Springer-Verlag.

Hawkins, John. 1990. A parsing theory of word order universals. *Linguistic Inquiry* 21, 223–261.

Hawkins, John. 1994. *A performance theory of order and constituency*. Cam-bridge: Cambridge University Press.

Hawkins, John. 1999. Processing complexity and filler-gap dependencies across grammars. *Language* 75, 244–285.

Heim, Irene. 1990. E-type pronouns and donkey anaphora. *Linguistics and Philosophy* 13, 137–177.

Hickok, Gregory. 2000. The left frontal convolution plays no special role in syntactic comprehension. *Behavioral and Brain Sciences* 23, 35–36.

Hirose, Yukio. 2002. Viewpoint and the nature of the Japanese reflexive *zibun*. *Cognitive Linguistics* 13, 357–401.

Hirsh-Pasek, Kathryn & Roberta Golinkoff. 1996. *The origins of grammar: Evidence from early language comprehension*. Cambridge, MA: MIT Press.

Hirtle, Walter. 1982. *Number and inner space: A study of grammatical number in English*. Quebec City: Presses de l'Université Laval.

Hoekstra, Eric. 1991. On double objects in English and Dutch. In K. Leffel & D. Bouchard (eds.). *Views on phrase structure*. Dordrecht: Kluwer.

Horn, Laurence. 1978. Remarks on Neg-Raising. In P. Cole (ed.), *Pragmatics (Syntax and Semantics 9)*, pp. 129–220. New York: Academic Press.

Hornstein, Norbert. 1999. Movement and control. *Linguistic Inquiry* 30, 69–96.

Hudson, Richard. 1992. So-called 'double objects' and grammatical relations. *Language* 68, 251–276.

Hulme, Charles & Vicki Tordoff. 1989. Working memory development: The effects of speech rate, word length, and acoustic similarity in serial recall. *Journal of Experimental Child Psychology* 47, 72–87.

Inoue, Atsu & Janet Dean Fodor. 1994. Information-based parsing of Japanese. In R. Mazuka & N. Nagai (eds.), *Japanese sentence processing*, pp. 9–63. Mahwah, NJ: Erlbaum.

Jackendoff, Ray. 2002. *Foundations of language*. New York: Oxford University Press.

Jackendoff, Ray & Peter Culicover. 2003. The semantic basis of control in English. *Language* 517–556.

Jacobsen, Pauline. 1990. Raising as functional composition. *Linguistics and Philosophy* 13, 423–475.

Jaeggli, Osvaldo. 1980. Remarks on *to*-contraction. *Linguistic Inquiry* 11, 239-245.

Jakubowicz, Celia. 1984. On markedness and binding principles. *Proceedings of the North East Linguistic Society* 14, 154–182.

Just, Marcel & Patricia Carpenter. 1992. A capacity theory of comprehension: Individual differences in working memory. *Psychological Review* 99, 122–149.

Just, Marcel, Patricia Carpenter, & Timothy Keller. 1996. The capacity theory of comprehension: New frontiers of evidence and arguments. *Psychological Review* 103, 773–780.

Just, Marcel & Sashank Varma. 2002. A hybrid architecture for working memory: Reply to MacDonald and Christiansen (2002). *Psychological Review* 109, 55–65.

Kaisse, Ellen. 1983. The syntax of auxiliary reduction in English. *Language* 59, 93-122.

Kamp, Hans & Uwe Reyle. 1993. *From discourse to logic: Introduction to modeltheoretic semantics of natural language, formal logic and Discourse Representation Theory*. Boston: Kluwer.

Kaufman, Diana. 1994. Grammatical or pragmatic: Will the real Principle B please stand up? In B. Lust, G. Herman, & J. Kornfilt (eds.), *Syntactic theory Cross-linguistic perspectives. Vol. 2: Binding, dependencies and learnability*, pp. 177–200. Mahwah, NJ: Erlbaum.

Kayne, Richard. 1994. *The antisymmetry of syntax*. Cambridge, MA: MIT Press.

Keenan, Edward. 1976. Towards a universal definition of 'subject'. In C. Li (ed.), *Subject and topic*, pp. 303-333. New York: Academic Press.

Keenan, Edward & Bernard Comrie. 1977. Noun phrase accessibility and Universal Grammar. *Linguistic Inquiry* 8, 63–100.

Kehler, Andrew. 2002. *Coherence, reference, and the theory of grammar*. Stanford University: Center for the Study of Language and Information.

Kemmerer, David. 1999. Impaired comprehension of subject-to-object raising constructions in Parkinson's disease. *Brain and Language* 66, 311–328.

Kempen, Gerard. 2000. Could grammatical encoding and grammatical decoding be subserved by the same processing module? *Behavioral and Brain Sciences* 23, 38–39.

Kempen, Gerard & Edward Hoenkamp. 1987. An incremental procedural grammar for sentence formation. *Cognitive Science* 11, 201–258.

Kempson, Ruth, Wilfried Meyer-Viol, & Dov Gabbay. 2001. *Dynamic syntax: The flow of language understanding.* Malden, MA: Blackwell.

Kim, Jong-Bok. 2004. Hybrid agreement in English. *Linguistics* 42, 1105-1128.

King, Harold. 1970. On blocking rules for contraction in English. *Linguistic Inquiry* 1, 134–136.

Kluender, Robert & Marta Kutas. 1993. Subjacency as a processing phenomenon. *Language and Cognitive Processes* 8, 573–633.

Kolk, Herman & Marion Weijts. 1996. Judgments of semantic anomaly in agrammatic patients: Argument movement, syntactic complexity, and the use of heuristics. *Brain and Language* 54, 86–135.

Krug, Manfred. 1998. String frequency: A cognitive motivating factor in coalescence, language processing and linguistic change. *Journal of English Linguistics* 26, 286–320.

Kuno, Susumu. 1987. *Functional syntax: Anaphora, discourse, and empathy.* Chicago: University of Chicago Press.

Kuno, Susumu & Ken-ichi Takami. 1993. *Grammar and discourse principles.* Chicago: University of Chicago Press.

Ladusaw, William and David Dowty. 1988. Toward a nongrammatical account of thematic roles. In W. Wilkins (ed.), *Thematic relations. (Syntax and Semantics 21),* pp. 61–73. San Diego: Academic Press.

Lakoff, George. 1970. Global rules. *Language* 46, 627–639.

Landau, Idan. 2003. Movement out of control. *Linguistic Inquiry* 34, 471–498.

Langacker, Ronald. 1995. Raising and transparency. *Language* 71, 1–62.

Larsen-Freeman, Diane & Michael Long. 1991. *An introduction to second language acquisition research.* New York: Longman.

Larson, Richard. 1988. On the double object construction. *Linguistic Inquiry* 19, 335–391.

Lasnik, Howard. 1989. *Essays on anaphora.* Dordrecht: Reidel.

Lasnik, Howard & Mamoru Saito. 1991. On the subject of infinitives. *Papers from the Twenty-Seventh Regional Meeting of the Chicago Linguistic Society,* 324–343.

Lasnik, Howard & Mamoru Saito. 1992. *Move alpha: Conditions on its application and output.* Cambridge, MA: MIT Press.

Levelt, Willem. 1989. *Speaking: From intention to articulation.* Cambridge: MIT Press.

Levine, Robert. 2002. Review of *Rhyme and reason: An introduction to minimalist syntax,* by J. Uriagareka. *Language* 78, 325-330.

Levinson, Stephen. 1987. Pragmatics and the grammar of anaphora: A partial pragmatic reduction of Binding and Control phenomena. *Journal of Linguistics* 23, 379-434.

Lieberman, Philip. 2000. *Human language and our reptilian brain: The subcortical bases of speech, syntax, and thought.* Cambridge, MA: Harvard University Press.

Lightfoot, David. 1991. *How to set parameters.* Cambridge, MA: MIT Press.

Linebarger, Marcia, Myrna Schwartz, & Eleanor Saffran. 1983a. Sensitivity to grammatical structure in so-called agrammatic aphasics. *Cognition* 13, 361–392.

Linebarger, Marcia, Myrna Schwartz, & Eleanor Saffran. 1983b. Syntactic processing in agrammatism: A reply to Zurif and Grodzinsky. *Cognition* 15, 207–213.

MacDonald, Maryellen. 1999. Distributional information in language comprehen-sion, production, and acquisition: Three puzzles and a moral. In B. MacWhinney (ed.), *The emergence of language,* pp. 177–196. Mahwah, NJ: Erlbaum.

MacDonald, Maryellen & Morten Christiansen. 2002. Reassessing working memory: Comment on Just and Carpenter (1992) and Waters and Caplan (1996). *Psychological Review* 109, 35–54.

MacDonald, Maryellen, Neal Pearlmutter, & Mark Seidenberg. 1994. The lexical nature of syntactic ambiguity resolution. *Psychological Review* 101, 676–703.

MacWhinney, Brian. 1987. Toward a psycholinguistically plausible parser. In S. Thomason (ed.), *Proceedings of the Eastern States Conference on Linguistics*. Columbus, OH: The Ohio State University.

MacWhinney, Brian. 1999. Preface. In B. MacWhinney (ed.), *The emergence of language*, pp. ix–xvii. Mahwah, NJ: Erlbaum.

MacWhinney, Brian. 2003. The emergence of grammar from perspective. Available at http://psyling.psy.cmu.edu/brian/.

MacWhinney, Brian. 2004. Multiple solutions to the logical problem of language acquisition. *Journal of Child Language* 31. In press.

Manzini, Rita. 1983. On control and control theory. *Linguistic Inquiry* 14, 421–446.

Marantz, Alec. 1984. *On the nature of grammatical relations*. Cambridge, MA: MIT Press.

Marantz, Alec. 1995. The Minimalist Program. In G. Webelhuth (ed.), *Government and Binding Theory and the Minimalist Program*, pp. 349–382. Cambridge, MA: Blackwell.

Marcus, Gary. 1998. Rethinking eliminative connectionism. *Cognitive Psychology* 37, 243–282.

Marcus, Gary. 2001. *The algebraic mind*. Cambridge, MA: MIT Press.

Marcus, Mitchell. 1980. *A theory of syntactic recognition for natural language*. Cambridge, MA: MIT Press.

Marslen-Wilson, William. 1975. Sentence perception as an interactive parallel process. *Science* 189, 226-228.

Mazuka, Reiko & Barbara Lust. 1990. On parameter setting and parsing: Predictions for acquisition. In L. Frazier & J. de Villiers (eds.), *Processing and acquisition*, pp. 163–206. Dordrecht: Kluwer.

McCawley, James. 1981. The syntax and semantics of English relative clauses. *Lingua* 53, 99–149.

McElree, Brian & Thomas Bever. 1989. The psychological reality of linguistically defined gaps. *Journal of Psycholinguistic Research* 18, 21–35.

McKee, Cecile. 1992. A comparison of pronouns and anaphors in Italian and English acquisition. *Language Acquisition* 2, 21–54.

McKinnon, Richard & Lee Osterhout. 1996. Constraints on movement phenomena in sentence processing: Evidence from event-related brain potentials. *Language and Cognitive Processes* 11, 495–523.

Menn, Lise. 2000. Babies, buzzsaws and blueprints: Commentary on review article by Sabbagh & Gelman. *Journal of Child Language* 27, 753–755.

Mitchell, D. C. 1987. Lexical guidance in human parsing: Locus and processing characteristics. In M. Coltheart (ed.), *Attention and performance XII: The psychology of reading*, pp. 601–618. Hillsdale, NJ: Erlbaum.

Miyake, Akira & N. Friedman. 1998. Individual differences in second language proficiency: Working memory as language aptitude. In A. Healy & L. Bourne (eds.), *Foreign language learning*, pp. 339–364. Mahwah, NJ: Erlbaum.

Morgan, Jerry. 1972. Verb agreement as a rule of English. *Proceedings of the Eighth Regional Meeting of the Chicago Linguistic Society*, 278–293.

Munn, Alan. 1999. First conjunct agreement: Against a clausal analysis. *Linguistic Inquiry* 30, 643–668.

Nathan, Geoffrey. 1981. What's these facts about? *Linguistic Inquiry* 12, 151–153.

Newmeyer, Frederick. 1998. *Language form and language function*. Cambridge, MA: MIT Press.

Newmeyer, Frederick. 2003a. Grammar is grammar and usage is usage. *Language* 79, 682–707.

Newmeyer, Frederick. 2003b. Review of *On nature and language*, by N. Chomsky. *Language* 79, 583–599.

Ni, Weija, Janet Fodor, Stephen Crain, & Donald Shankweiler. 1998. Anomaly detection: Eye movement patterns. *Journal of Psycholinguistic Research* 27, 515–539.

Nicol, Janet & David Swinney. 1989. The role of structure in coreference assignment during sentence comprehension. *Journal of Psycholinguistics Research* 18, 5–19.

Ninio, Anat. 1988 On formal grammatical categories in early child language. In Y. Levy, I. Schlesinger, & M. Braine (eds.), *Categories and processes in language acquisition*. Hillsdale, NJ: Erlbaum. 99–119.

O'Grady, William 1997. *Syntactic development*. Chicago: University of Chicago Press.

O'Grady, William. 1998. The syntax of idioms. *Natural Language and Linguistic Theory* 16, 279–312.

O'Grady, William. 2003. Issues in language acquisition and language loss. *Studies in Language Sciences* 3, 3–33.

O'Grady, William, Miseon Lee, & Miho Choo. 2003. A subject-object asymmetry in the acquisition of relative clauses in Korean as a second language. *Studies in Second Language Acquisition* 25, 433–448.

Oakhill, Jane & Alan Garnham. 1989. The on-line construction of discourse models. *Language and Cognitive Processes* 4, 263–286.

Osterhout, Lee & Phillip Holcomb. 1993. Event-related potentials and syntactic anomaly: Evidence of anomaly detection during the perception of continuous speech. *Language and Cognitive Processes* 8, 413–437.

Osterhout, Lee & Linda Mobley. 1995. Event-related potentials elicited by failure to agree. *Journal of Memory and Language* 34, 739–773.

Otsu, Yukio. 1981. Universal Grammar and syntactic development in children: Toward a theory of syntactic development. Doctoral dissertation, MIT.

Palmer-Brown, Dominic, Jonathan Tepper, & Heather Powell. 2002. Connectionist natural language parsing. *Trends in Cognitive Science* 6, 437–442.

Pearlmutter, Neal, Susan Garnsey, & Kathryn Bock. 1999. Agreement processes in sentence comprehension. *Journal of Memory and Language* 41, 427–456.

Pesetsky, David. 1982. Paths and categories. Ph.D. dissertation, MIT.

Phillips, Colin. 1996. Order and structure. Ph.D. dissertation, MIT.

Phillips, Colin. 2003. Linear order and constituency. Linguistic Inquiry 34, 37–90.

Phillips, Colin, Nina Kazanina, & Shani Abada. 2004. ERP effects of the processing of syntactic long-distance dependencies. Manuscript, Department of Linguistics, University of Maryland.

Pickering, Martin. 1999. Sentence comprehension. In S. Garrod & M. Pickering (eds.), *Language processing*, pp. 123–153. East Sussex, UK: Psychology Press.

Piñango, Maria, Petra Burkhardt, Dina Brun & Sergei Avrutin. 2001. The psycho-logical reality of the syntax-discourse interface: The case of pronominals. Paper presented at the workshop 'From sentence processing to discourse interpretation: Crossing the borders,' Utrecht University.

Pinker, Steven. 1989. *Learnability and cognition: The acquisition of argument structure*. Cambridge, MA: MIT Press.

Pinker, Steven. 1994. *The language instinct*. New York: William Morrow & Co.

Pollard, Carl & Ivan Sag. 1987. *Information-based syntax and semantics. Vol. 1: Fundamentals*. Stanford University: CSLI Publications.

Pollard, Carl & Ivan Sag. 1992. Anaphora in English and the scope of binding theory. *Linguistic Inquiry* 23, 261–303.

Pollard, Carl & Ping Xue. 1998. Chinese reflexive *ziji*: Syntactic reflexives vs. non-syntactic reflexives. *Journal of East Asian Linguistics* 7, 287–318.

Postal, Paul. 1974. *On raising: One rule of grammar and its theoretical implications*. Cambridge, MA: MIT Press.

Postal, Paul & Geoffrey Pullum. 1982. The contraction debate. *Linguistic Inquiry* 13, 122–138.

Pritchett, Bradley. 1992. *Grammatical competence and parsing performance*. Chicago: University of Chicago Press.

Pullum, Geoffrey. 1996. Learnability, hyperlearning and the poverty of stimulus. *Proceedings of the Berkeley Linguistics Society* 22, 498–513.

Pullum, Geoffrey. 1997. The morpholexical nature of English *to*-contraction. *Language* 73, 79–102.

Pullum, Geoffrey & Barbara Scholz. 2002. Empirical assessment of stimulus poverty arguments. *Linguistic Review* 19, 9–50.

Pullum, Geoffrey & Arnold Zwicky. 1986. Phonological resolution of syntactic feature conflict. *Language* 62, 751–773.

Radford, Andrew. 1990. *Syntactic theory and the acquisition of English.* Oxford: Blackwell.

Radford, Andrew. 1997. *Syntax: A minimalist introduction.* Cambridge University Press.

Read, Charles & Victoria Hare. 1979. Children's interpretation of reflexive pro-nouns in English. In F. Eckman & A. Hastings (eds.), *Studies in first and second language acquisition,* pp. 98–116. Rowley, MA: Newbury House.

Reid, Wallis. 1991. *Verb and noun in English: A functional explanation.* London: Longman.

Reinhart, Tanya. 1981. Definite NP anaphora and c-command domains. *Linguistic Inquiry* 12, 605–635.

Reinhart, Tanya. 1983. *Anaphora and semantic interpretation.* Chicago: University of Chicago Press.

Reinhart, Tanya & Eric Reuland. 1991. Anaphors and logophors: An argument-structure perspective. In J. Koster & E. Reuland (eds.), *Long-distance anaphora,* pp. 283–321. Cambridge, UK: Cambridge University Press.

Rice, Mabel & Ken Wexler. 1996. Tense over time: The persistence of optional infinitives in English in children with SLI. *Proceedings of the 20th Boston University Conference on Language Development,* 610–621.

Richards, Norvin. 1997. What moves where when in which language? Ph.D. dissertation, MIT.

Rizzi, Luigi. 1990. *Relativized minimality.* Cambridge, MA: MIT Press.

Robinson, Peter. 2002. Effects of individual differences in intelligence, aptitude and working memory on incidental SLA. In P. Robinson (ed.), *Individual differences and instructed language learning,* pp. 211–251. Philadelphia: John Benjamins.

Rosenbaum, Peter. 1967. *The grammar of English predicate complement construc-tions.* Cambridge, MA: MIT Press.

Runner, Jeffrey. 2003. Freeing possessed NPs from binding theory. Unpublished ms., Department of Linguistics, University of Rochester.

Runner, Jeffrey, Rachel Sussman, & Michael Tanenhaus. 2003. Assignment of reference to reflexives and pronouns in picture noun phrases: Evidence from eye movements. *Cognition* 89, B1–13.

Safir, Kenneth. 1985. *Syntactic chains.* Cambridge, UK: Cambridge University Press.

Sag, Ivan & Carl Pollard. 1991. An integrated theory of complement control. *Language* 67, 63–113.

Sag, Ivan & Thomas Wasow. 1999. *Syntactic theory: A formal introduction.* Stanford, CA: Center for the Study of Language and Information.

Sakai, Kuniyoshi, Ryuichiro Hashimoto, & Fumitaka Homae. 2001. Sentence processing in the cerebral cortex. *Neuroscience Research* 39, 1–10.

Samuels, Richard. 2004. Innateness in cognitive science. *Trends in Cognitive Science* 8.3, 136–141.

Sampson, Geoffrey. 1989. Language acquisition: Growth or learning? *Philosophical papers* 18, 203–240.

Sanford, Anthony & Simon Garrod. 1989. What, when and how? Questions of immediacy in anaphoric reference resolution. *Language and Cognitive Processes* 4, 335–362.

Sanford, Anthony & Patrick Sturt. 2002. Depth of processing in language comprehension: Not noticing the evidence. *Trends in Cognitive Sciences* 6. 382–386.

Sangster, Rodney. 1982. *Roman Jakobson and beyond: Language as a system of signs.* Berlin: de Gruyter.

Sauerland, Uli & Paul Elbourne. 2002. Total reconstruction, PF movement, and derivational order. *Linguistic Inquiry* 33, 283–319.

Saxton, Matthew. 1997. The contrast theory of negative input. *Journal of Child Language* 24, 139–161.

Saxton, Matthew, Bela Kulscar, Greer Marshall, & Mandeep Rupra. 1998. Longer-term effects of corrective input: An experimental approach. *Journal of Child Language* 25, 701–721.

Schütze, Carson. 1999. English expletive constructions are not infected. *Linguistic Inquiry* 30, 467–484.

Searle, John. 2002. End of the revolution. *The New York Review of Books,* February 28, 2002, 33–36.

Sekerina, Irina, Karin Stromswold, & Arild Hestvik. 2004. How do adults and children process referentially ambiguous pronouns? *Journal of Child Language* 31, 123–152.

Selkirk, Elizabeth. 1982. *The syntax of words.* Cambridge, MA: MIT Press.

Selkirk, Elizabeth. 1984. *Phonology and syntax: The relation between sound and structure.* Cambridge, MA: MIT Press.

Sherman, Janet & Janell Schweickert. 1989. Syntactic and semantic contributions to sentence comprehension in agrammatism. *Brain and Language* 37, 419–439.

Slobin, Dan. 1985. Crosslinguistic evidence for the language-making capacity. In D. Slobin (ed.), *The crosslinguistic study of language acquisition. Vol. 2*, pp. 1157–1256. Hillsdale, NJ: Erlbuam.

Slobin, Dan & Thomas Bever. 1982. Children use canonical sentence schemas: A crosslinguistic study of word order and inflections. *Cognition* 12, 229–265.

Smith, Edward & John Jonides. 1997. Working memory: A view from neuroimaging. *Cognitive Psychology* 33, 5–42.

Smith, Neil & Ianthi-Maria Tsimpli. 1995. *The mind of a savant: Language learning and modularity.* Cambridge, MA: Blackwell.

Smolensky, Paul. 1999. Grammar–based connectionist approaches to language. *Cognitive Science* 23, 589–613,

Snow, Catherine & Charles Ferguson. 1977. *Talking to children: Language input and acquisition.* Cambridge, UK: Cambridge University Press.

Snyder, William. 2000. An experimental investigation of syntactic satiation effects. *Linguistic Inquiry* 31, 575–582.

Sobin, Nicolas. 1987. The variable status of COMP-trace phenomena. *Natural Language and Linguistic Theory* 5, 33–60.

Sobin, Nicolas. 1997. Agreement, default rules, and grammatical viruses. *Linguistic Inquiry* 28, 318–343.

Solan, Lawrence. 1987. Parameter setting and development of pronouns and reflexives. In T. Roeper & E. Williams (eds.), *Parameter setting*, pp. 189–210. Boston: Reidel.

Sparks, Randall. 1984. Here's a few more facts. *Linguistic Inquiry* 15,179–183.

Speas, Margaret. 1990. Phrase structure in natural language. Boston: Kluwer.

Speas, Peggy & Carol Tenny. 2003. Configurational properties of point of view roles. In A. Di Sciullo (ed.), *Asymmetries in grammar*, pp. 345–371. Philadelphia: John Benjamins.

Sproat, Richard. 1984. Infl and the configurationality of VSO languages. *Proceedings of the North East Linguistic Society* 14, 418–431.

St. John, Mark & Morton Ann Gernsbacher. 1998. Learning and losing syntax: Practice makes perfect and frequency builds fortitude. In A. Healy & L. Bourne, Jr. (eds.), *Foreign language learning: Psycholinguistic studies on training and retention*, pp. 231–255. Mahwah, NJ: Erlbaum.

Starosta, Stanley. 1994. Lexicase. In R.E. Asher & J.M.Y. Simpson (eds.), *The encyclopedia of language and linguistics. Vol. 4*, pp. 2167–2174. Oxford: Pergamon Press.

Starosta, Stanley. 1997. Control in constrained dependency grammar. In A. Simon-Vandenbergen, K. Davidse, & D. Noël (eds.), *Reconnecting language: Morphology and syntax in functional perspectives*, pp. 99–138. Amsterdam: John Benjamins.

Steedman, Mark. 1996. *Surface structure and interpretation.* Cambridge, MA: MIT Press.

Steedman, Mark. 1999. Connectionist sentence processing in perspective. *Cog-nitive Science* 23, 615–634.

Steedman, Mark. 2000. *The syntactic process.* Cambridge, MA: MIT Press.

Stowe, Laurie. 1986. Parsing wh-constructions. *Language and Cognitive Processes* 1, 227–246.

Stowe, Laurie. 2000. Sentence comprehension and the left inferior frontal gyrus: Storage, not computation. *Behavioral and Brain Sciences* 23, 51.

Stowell, Timothy. 1981. Origins of phrase structure. Ph.D. dissertation, MIT.

Stroik, Thomas. 1990. Adverbs as sisters. *Linguistic Inquiry* 21, 654–661.

Sturt, Patrick. 2003. The time course of the application of binding constraints in reference resolution. *Journal of Memory and Language* 48, 542–562.

Sturt, Patrick & Matthew Croker. 1998. Generalized monotonicity for reanalysis models. In J. D. Fodor & F. Ferreira (eds.), *Reanalysis in sentence processing,* pp. 365–400. Dordrecht: Kluwer.

Swinney, David, Marilyn Ford, Uli Frauenfelder, & Joan Bresnan. 1988 On the termporal course of gap-filling and antecedent assignment during sentence comprehension. In B. Grosz, R. Kaplan, M. Macken, & I. Sag (eds.), *Language structure and processing.* Stanford, CA: CSLI.

Tavakolian, Susan. 1978. The conjoined-clause analysis of relative clauses and other structures. In H. Goodluck & L. Solan (eds.), *Papers in the structure and development of child language,* pp. 37–83. Amherst, MA: University of Massachusetts Linguistics Department, GLSA Publications.

Thal, Donna & Melanie Flores. 2001. Development of sentence interpretation strategies by typically developing and late-talking toddlers. *Journal of Child Language* 28, 173–193.

Thornton, Rosalind. 1990. Adventures in long-distance moving: The acquisition of complex Wh-questions. Ph.D. dissertation, University of Connecticut.

Tomasello, Michael. 1995. *Beyond names for things: Young children's acquisition of verbs.* Mahwah, NJ: Erlbaum.

Tomasello, Michael. 2003. *Constructing a language: A usage-based theory of language acquisition.* Cambridge, MA: Harvard University Press.

Townsend, David & Thomas Bever. 2001. *Sentence comprehension: The integra-tion of habits and rules.* Cambridge, MA: MIT Press.

Ullman, Michael. 2001. A neurocognitive perspective on language: The declarative/ procedural model. *Nature Reviews | Neuro-science* 2, 717–726.

van der Lily, Heather & Linda Stollwork. 1997. Binding theory and grammatical specific language impairment in children. *Cognition* 62, 245–290.

Walther, Catherine. 1995. Processing of reflexives in coordinate NPs: A question of point of view. *Journal of Psycholinguistic Research* 24, 39–78.

Wanner, Eric & Michael Maratsos. 1978. An ATN approach to comprehension. In M. Halle, J. Bresnan, & G. Miller (eds.), *Linguistic theory and psychological reality,* pp. 119–161. Cambridge, MA: MIT Press.

Warren, Paul, Shari Speer, & Amy Schafer. 2003. *Wanna-*contraction and prosodic disambiguation in US and NZ English. *Wellington Working Papers in Linguistics* 15, 31–49.

Wasow, Thomas. 1997. End-weight from the speaker's perspective. *Journal of Psycholinguistic Research* 26, 347–361.

Wechsler, Stephen & Lorna Zaltic. 2000. A theory of agreement and its application to Serbo-Croatian. *Language* 76, 799–832.

Weinberg, Amy. 1999. A minimalist theory of human sentence processing. In S. Epstein & N. Hornstein (eds.), *Working minimalism,* pp. 283–315. Cambridge, MA: MIT Press.

Weinberg, Steven. 2000. Will we have a final theory of everything? *Time,* April 10, 2000, 86–87.

Wexler, Kenneth. 1996. The development of inflection in a biologically based theory of language acquisition. In M. Rice (ed.), *Toward a genetics of language,* pp. 113–144. Mahwah, NJ: Erlbaum.

Wexler, Kenneth. 1998. Maturation and growth of grammar. In W. Ritchie & T. Bhatia (eds.), *Handbook of child language acquisition,* pp. 55–105. San Diego: Academic Press.

Wexler, Kenneth & M. Rita Manzini. 1987. Parameters and learnability in binding theory. In T. Roeper & E. Williams (eds.), *Parameter setting,* pp. 41–76. Dordrecht: Reidel.

Winograd, Terry. 1972. *Understanding natural language.* San Diego: Academic Press.

Wolf, Florian, Edward Gibson, & Timothy Desmet. 2004. Discourse coherence and pronoun resolution. *Language and Cognitive Processes.* In press.

Wood, Mary. 1993. *Categorial grammars.* New York: Routledge.

Zurif, Edgar. 1998. The neurological organization of some aspects of sentence comprehension. *Journal of Psycholinguitic Research* 27, 181–190.

Zwicky, Arnold & Geoffrey Pullum. 1983. Cliticization vs. inflection: English *n't. Language* 59, 502-513.

Index